The *Dred Scott* Case

Ohio University Press Series on
Law, Society, and Politics in the Midwest

SERIES EDITORS: PAUL FINKELMAN AND L. DIANE BARNES

The History of Ohio Law, edited by Michael Les Benedict and John F. Winkler

Frontiers of Freedom: Cincinnati's Black Community, 1802–1868, by Nikki M. Taylor

A Place of Recourse: A History of the U.S. District Court for the Southern District of Ohio, 1803–2003, by Roberta Sue Alexander

The Black Laws: Race and the Legal Process in Early Ohio, by Stephen Middleton

The History of Indiana Law, edited by David J. Bodenhamer and Hon. Randall T. Shepard

The History of Michigan Law, edited by Paul Finkelman and Martin J. Hershock

The Rescue of Joshua Glover: A Fugitive Slave, the Constitution, and the Coming of the Civil War, by H. Robert Baker

The History of Nebraska Law, edited by Alan G. Gless

American Pogrom: The East St. Louis Race Riot and Black Politics, by Charles L. Lumpkins

No Winners Here Tonight: Race, Politics, and Geography in One of the Country's Busiest Death Penalty States, by Andrew Welsh-Huggins

The Dred Scott *Case: Historical and Contemporary Perspectives on Race and Law,* edited by David Thomas Konig, Paul Finkelman, and Christopher Alan Bracey

EDITED BY DAVID THOMAS KONIG,
PAUL FINKELMAN, AND CHRISTOPHER ALAN BRACEY

The *Dred Scott* Case

HISTORICAL AND CONTEMPORARY
PERSPECTIVES ON RACE AND LAW

Ohio University Press ー Athens

Ohio University Press, Athens, Ohio 45701
www.ohioswallow.com
© 2010 by Ohio University Press
All rights reserved

Printed in the United States of America
Ohio University Press books are printed on acid-free paper ⊗ ™

17 16 15 14 13 12 11 10   5 4 3 2 1

Library of Congress Cataloging-in-Publication Data
The Dred Scott case : historical and contemporary perspectives on race and law /
edited by David Thomas Konig, Paul Finkelman, and Christopher Alan Bracey.
    p. cm.
  Includes bibliographical references and index.
  ISBN 978-0-8214-1911-3 (cloth : alk. paper) — ISBN 978-0-8214-1912-0 (pbk. :
alk. paper)
  1. Scott, Dred, 1809–1858—Trials, litigation, etc. 2. Slavery—Law and
legislation—United States—History. 3. Slavery—United States—Legal
status of slaves in free states—History. 4. Constitutional history—United
States. 5. United States—Race relations—History. 6. United States—
History—1849–1877. I. Konig, David Thomas, 1947– II. Finkelman, Paul,
1949– III. Bracey, Christopher Alan, 1970–
  KF228.S27D74 2010
  342.7308'7—dc22

2010002129

This book is dedicated to the memory of

Walter Ehrlich and John A. Madison Jr.,

who kept the story alive

CONTENTS

ACKNOWLEDGMENTS

Bringing together the symposium that produced these essays was a collaborative effort. We are especially grateful for the financial support provided by Dean Kent Syverud of the Washington University Law School and Dean Edward Macias of the Faculty of Arts and Sciences and by generous alumni. Linda McClain and Jo Hobbs supplied the support that assured the success of the symposium and the production of this volume. Kevin Butterfield provided the fine hand of editorial expertise to the manuscript. We are deeply indebted, too, to our colleagues whose essays have brought to this project the historical and contemporary perspectives and broad knowledge that it demands. We hope that our work here does justice to the subject.

David Thomas Konig
St. Louis, Missouri

Paul Finkelman
Albany, New York

Christopher Alan Bracey
Washington, D.C.

American Confluence

History, Race, and Law

David Thomas Konig, Paul Finkelman, and Christopher Alan Bracey

NO SYMBOL of St. Louis looms more dominant than its famous Gateway Arch, which since its opening in 1967 has afforded more than forty million visitors an expansive view of the middle of the North American continent. It was at the confluence of two great river systems—the Missouri and the Mississippi—that modern America came together: the addition of the Louisiana Purchase in 1803 linked the ideals of the nation's Revolutionary past with the promise of its future. But the confluence also made real the unresolved Revolutionary debate over that future and led to its coming apart. Indeed, the Arch is only one structure in what officially constitutes the Jefferson National Expansion Memorial. Much smaller and literally overshadowed by the Arch is the Old Courthouse, erected as the Circuit Court of St. Louis County in the middle of the nineteenth century. The Arch provides symbolic representation of the nation's expansion westward, but the Old Courthouse embodies in its actual presence the struggle over the nation's destiny that such expansion produced. It was in the Old Courthouse in 1846 that Dred and Harriet Scott filed petitions for their freedom in the St. Louis Circuit Court, beginning litigation that eventually made its way to the Supreme Court of the United States. While the Arch represents a triumphalist view of the nation's history, the legal struggles that began in the Old Courthouse contain within them a far more problematic legacy. Visitors to the Arch will see an expanse of prairie stretching westward, where Meriwether Lewis and William Clark began a journey that ended in their arrival at the Pacific Ocean, but they need to be reminded that the Scotts' legal odyssey ended in failure. The Scotts gained their freedom only through private manumission, because legal redress failed them.

It also failed generations of their descendants, despite the human toll of the Civil War, the passage of three amendments to the Constitution, and the enactment of numerous civil rights laws. Inequality remains a stubborn historical legacy, deeply rooted in racism and often abetted by law, but also sustained by unthinking decisions and benign indifference. The struggle for equality did not begin with the Scotts' petition in 1846, of course; rather, it is as old as the Republic itself. Abraham Lincoln recognized this fact, and Americans today need to be reminded of it just as did those who stood and heard Lincoln denounce the *Dred Scott* decision in his famous debates with Stephen A. Douglas in their Senate race in 1858.

The history of St. Louis is inextricably tied to its own ambivalence over slavery: representing the promise of the future, it drew settlers wishing to bring slavery to the West as a basis for its wealth and power but also those who sought to escape an institution that they regarded as a curse that had blighted the past and would corrupt the future. Hundreds of slaves gained their freedom in St. Louis, some through lawsuits, others through masters who simply decided it was time to end their involvement in the institution. In many ways, antebellum St. Louis was an island off the coast of Missouri, where free blacks lived and where fugitive slaves escaped, relying on the anonymity of the city to secure some personal freedom even in the heart of a slave city. Additionally, just as Dred and Harriet Scott were first suing for their own freedom, St. Louis became the new home for thousands of German refugees from the failed revolutions of 1848. Escaping the tyranny of the Old World for the liberty of the New, they flocked to St. Louis and later rallied behind another immigrant, the antislavery General Franz Sigel, to preserve the Union and, in the process, end slavery.

William Greenleaf Eliot, who founded Washington University as an antislavery outpost to civilize the West amid the increasing violence of the 1850s, commented that divisions over slavery were most heated in cities such as his. Eliot's successors at Washington University thus welcomed the opportunity to use the 150th anniversary of the *Dred Scott* decision to hold a scholarly symposium that would continue its own legacy of involvement in its community, both local and national. The symposium, which was held at the Washington University Law School on March 1, 2, and 3, 2007, had the unqualified support of Dean Kent Syverud of the Washington University Law School and Dean Edward S. Macias of the College of Arts and Sciences as well as the entire university community and numerous generous supporters from the alumni, legal, and business communities who recognized the importance of the city's identification with such an important message.

The commemoration also received the support of other St. Louisans who embody the struggle of Dred and Harriet Scott, most significantly their own descendants, whose lives in St. Louis since 1857 give meaning to the continuing struggle begun here in 1846. Renewed attention to the Scotts and their legacy led to the discovery that Dred and Harriet's daughter Lizzie Scott lived in St. Louis until 1945, so quietly that she slipped from historical notice. Yet Lizzie's quiet life and her support for the family of her sister, Eliza Scott Madison, testify to the continuity of struggle that makes such "inarticulate" historical actors so ultimately significant.[1] Thanks to their greatgranddaughter Lynne Madison Jackson, who has founded the Dred Scott Heritage Foundation, the efforts of Dred and Harriet Scott, Lizzie Scott, and Eliza Scott Madison will now receive the attention they merit.

Since the time of Dred Scott, St. Louis has been the site of ongoing legal battles for justice and equality. The Gateway Arch was not the only structure nearing completion as it rose above the Mississippi River in 1966. That year Joseph Lee Jones and his wife, Barbara Jo Jones, brought a civil rights suit in federal court against the real estate developer who had refused to sell them a new home being built on the grounds of the Paddock Country Club in St. Louis County. That case, which reached the United States Supreme Court two years later, held that the denial of the Joneses' right to purchase a home in the Paddock Wood subdivision was one of the "badges and incidents of slavery" prohibited by law.[2]

In May of that same year, within the shadow of the Arch, the St. Louis Cardinals began play at the newly completed Busch Memorial Stadium, and in July hosted the Major League All-Star Game, where Curt Flood played center field for the National League with the same flawless skill that saw him play that entire 1966 season for the Cardinals without making an error. No one could have predicted that the Cardinals would trade Flood, much less that when they did trade him after the 1969 season Flood would challenge their right to do so and take his case all the way to the Supreme Court. Yet, the perspective of history reveals embedded in Flood's refusal to report to his new team the historic legacy of African American assertion of full citizenship. Defending his right, Flood compared his status to that of a slave—by his own admission a very well paid slave, but a slave no less. "After twelve years in the major leagues," he wrote to baseball commissioner Bowie Kuhn, "I do not feel I am a piece of property to be bought and sold irrespective of my wishes. I believe that any system which produces that result violates my basic rights as a citizen and is inconsistent with the laws of the United States and of the several States." Flood made no allegation of racial discrimination behind the trade or the reserve clause that bound every player to the team that held his contract. Nonetheless, the fact that it was an African American bringing this suit attested to the continuing quest for "basic rights as a citizen" that remained unfulfilled more than a century after the Civil War.

Those who attended the symposium in St. Louis needed no reminding that, for many, enjoyment of the "basic rights of a citizen" sought by Dred and Harriet Scott remains an unrealized goal. But the scholars who convened there, and the essays they have produced for this volume, demonstrate how the complicated, nuanced, and contradictory history of the Scotts' struggle can still contribute to understanding the nation's problematic commitment to legal equality. For that reason, it is hoped that their scholarly essays will accomplish what Justice Thurgood Marshall called for in his dissent from the Court's denial of Curt Flood's claim: that as Americans "we must admit our error and correct it."[3]

Like Flood and the Joneses, the Scotts focused national attention on an issue that arose in St. Louis but embodied a national problem. By 1854, when the Scotts' case reached the Supreme Court, it was no longer a simple freedom suit like the hundreds that had preceded it, and the issues it raised were recognized as having far more than local impact. The legal talent assembled on each side reflected those realities, just as the stature of those who met for the symposium demonstrated the historical and contemporary importance of that unsettled legacy and drew national attention to the continuing efforts to understand and solve it.

Notes

1. For recent discoveries on the lives of Dred and Harriet's daughters, see Ruth Ann Hager, *Dred and Harriet Scott: Their Family Story* (St. Louis: St. Louis County Library, 2010).

2. Jones v. Alfred H. Mayer Co., 255 F. Supp. 115 (1966); 390 U.S. 409, 439–40 (1968).

3. Flood v. Kuhn, 407 U.S. 258, 289, 293 (1972). For a full account of the case, see Brad Snyder, *A Well-Paid Slave: Curt Flood's Fight for Free Agency in Professional Sports* (New York: Viking, 2006).

PART ONE

Historical Perspectives
The Power of the Past

ONE

Constitutional Law
and the Legitimation of History

The Enduring Force of Roger Taney's "opinion of the court"

David Thomas Konig

ROGER TANEY was not the first judge to seek legitimacy for an opinion by drawing on the authority of the past, and his "opinion of the court" in *Dred Scott v. Sandford* only continued a long tradition of applying— some would say, manipulating—the historical method to reach desired results. Current academic criticism of the "historical method of adjudication" remains framed by a 1965 article by historian Alfred H. Kelly that stands as a classic censure of the fallacies of reasoning and decontextualized evidence that lead judges to use historical argument to reach conclusions that are wrong or historically impossible to prove. Kelly, however, was only giving voice to a long tradition of criticism and providing additional argument to strictures made that same year by legal scholar Mark DeWolfe Howe, who had observed that such corruption of the historical method had "very probably always marked the divisions within the Court." Those who disparage the way history has been used in adjudication acknowledge, of course, that the historical recovery of the past and the judicial resolution of legal disputes can work at cross-purposes. There exists an inherent dilemma of method and goal, what Howe called the "tension between the complexities of a confused reality and the simplicities of sure conviction." Acknowledging the different professional imperatives of the lawyer, historian Kelly conceded that the object of the adversarial process of advocacy litigation "is, after all, not history, but the resolution of a lawsuit, and the judges are supposed to resolve opposing claims of counsel in such a way as to produce something coherent in terms of justice, legal continuity, or ascertainable law. It is not for a historian to choose." Just as judges must choose between competing legal narratives, so too must they choose between competing historical narratives in order to arrive at the "simplicities of conviction" needed for adjudicating disputes.[1]

This essay argues that the impact of rejecting a particular legal doctrine differs materially from that of rejecting a particular version of history, which ultimately poses a much greater harm in a democracy. Consigning a legal doctrine to extinction is not the same as rejecting the "the complexities of a confused reality" of the past, which may do serious harm beyond what the legal decision produces. While "bad history" can lead to bad decisions, such damage may affect only the parties to a particular case. Even if, as in the case of *Dred Scott,* its decision has an immediate impact on millions and accelerates a national crisis, its impact can be reversed by constitutional amendment. Thus, the law announced in Chief Justice Roger B. Taney's "opinion of the court" (*his* term, anointing what was, actually, only his own opinion among a thicket of contradictory concurring and dissenting opinions)[2] was altered by three amendments to the Constitution, but its greater and much longer term damage lies outside the law and continues to the present day. Taney's simplistic version of a complex past, announced and anointed as "too clear to dispute,"[3] was a form of collateral damage that has outlived its primary constitutional harm by corrupting our nation's historical memory and creating a false normative narrative of the American experience. The "opinion of the court" thus placed the imprimatur of a vastly respected institution on an interpretation of history whose fallacies continue to undermine the historical foundations of core constitutional beliefs.

Taney's history was a classic example of how a judge uses history "not to learn about the past, but merely to support an outcome."[4] The purpose of his historical analysis—to which Taney devoted more space in his opinion than any other issue—was to exclude all African Americans, slave or free, from any rights specified in the Constitution.[5] To do so required establishing that even free blacks were not among those "who were citizens of the several States when the Constitution was adopted. And in order to do this," he stated, "we must recur" to the political institutions of the time and "inquire who, at that time, were recognized as the people or citizens of a State, whose rights and liberties had been outraged by the English Government; and who declared their independence, and assumed the powers of Government to defend their rights by force of arms." His denial of African American citizenship was unequivocal: "In the opinion of the court, the legislation and histories of the times, and the language used in the Declaration of Independence, show, that neither the class of persons who had been imported as slaves, nor their descendants, whether they had become free or not, were then acknowledged as a part of the people, nor intended to be included in the general words used in that memorable instrument."[6]

The historical account supporting this opinion was unmediated by context, nuance, or contradictory example and was marked by sweeping and global generalizations of confident correctness. Taney's only concession to doubt was to acknowledge that "it is difficult at this day to realize the state of opinion in relation to that unfortunate race" in the past, but he quickly pointed out that "the public history of every European nation displays it in a manner too plain to be mistaken." In terms admitting of no uncertainty, Taney maintained that Africans "had for more than a century before been regarded as beings of an inferior order, and altogether unfit to associate with the white race, either in social or political relations; and so far inferior, that they had no rights which the white man was bound to respect." Anticipating challenge to such a statement, Taney supported it as "an axiom in morals as well as in politics, which no one thought of disputing, or supposed to be open to dispute," so universally held that "no one seems to have doubted the correctness of the prevailing opinion of the time." As to the principle that "all men are created equal," Taney flatly stated that "it is too clear for dispute" that no one intended it to apply either to enslaved *or free* blacks. For emphasis, Taney stated that by the "common consent" of all "civilized Governments and the family of nations" *all* Africans were "doomed to slavery." "The unhappy black race," he concluded, "were separated from the white by indelible marks, and laws long before established, and were never thought of or spoken of except as property."[7]

Taney's opinion, however, did more than call on history to solidify slavery by showing it to be embedded in the American past, essential to its origins, justified by its religion, and inseparable from its present commitment to liberty. Those arguments had been made for decades, and by the 1850s there existed a widespread and deeply entrenched Southern tradition of using history to show the universality of slavery as a system and the suitability of Africans for it. Proslavery apologists, that is, already had constructed an "inescapable past" for American slavery and had used "history as moral and political instruction" to describe slavery as normal and racism natural.[8]

Such a proslavery historical narrative brought the institution to the center of the national narrative and justified it against the rising din of antislavery argument, but it did not fully answer a new challenge emerging as Dred and Harriet Scott's petition for freedom, commenced in the 1840s, moved slowly through the next decade. If history was to continue to provide the narrative basis for a jurisprudence of slavery and racial control, it had to address more than slavery and slaves: it had to respond to the historical reality of free African Americans whose past belied the conventional narrative, and whose vocal assertion of that fact contradicted the very foundations of proslavery jurisprudence. Taney had ample support for his version of the history of slavery; he had to create it for his version of free African Americans.

Taney's opinion, to be sure, expressed the widespread and prevailing historical understanding among whites of the debased and excluded position of African Americans in the nation's history. But it is vital for subsequent generations to be aware that such a view, however widely held in the nineteenth century, was nonetheless only one interpretation of that past available at the time, one that by the 1850s was coming under repeated attack as orthodoxy. It was, in fact, constructed to deny what Robert Cover, a legal scholar sensitively attuned to the humanistic dimensions of the law, has identified as the "multiplicity of the legal meanings created out of the exiled narratives and divergent social bases for their use."[9] Indeed, Taney's history must be read as a carefully selective response to an ever louder assertion of black citizenship, which was presenting its own powerfully articulated historical counternarrative. That alternative narrative did not represent mainstream history, but neither was it obscure or inaccessible to anyone making even a half-hearted attempt to recover the past. The seriousness with which Taney and others had to deny it, as well as the attention given it by other proslavery apologists, makes it unlikely that Taney was unaware of it.[10] He had to assert a narrative that would erase African Americans from membership in the political community that had founded the republic and thus had earned the enjoyment of the rights announced in the Declaration of Independence and set out in the Constitution's creation of a "more perfect union." To understand Taney's process of historical construction, it is necessary to recover what he was responding to.

Almost as soon as the incompatibility of slavery and freedom became apparent in the 1780s there arose explanations to resolve it by denying African Americans membership in the generation that founded the republic. David Ramsay, a Pennsylvania native who married into the elite of South Carolina, had advocated arming slaves during the War for Independence—a step taken by several northern states, including his native Pennsylvania—but he gradually felt the pressure of the slaveholding society around him, abandoned the attempt, and moved steadily away from his tentative antislavery position. By the time he wrote his *History of the American Revolution* (1789), his muted criticism of the "evil" of slavery was largely limited to the "mischievous effects" of the institution on white society and the danger of slave insurrection. To reinforce the idea that Africans were both unwilling and unable to claim membership in a free nation, Ramsay described their military service with Lord Dunmore in Virginia as "more prejudicial to their British employers than to the provincials." Acculturated to enslavement, he wrote, they "are so well satisfied with their condition, that several have been known to reject proffered freedom . . . and emancipation does not appear to be the wish of the generality of them." The longer he lived in South Carolina, the more Ramsay absorbed the prevailing white view of slavery. Though he lamented the ill effects of the system, "necessity" compelled it, because the coastal low country "could only be cultivated by black men." With slavery assumed as a natural fact of life, his history of the Revolution removed the slave "from the realm of moral discourse," in the words of Ramsay's definitive biographer, while his 1809 *History of South Carolina,* a state whose population was more than 50 percent black, simply "ignored the African. The oversight could not have been accidental," writes Arthur Shaffer. "If he could not positively endorse slavery, he would remain silent."[11] Ramsay was helping to shape the paradigm of the African American experience in the United States: enslavement as a natural fact, debasing the African colonists to a lesser status and excluding them from the body politic.

John Marshall, though hardly known as an advocate of the slave regime, provided constitutional and historical support for this model. His court showed "caution" in dealing with the few cases involving slavery that came before it, assuming an unaccustomed formalist style in its decision making. Throughout his public career Marshall sided with those working to preserve the institution. As a nationalist who hoped to avoid sectional conflict, he "wished that slavery would somehow go away," and as a protector of property rights he avoided choosing between "the sacred rights of liberty and property" when in conflict. Despite his nationalism, however, Marshall believed that slavery was a matter to be left to the states, and in 1829 he agreed to serve in the Virginia constitutional convention primarily to promote a new constitution that would better protect slavery as property against the possibility of a democratic western majority that might threaten its existence.[12]

Marshall's writing of history complemented his jurisprudence. His magnum opus, a five-volume biography of George Washington with the nation's colonial history as backdrop, gave little attention to Africans, whether enslaved at Mount Vernon or serving with his army, despite the deep and lasting impact that African American military service had on Washington's thinking about slavery. Their only role in the historical image Marshall constructed was as slaves or potential incendiaries. The inauguration of "commercial liberty" that followed the collapse of the Virginia Company attracted a Dutch ship that "brought into James River twenty Africans, who were immediately purchased as slaves." No contingency, no period of unfree indenture, no discussion of economic forces diminished the naturalness of enslavement. His first volume also described the Stono Rebellion of 1739, in which self-emancipated Africans demonstrated their unfitness for freedom with a murderous rampage of whites. "Intoxicated with ardent spirits, and with their short lived success," Marshall continued, "they considered their work as already achieved and halted in an open field, where the time which might have been employed in increasing their numbers, and extending their devastation, was devoted to dancing and exultation."

Surprised by armed whites, their insurrection collapsed, and their leaders were executed. Africans appear again in his second volume, once more a menace to Americans as part of Lord Dunmore's "force of the disaffected and negroes." To make clear their incapacity for membership among civilized peoples, Marshall returned to the subject in his final volume, describing the Haitian revolution as a bloody race war and "one indiscriminate massacre, from which neither age nor sex could afford an exemption."[13]

Marshall's stature conferred legitimacy on his history and had a profound impact in advancing a particular version of American history. The reading public was unaware that Marshall had done little research and was in some cases virtually quoting without attribution from others, but, observes one commentator, "It was natural to believe that a history written by the great jurist would be marked by soundness, high scholarly qualities, and reliability."[14] Marshall's account of the American past helped imprint in the national mind an identity that emerged from its experience and helped justify continuity with the ideas and actions imputed to it. His writing of history also relegated the indigenous native population to a subordinate position and legitimated the assertion of legal title over their lands. In *Johnson v. M'Intosh* Marshall asserted the legality of the acquisitions by constructing a principle of "discovery" that, he insisted, had always been an acknowledged basis for "the exclusive right of the discoverer to appropriate the lands occupied by Indians." "The history of America," he wrote without fear of contradiction, "from its discovery to the present day, proves, we think, the universal recognition of these principles." The doctrine allowed Marshall to strip the Indians of their rights and degrade them to a legally insignificant status of "occupants, to be protected," rather than as owners. Indian rights were not, he insisted, "entirely disregarded; but were, to a considerable extent, impaired."[15]

Marshall, it has been shown, was well aware that his historical sources had serious deficiencies, just as he was aware of other sources that contradicted his version of history. But his forensic history required such an account. Even what another scholar calls his "demeaning and insulting" statements about the Indian "were not simply gratuitous insults" but were prescriptively inserted "value judgments" that served the important forensic purpose of creating a powerful metaphor with which to rationalize and justify dispossession of a people considered unworthy of land ownership.[16]

Marshall's use of history to label Native Americans incapable of civilized life and to reduce them to a subordinate status with rights not worthy of respect has strong parallels with the way history served to legitimate a similar, though even more extreme, treatment of African Americans. In both cases, moreover, there existed powerful alternative narratives that had to be denied. That impulse culminated in Taney's expunging of black citizenship from American history.

African American participation in the achievement of nationhood and in sharing the rights of citizenship were facts that in the 1840s and 1850s black abolitionists were ever more insistently presenting to the American public, laying claim to the legal rights they were entitled to by virtue of that historical experience. Such claims emerged more vocally in the 1840s, as many free blacks rejected colonization and demanded citizenship rights in the land of their birth. Meeting in convention, they urged emancipation of the enslaved and equal rights for those African Americans who already had their freedom. Although the conventions had little political impact, their "addresses" and "memorials" nevertheless had a significant effect in altering the discourse over rights. Directed at the white public and legislators, these manifestos made claim to full membership as citizens and supported their claim with historical evidence of black participation in the Revolution.[17] "*We are Americans,*" asserted the New York State Convention of Colored Citizens in 1840, arguing that "the right of our birthdom, our service in behalf of the country," justified "the claims and rights of a disfranchised people." Clearly stating a point that Taney would have to refute, it declared, "We can find no nation that has the temerity to insult the common sense of mankind" by basing rights on skin color or body shape. Though the legal position of blacks had suffered badly since the Revolution, it called upon the people of New York to "restore the fountains of political justice in this State to their pristine purity. . . . We call upon you to return to the pure faith of your republican fathers."[18]

The Ohio convention of 1851 drew on statements by major white figures to make the same plea to that state's constitutional convention. It included Roger Sherman Baldwin's speech on the Senate floor in which he pointed out that "colored men voted" in most states in 1789. "All free people then stood upon the same platform in regard to their political rights," he argued, "and were so recognized in most of the States of the Union." Even

Andrew Jackson provided support, as the convention cited his addressing free black soldiers before the Battle of New Orleans as "Sons of Freedom" and as "Americans." He assured them that "through a *mistaken policy* they had been deprived of a participation in the glorious struggle for national rights, in which our country was engaged," and that the policy was now ended.[19]

Among the most active black abolitionists keeping this narrative before the public at large was William Cooper Nell, a Bostonian who worked for Frederick Douglass's *Northern Star* and William Lloyd Garrison's *Liberator*. Nell had also been among the founders of the short-lived "American Reform Board of Disfranchised Commissioners," but his most lasting achievement was the publication of two books that presented example after example of black participation in the founding of the nation. Nell's books, written with the support of Frederick Douglass, explicitly associated such a history with entitlement to citizenship, and it is no coincidence that such claims came in the wake of the passage of the Fugitive Slave Act, whose provisions denied alleged fugitives of their most basic due process rights, including the Constitutional guarantee of habeas corpus. His *Service of Colored Americans in the Wars of 1776 and 1812* began with the shooting of Crispus Attucks at the Boston Massacre, an event whose importance went beyond the personal martyrdom or heroism it was commonly cited for. Instead, Nell makes it clear "that the colored man, Attucks, was *of* and *with* the people, and was never regarded otherwise." He noted, too, that "the Colored Soldiers called the 'Bucks of America'" had served in the war, and that John Hancock had presented them with a silk banner "as a tribute to their courage and devotion to the cause of American Liberty, through a protracted and bloody struggle."[20]

Nell was aware of the power of corroboration by eminent whites, and when he continued his project four years later with *The Colored Patriots of the American Revolution* he included remarks by Harriet Beecher Stowe, Wendell Phillips, and John Greenleaf Whittier. In his "Author's Preface," Nell quoted from an Independence Day speech made in 1847 by the Garrisonian Whittier, who had pointed out the historical injustice of "a whole nation doing honor to the memories of one class of its defenders, to the total neglect of another class, who had the misfortune to be of darker complexion." Whittier then took satisfaction in "inviting notice to certain historical facts, which, for the last half century, have been quietly elbowed aside." "They have no historian," Whittier lamented, but "enough is known to show that the free colored men of the United States bore their full proportion of the sacrifices and trials of the Revolutionary War." Stowe understood the power of collective memory in recognizing the "record of worth in this oppressed and despised race," because it would reverse the "cruel and unjust public sentiment, which has so long proscribed them." Philips, too, saw the need to redirect public memory toward an inclusive narrative, which would "stem the tide of prejudice against the colored race."[21]

Nell had enlisted such support to "rescue many gallant names from oblivion" in one battle of what had become an escalating "history war." In his description of the Battle of Cowpens, for example, John Marshall had made specific reference that "a waiter, too small to wield a sword," saved a patriot officer by shooting a British officer about to kill him. When William Ranney painted the scene in 1845, he showed the young black man who had wielded the pistol. Black participation at Bunker Hill, by contrast, was effaced. John Trumbull's painting of *The Battle of Bunker Hill* shows a black soldier (Peter Salem, a free man) holding a musket next to Lieutenant Thomas Grosvenor, as does a 1798 engraving made from it. But, as Nell pointed out in 1855, later engravings removed Salem. So, too, a petition to the Massachusetts legislature to appropriate $1,500 for a statue in memory of Crispus Attucks, "the first martyr in the Boston Massacre," was rejected, on the grounds that "a boy, Christopher Snyder, was previously killed."[22]

Commemorating Crispus Attucks became a central issue in the demand for black citizenship, and it intensified in the wake of Taney's opinion. The next year, Nell and other black abolitionists celebrated the first annual "Crispus Attucks Day" in Boston, for which they assembled numerous reminders of the Revolution, including an engraving of Emmanuel Leutze's painting *Washington Crossing the Delaware* (1851), which featured Prince Whipple, a black man, among the oarsmen.[23] The speed with which Taney's narrative was countered attests to the active and ongoing efforts already in place promoting a counternarrative. It did not require mobilization of new efforts or the search for new data, that is, but rather could count on an existing fund of knowledge well known in black and abolitionist circles.

But it was not abolitionists alone who were offended by Taney's manipulation of history, for abolitionism constituted only part of the opposition to slavery. Free-soil whites who had little interest in the rights of African Americans also challenged what Taney claimed "no one seems to have doubted" at the founding of the republic. Angrily replying to Taney, former U.S. Senator Thomas Hart Benton emphatically disagreed in a manner befitting a man who shot Andrew Jackson in a brawl. Despite apologies that he "was breaking down under the approaches of a terrible attack, while he was still writing it, and was prostrate before it was finished," Benton managed to produce a robust (and repetitive) *Historical and Legal Examination of That Part of the Decision of the Supreme Court of the United States in the Dred Scott Case, Which Declares the Unconstitutionality of the Missouri Compromise Act, and the Self-Extension of the Constitution to Territories, Carrying Slavery along With It.* Steadfastly affirming the constitutionality of the Missouri Compromise, Benton asserted that he would "limit myself, as the Court did, to the strict legal inquiry which the subject exacts," but, like Taney, he roamed freely into historical argument. Any inquiry into "the origin and design" of the background of the case, he insisted, "belongs to history, veracious [*sic*] and fearless." But it was to history that he returned in his reproach of the Court, claiming that he was expressing "the history of the times" on congressional authority and revealing the "daily current knowledge" of the Philadelphia Convention, explaining the "history, and the obvious meaning of language," in the text. He also produced the "record[ed] history of the day" concerning the Compromise, and when a Northern senator asserted his state's importance in passing the Northwest Ordinance Benton dismissed it as "a prominence excusable in oratory, but not justified in history."[24]

Benton's attack on Taney's version of history, though it did not address the rights of African Americans, contained within it more subtle points worth emphasizing today. A Democrat who believed in the sovereignty of the people as expressed at the ballot box, he assailed the inherent "evil" of politicizing the courts by "bringing the federal judiciary into the vortex of federal politics." His belief in the sovereignty of the people also led him to a much more profound matter. In challenging Taney's interpretation of the Missouri Compromise, Benton noted that because the Compromise was "an event long since passed, and its history inaccessible to the community, many are persuaded to believe in the fable" spun by Taney and widely believed by the public.[25]

Benton, therefore, was making common—if highly ironic—cause with Nell and the black abolitionists who also recognized the power of public memory as a force in law and politics. They both appreciated that popular historical consciousness expounded by judges has more than judicial impact. Endorsed by the prestige of the court, it elevates one interpretation above others in a culture in which historical knowledge is deeply contested and its messages up for grabs. In a volume that grew out of an effort to answer the question "How do Americans understand their past?" two distinguished historians came to the conclusion that "the real issue was not as the pundits were declaring, what Americans did not know about the past, but what they *did* know and think"—that is, that the nation's "historical consciousness" or "historical memory" consisted of discordant and often wildly incorrect accounts of the past. The result is that the historical past becomes a tool with which to advance a "heritage." Defining "heritage," David Lowenthal comes close to describing forensic history and the historical process as evident in Taney's "opinion of the court": "not an effort to know what actually happened but a profession of faith in a past tailored to present-day purposes."[26]

Judicially endorsed versions of the past can spread widely into the political culture, flowing back into the courthouse and legislature to exert enormous extrajudicial pressure on our legal and political systems. The use of historical materials by a judiciary in a liberal democracy therefore has often served, as it did for Taney, to justify law's authority as a "modality of rule" by invoking what it anoints as the normative experience of the people.[27]

This process has had especially damaging effects in shaping the collective memory of the nation's racialized past. One effect is the widespread denial "that slavery was a major cause of the Civil War." A proper encounter with the past requires engaging its contradictions and complexities, but, as another study of public memory concludes, historians and museum interpreters "encounter a public often unwilling to hear a story that calls into question comfortable assumptions about the nation's past."[28] Taney's historical "opinion of the court" endorsed and solidified an enduring stigma that has normalized racial hierarchy and impeded the struggle for equality long after ratification of the Fourteenth Amendment. Norman Spaulding expresses this general process well: "In liberal democracies, where sovereign power operates on the principle of consent, public accountability, and constitutional restraint, national narratives also confer political legitimacy—they define the discursive space for the negotiation and justification of political power by regulating the collective memory of a nation's fundamental commitments."[29] In a democracy where popularly held notions of what relations "ought" to be and how law "ought" to formalize norms, judges' forensic history simplifies the complexities of the past and announces a definitive interpretation that takes on the quality of an "official" history. So great is the prestige of the judicial role that its pronouncements on history are assumed to be based on the very ideal of objectivity that the historian follows only in the breach. Historian Peter Novick, in explaining how American historians seek an unachievable goal of "objectivity," contrasts them unfavorably with judges, who, he maintains, more self-consciously embody that unmet ideal: "The historian's conclusions are expected to display the standard judicial qualities of balance and evenhandedness," Novick writes. "As with the judiciary, these qualities are guarded by the insulation of the historical profession from social pressures or political influence, and by the individual historian avoiding partisanship or bias—not having any investment in arriving at one conclusion rather than another."[30]

Constitutional litigation in the years since Kelly wrote has drawn historical argument more fully into legal debate, making necessary a heightened level of scrutiny. The growth of an intellectually vigorous and diverse academy has brought new disciplinary perspectives into legal argument and presented the courts with innovative challenges drawing heavily on material not found in "authoritative legal materials" and "emphasizing abstract theory at the expense of practical scholarship."[31] History, when simplified and stripped of complexity for the purpose of adjudication, can provide precisely the kind of "practical scholarship" that judges prefer when they look to it for its familiarity as a traditional source of authority, its relative accessibility to nonspecialists, and its avowed commitment to the recovery and interpretation of "fact." But in deceiving the public about the past, such history deceives us about the present.

Notes

1. Dred Scott v. John F. A. Sandford, 60 U.S. (19 How.) 393 (1857) (Taney's "opinion of the court" is at 399–529, and dissents by John McLean and Benjamin R. Curtis are at 529–633); Alfred H. Kelly, "Clio and the Court: An Illicit Love Affair,"

Supreme Court Review 1965 (1965): 119 (citing Howe), 156. Kelly was expanding on Mark DeWolfe Howe, "Split Decisions," *New York Review of Books,* July 1, 1965. John Phillip Reid, "Law and History," *Loyola of Los Angeles Law Review* 27, no. 1 (1998–99): 201nn35–36, provides pertinent citations to the academic faultfinding. The protracted historical debate between Sir Edward Coke and his opponents in the constitutional disputes of the seventeenth century is the subject of J. G. A. Pocock, *The Ancient Constitution and the Feudal Law: A Study of English Historical Thought in the Seventeenth Century* (Cambridge: Cambridge University Press, 1957).

2. On the lack of a single, coherent "opinion" in *Dred Scott,* see Don E. Fehrenbacher, *The Dred Scott Case: Its Significance in American Law and Politics* (New York: Oxford University Press, 1978), 305–404.

3. Scott, 60 U.S. at 410.

4. Reid, "Law and History," 203.

5. Fehrenbacher points out that Taney devoted twenty-four pages (or 44 percent) of the fifty-five pages of his opinion to this point (*Dred Scott Case,* 337). Of the more than two hours it took to read the opinion, this section probably consumed more than an hour.

6. Scott, 60 U.S. at 407.

7. Ibid. at 407–10.

8. Elizabeth Fox-Genovese and Eugene D. Genovese, *The Mind of the Master Class: History and Faith in the Southern Slaveholders' Worldview* (New York: Cambridge University Press, 2005), esp. pt. 2, "The Inescapable Past," 125–246. The literature of proslavery thought is vast, and its impact enormous. For other studies, see also Winthrop D. Jordan, *White over Black: American Attitudes toward the Negro, 1550–1812* (Chapel Hill: University of North Carolina Press, 1968), and George M. Fredrickson, *The Black Image in the White Mind: The Debate on Afro-American Character and Destiny, 1817–1914* (New York: Harper and Row, 1971).

9. Robert M. Cover, "Nomos and Narrative," in *Narrative, Violence, and the Law: The Essays of Robert Cover,* ed. Martha Minow, Michael Ryan, and Austin Sarat (Ann Arbor: University of Michigan Press, 1993), 113.

10. Not coincidentally, T. R. R. Cobb chose to preface *An Inquiry into the Law of Negro Slavery in the United States of America* (Philadelphia: T. and J. W. Johnson, 1858; repr., ed. Paul Finkelman, Athens: University of Georgia Press, 1999) with "An Historical Sketch of Slavery" that included descriptions of how emancipated blacks had shown themselves unfit for citizenship (cci–ccv).

11. David Ramsay, *The History of the American Revolution* (Philadelphia: R. Aitken and Son, 1789; repr., ed. Lester H. Cohen, Indianapolis: Liberty Classics, 1990), 14, 496, 229, 20–25; Arthur H. Shaffer, *To Be an American: David Ramsay and the Making of the American Consciousness* (Columbia: University of South Carolina Press, 1991), 176, 187.

12. Donald M. Roper, "In Quest of Judicial Objectivity: The Marshall Court and the Legitimation of Slavery," *Stanford Law Review* 21, no. 3 (1969): 533, 535,

quoting his opinion in *The Antelope,* 23 U.S. (10 Wheat.) 66, 114 (1825); R. Kent Newmyer, *John Marshall and the Heroic Age of the Supreme Court* (Baton Rouge: Louisiana State University Press, 2001), 330, 389–91.

13. John Marshall, *The Life of George Washington, Commander in Chief of the American Forces, during the War Which Established the Independence of His Country, and First President of the United States,* 5 vols. (Philadelphia: C. P. Wayne, 1804–7), 1:63, 330–32, 2:372, 5:368. On the regard in which Washington held his black soldiers and their entitlement to freedom, see Henry Wiencek, *An Imperfect God: George Washington, His Slaves, and the Creation of America* (New York: Farrar, Straus and Giroux, 2003).

14. William A. Foran, "John Marshall as Historian," *American Historical Review* 43, no. 1 (1937): 51.

15. Johnson v. M'Intosh, 21 U.S. (8 Wheat.) 543, 573–74, 584 (1823). On Marshall's manipulation of history, see Lindsay G. Robertson, *Conquest by Law: How the Discovery of America Dispossessed Indigenous Peoples of Their Lands* (New York: Oxford University Press, 2005).

16. Robertson, *Conquest by Law,* 103; Philip J. Prygoski, "War as Metaphor in Federal Indian Law Jurisprudence: An Exercise in Judicial Activism," *Thomas M. Cooley Law Review* 14, no. 3 (1997): 501.

17. Philip S. Foner and George E. Walker, eds., *Proceedings of the Black State Conventions, 1840–1865* (Philadelphia: Temple University Press, 1979), xii–xvi. See also Howard Holman Bell, ed., *Minutes of the Proceedings of the National Negro Conventions, 1830–1865* (New York: Arno Press, 1969); and Bell's *A Survey of the Negro Convention Movement, 1830–1861* (New York: Arno Press, 1969).

18. "Address of the New York State Convention of Colored Citizens, to the People of New York," in *Proceedings,* 21, 23.

19. "Hear Us for Our Cause," ibid., 271.

20. William C. Nell, *Services of Colored Americans in the Wars of 1776 and 1812* (Boston: Prentiss and Sawyer, 1851; repr., New York: AMS Press, 1976), 5, 9. For more on Nell, who is considered among the first African American historians, see Earl Smith, "William Cooper Nell on the Fugitive Slave Act," *Journal of Negro History* 66, no. 1 (1981): 37–40. For an appreciation of Nell's significance and that of other black abolitionists in redirecting the dialogue on freedom, see Scott Hancock, "'Tradition Informs Us': African Americans' Construction of Memory in the Antebellum North," in *Slavery, Resistance, Freedom,* ed. Gabor S. Boritt and Scott Hancock (New York: Oxford University Press, 2007), 51–56; and David W. Blight, "They Knew What Time It Was: African-Americans and the Coming of the Civil War," in *Why the Civil War Came,* ed. Gabor S. Boritt (New York: Oxford University Press, 1996), 51–77. On the "Bucks of America," see Sidney Kaplan and Emma Nogrady Kaplan, *The Black Presence in the Era of the American Revolution,* rev. ed. (Amherst: University of Massachusetts Press, 1989), 65–66.

21. William Cooper Nell, *The Colored Patriots of the American Revolution* (Boston: Robert F. Wallcut, 1855; repr., New York: Arno Press, 1968), 9 (Nell), 6 (Stowe), 9 (Whittier).

22. Nell, *Services of Colored Americans,* 12, 5; *Colored Patriots of the American Revolution,* 21. For an extensive and illuminating study of the erasure of the black presence, see Kaplan and Kaplan, *Black Presence in the Era of the American Revolution,* esp. 21–23.

23. Kaplan and Kaplan, *Black Presence in the Era of the American Revolution,* 10, 49–50.

24. Thomas Hart Benton, *Historical and Legal Examination of That Part of the Decision of the Supreme Court of the United States in the Dred Scott Case, which Declares the Unconstitutionality of the Missouri Compromise Act, and the Self-Extension of the Constitution to Territories, Carrying Slavery along With It* (New York: D. Appleton, 1857), 3, 11, 51, 54, 94, 44.

25. Ibid., 130, 103.

26. Roy Rosenzweig and David P. Thelen, *The Presence of the Past: Popular Uses of History in American Life* (New York: Columbia University Press, 1998), 1–3; David Lowenthal, *The Heritage Crusade and the Spoils of History* (New York: Cambridge University Press, 1998), x.

27. Christopher L. Tomlins describes how, historically, interdisciplinarity in legal scholarship reflects law's "disciplinary insufficiency as a modality of explanation and legitimation of the results in its interactions with audiences it must convince," and he argues forcefully that when law intersects with other disciplines, "Mostly . . . law wins." "Framing the Field of Law's Encounters: A Historical Narrative," *Law and Society Review* 34, no. 4 (2000): 911, 967.

28. Editors' introduction, *Slavery and Public History: The Tough Stuff of American Memory,* ed. James Oliver Horton and Lois E. Horton (New York: New Press, 2006), xi.

29. Norman W. Spaulding, "Constitution as Countermonument: Federalism, Reconstruction, and the Problem of Collective Memory," *Columbia Law Review* 103, no. 8 (2003): 1998–99.

30. Peter Novick, *That Noble Dream: The "Objectivity Question" and the American Historical Profession* (New York: Cambridge University Press, 1988), 2.

31. For judicial critique and a call for "more practical scholarship," see Harry T. Edwards, "The Growing Disjunction between Legal Education and the Legal Profession," *Michigan Law Review* 91, no. 1 (1992): 47, 34. For a survey of how the newer trends in historical inquiry have influenced other disciplines, see Terrence J. McDonald, ed., *The Historic Turn in the Human Sciences* (Ann Arbor: University of Michigan Press, 1999), especially Robert W. Gordon, "The Past as Authority and as Social Critic: Stabilizing and Destabilizing Functions of History in Legal Argument," 339–78. For a warning that such a direction in the writing of history threatens to alienate its users and become irrelevant, see Gordon S. Wood, *The Purpose of the Past: Reflections on the Uses of History* (New York: Penguin Press, 2008).

TWO

Dred Scott versus the *Dred Scott* Case

The History and Memory of a Signal Moment in American Slavery, 1857–2007

Adam Arenson

NEWS OF the decision reached St. Louis before the end of the day. On March 6, 1857, Chief Justice Roger Brooke Taney gathered the U.S. Supreme Court to deliver the decision in *Dred Scott v. Sandford.* The result was telegraphed throughout the country all afternoon: "The act of Congress which prohibits citizens from holding property of this character north of a certain line is not warranted by the constitution, and is therefore void," Taney announced, "and neither Dred Scott nor any one of his family were made free by their residence in Illinois."[1]

The complexities of law embedded in the *Dred Scott* case were immediately controversial, and they remain the focus of intense legal and historical scholarship. Yet something very peculiar often happens in these accounts. The Scott family—Dred, Harriet, and their daughters, Eliza and Lizzie— often disappear. In each round of the case, the location, occupation, and journeys of the Scott family were at issue. But in the recorded history, after March 6, 1857, the Scotts suddenly fade, as if their lives ended that day in the courthouse. They did not.

The one hundred and fifty years between the *Dred Scott* decision and the most recent round of commemorations has been a period of tumult in the United States. After a brief window of opportunity during the Civil War and Reconstruction, the lives of African Americans remained scarred by the legacies of slavery and the doctrines of white supremacy, an atmosphere of vitriol that has lifted only in the past half century. Stripping back the inaccuracies to recover the true lives of slaves is only recently a scholarly priority, and finding Dred Scott and his family has been an ongoing task.[2]

In his Pulitzer Prize–winning analysis of the *Dred Scott* case, historian Don Fehrenbacher noted that "what has been believed about the Dred Scott case . . . became in itself a discernible historical force," but he only gestured to these "pseudo-recollections" before framing the case's significance in the realm of precedents and civil rights. In the same year, Walter Ehrlich published an insightful look at the Scotts' lives and the course of the case but openly admitted how "the impact of the decision is not within the scope of this monograph."[3] While a few recent articles have engaged both elements, the separation of the history of the Scott family from the memory of the *Dred Scott* case has generally been perpetuated.[4]

Elsewhere I have examined how the *Dred Scott* decision catalyzed the transformation of St. Louis politics, turning Missouri toward gradual emancipation just as the South's proslavery advocates were declaring victory.[5] And I have described how the Scotts' lives were recovered to memory through the actions spearheaded by their descendants.[6] Here I chronicle how the legacies of the *Dred Scott* case were long divorced from the fate and commemoration of the Scott family, in political rhetoric as well as scholarly dialogue. To reunite the Scott family and the *Dred Scott* case is to add the human cost to the legal significance of this signal moment in American history.

Taney's decision in the *Dred Scott* case did not change the legal status of the Scott family; it merely reaffirmed the Missouri Supreme Court's judgment in *Scott v. Emerson*. Neither was it a surprise, as the outcome—including which justices dissented—had been leaked months before (see fig. 2.1).[7] Yet the decision did catapult the words "Dred Scott" into political shorthand, placing the name of an unknown African American at the center of the controversy over slavery. As Donn Pratt, a political observer in Cincinnati,

> We give this morning a report that the Judges of the U. S. Supreme Court have agreed upon their decision in the case of Dred Scott, and that on the point of the Missouri compromise the opinion of a majority of the Judges is adverse to the constitutionality of the act of 1820. The report, however, can scarcely be regarded as authentic. It is not probable that the Judges have made their decision as yet, or that they would allow the result of their deliberations to reach the public in the present stage of the subject.

FIGURE 2.1. Despite the political controversy caused by the *Dred Scott* decision, the outcome was not a surprise to legal observers; it had been revealed in newspaper articles such as this, months before the official announcement. "Case of Dred Scott," *Boston Daily Advertiser,* January 2, 1857, issue 2, col F. Image provided by 19th Century U.S. Newspapers, a Gale Digital Collection, a part of Cengage Learning

observed to his antislavery ally George R. Harrington ten days after the decision was made, "The Dred Scott decision . . . sinks deep into the minds of the American people."[8]

What did the *Dred Scott* decision mean for the Scott family, and for St. Louis? Despite the increasingly heated rhetoric in national newspapers, the *Dred Scott* decision seemed hardly to change anything in St. Louis. Manumissions and filings for freedom bonds did not significantly increase or decrease.[9] The St. Louis University Philalethic Society proposed the question, "Has congress the ~~power~~ right to abolish slavery in the territories?" at their first meeting after the decision was announced, but then they did not debate it for months.[10] In local newspapers, other concerns predominated, but the true reaction came during St. Louis's April elections, when the emancipationist ticket shocked the nation with its victory.[11]

After the decision the Scott family remained slaves, but the notoriety of the case raised them up from the anonymity of their race, their condition, and their menial work.[12] Reporters sought Scott out, and one who seemingly received Dred Scott's cooperation noted that escape to freedom had often been available, but that Dred Scott was now "insisting on abiding by the principles involved in the decision." In the only known words attributed directly to Dred Scott, he described how the prolonged nature of the case had provided him "a 'heap o' trouble,' he says, and if he had known that 'it was gwine to last so long,' he would not have brought it." Scott was "tired of running about" and anxious to secure the purchase of his family. In the final sentence, "he says grinningly, that he could make thousands of dollars, if allowed, by traveling over the country and telling who he is."[13] This brief speech of Dred Scott's accentuates how even the most famous slaves were lost to history.

On May 26, 1857, the Scott family attained its freedom. In the national news, Irene Emerson's second husband Calvin Chaffee, now a Republican representative from Massachusetts, claimed horror to learn that he might be the owner of Dred Scott. Yet his fright may have been staged, perhaps an aftereffect of allowing his wife's St. Louis allies to continue the case with his tacit approval and simply hoping for the opposite result.[14] The Blow family had worked to gain title and purchase the family's freedom. Yet, after the *Dred Scott* decision, what could freedom mean for the family or anyone of African descent? The *Hartford Daily Courant* stated the contradiction directly: "Dred Scott is a slave no more," the editors wrote. "Being a freeman, in spite of Chief Justice Taney, we suppose he now has no rights which white men are bound to respect."[15]

Despite the legal limits, celebrity status attached to the Scott family. Dred Scott "is well known to many of our citizens, and may frequently be seen passing along Third Street," the *St. Louis News* reported.[16] Travelers noted meeting him in the street or at church.[17] A *Leslie's Illustrated* correspondent inquiring at the Scotts' alley address brought a rebuke from Harriet—her only recorded words—that suggested she was tired of the attention. "What white man arter dad nigger for?" the dialect depiction read. "Why don't white man 'tend to his business, and let dat nigger 'lone?" Harriet was adamant that Dred would do no touring and that "she'd always been able to yarn her own livin, thank God." The *Leslie's* reporter succeeded in cajoling the Scott family into the local photography studio, and the result made the front cover of the newsmagazine (see figs. 2.2, 2.3, and 2.4).[18] That June, Abraham Lincoln addressed the Republican State Convention in Springfield and discussed the *Dred Scott* decision. He denied that "because I do not want

FIGURES 2.2, 2.3, AND 2.4. Despite the legal limits, celebrity status attached to the Scott family. After the loss in the U.S. Supreme Court and the family's emancipation by Taylor Blow, Dred and Harriet Scott, with their daughters Lizzie and Eliza, were cajoled into the local photography studio by a *Leslie's* reporter, and the resulting engraving appeared on the magazine cover. They entered the visual record dignified, but without joy. Dred Scott, Harriet Scott, and Eliza and Lizzie Scott, *Leslie's Illustrated,* June 1857. Image provided by 19th Century U.S. Newspapers, a Gale Digital Collection, a part of Cengage Learning

a black woman for a *slave* I must necessarily want her for a *wife.*" Rather, he said, "I can just leave her alone . . . in her natural right to eat the bread she earns with her own hands."[19] To work and be left alone—this is what Harriet Scott sought. Yet, even unbound, the *Dred Scott* decision stood in her way.

"I look forward to a great reaction in regard to the Slavery question," George Caleb Bingham, the master painter and sometime Whig politician of Missouri, wrote home from the art studios in Düsseldorf in June 1857, keeping up on local politics. In the same letter Bingham discussed his latest painting, "a large picture of 'life on the Mississippi' . . . far ahead of any work of that Class which I have yet undertaken."[20] The painting, *Jolly Flatboatmen at Port* (1857), reflects the impact of the *Dred Scott* case (see fig. 2.5).[21] In the earlier *The Jolly Flatboatmen* (1846), a young man danced on the top of the flatboat, arms spread carefree over the wide expanse of river.[22] Now Bingham constricted the river panorama, multiplied the hints of nostalgia, and heightened the contrasts by placing a black dockworker among the new figures. He stood with a relaxed pose, his face breaking into a smile, his height equal to that of the fiddle player on the opposite side of the compositional pyramid.

This was no casual decision. The work of William Sidney Mount, an earlier master of American genre painting whom Bingham admired, used the sharing of music to suggest connections between workers across the barriers of race and class.[23] For an expatriate Missourian sympathetic to antislavery, the *Dred Scott* decision intimated narrowed horizons and change along the river. It seems no coincidence that the white man's pole, coming up between the dancer and the African American enjoying his performance, gives the silhouette of a rifle pointed to the sky.

Closer to home, former Senator Thomas Hart Benton took a keen interest in the *Dred Scott* decision, declaring it no victory for either side. "Far from settling the question, the opinion itself has become a new question,"

FIGURE 2.5. Though he was in Düsseldorf when the *Dred Scott* case was decided, the politically active Missouri painter George Caleb Bingham returned to his signature works, but with an eye to the changed times. Adding an African American to the scene of dancing flatboatmen, Bingham commented on the *Dred Scott* decision as a moment of narrowed horizons and change along the river. George Caleb Bingham, *Jolly Flatboatmen at Port,* 1857, St. Louis Art Museum

Benton wrote.[24] As David Konig has noted in this volume, Benton's questions joined those of African Americans, resisting the *Dred Scott* decision by insisting on the importance of historical events as they remembered them, not only as glossed by Taney and other judges.[25] "We shall not, in this place, call in question the judgment of the learned Chief Justice," local African American chronicler Cyprian Clamorgan wrote of the *Dred Scott* decision in his pamphlet *The Colored Aristocracy of St. Louis*—but then proceeded to suggest it was because Taney "has in this State kindred of a darker hue than himself."[26] Beginning in 1858, black community leaders in Boston took the *Dred Scott* decision as an impetus to protest and celebrate the martyrdom of Crispus Attucks, killed March 5, 1770. As they took to the streets that week, they kept in mind the martyrdom under way for Dred Scott as well.[27] Defiant pride mixed with mournful nostalgia as free African Americans were buffeted by the same forces that limited their slave brethren.

On September 17, 1858, Dred Scott died. The most prominent political newspapers all noted his passing: "Few men who have achieved greatness have won it so effectually as this black champion," the *New York Times* declared, reviewing his life circumstances, the family left behind, and the sour way in which Dred Scott became "accidentally but ineffaceably associated" with Taney's decision. The editors were sure that "the adverse decision he encountered here will there meet with reversal," in "the Supreme Court above."[28] Left earthbound, however, was the *Dred Scott* case. The *Daily National Intelligencer* knew most would welcome it if "all the useless strife connected with his name . . . also died," yet the editors understood that was fruitless, as "at present the whole State of Illinois is agitated by the question what does Senator DOUGLAS say of Dred?"[29] As the Lincoln-Douglas debates turned on parsing of the *Dred Scott* case, the Scotts themselves were ever more abstracted.

Even as the *Dred Scott* case remained central to the struggles of the Civil War and Reconstruction, Harriet Scott, her daughters, sons-in-law, and grandchildren kept out of the news. When Wesleyan Cemetery in St. Louis was closed in 1867, Taylor Blow arranged for Dred Scott's reinterment in Calvary Cemetery.[30] Though the ex-slave community had begun a fund to erect a monument, "its originators failed in their project," a newspaper article would recall, and the grave remained unmarked.[31] On June 17, 1876, Harriet Scott passed away at the home of her daughter and son-in-law, Eliza and

Wilson Madison. She was buried in the Greenwood Cemetery, her grave also without a headstone.[32] The blank graves mirrored the greater effacing: As the white communities north and south worked to reunify the country in the wake of Reconstruction, they worked to put the *Dred Scott* case behind them.[33] Now memory too could bury Dred and Harriet Scott.

As I have examined elsewhere, a small number of white St. Louisans resisted the general amnesia about the Scotts during the Jim Crow era.[34] In 1882, Mary L. Barnum, whose husband had owned the hotel where Dred Scott had worked, commissioned Scott's portrait for the Missouri Historical Society.[35] For the dedication of the portrait, the historical society turned to James Milton Turner, a St. Louis County freedman politician who had been the Grant administration's ambassador to Liberia. The dedication of this portrait, Turner argued, demonstrated "the strict impartiality of all true history," integrating the story of how "the Negro has been with us . . . from the very beginning of the history of our State, and, indeed, of the nation itself." Turner saw in Dred Scott an African American having "carved his humble niche in the temple of time."[36] (*His* indeed; this was for Dred Scott alone. For the next century, Harriet Scott was to fall victim to the double bind of race and sex. Her presence and her actions in filing and then encouraging her husband in the case were hardly mentioned again until the late twentieth century.[37])

Turner congratulated not a true acknowledgment of Dred Scott but his own dreams for opening a racially segregated American society, which would come to naught. The *Dred Scott* case was a known quantity in Jim Crow America, but its specifics were denatured to the point where they could serve as fodder for humor. "What's this Dead Scott decision about?" a Mrs. Wigglesworth asked her husband, according to a vignette in the 1883 *San Francisco Daily Evening Bulletin.* "Dread Scott—not Dead Scott," Mr. Wigglesworth said, but with this correction of sorts made, his knowledge also ran out. He is recorded adding, "Something to do with the Mexican War."[38] In Gilded Age America, facts began to slip away as the social standing of African Americans declined.

In 1886, the *St. Louis Daily Globe* marked the thirtieth anniversary of the *Dred Scott* case by reengraving the images of Dred, Harriet, and Eliza Scott and adding a portrait of John Madison, one of two surviving grandsons (see figs. 2.6, 2.7, 2.8, and 2.9). Yet no quotes from Scott descendants accompanied the images. Instead, the reporter questioned Thomas C. Reynolds, a former secessionist governor of Missouri who in 1857 had been U.S. district attorney in St. Louis. "Scott was a very respected negro," Reynolds

FIGURES 2.6, 2.7, 2.8, AND 2.9. On the thirtieth anniversary of the *Dred Scott* decision, the *St. Louis Daily Globe* reengraved the daguerreotypes of Dred, Harriet, and Eliza Scott and added an image of John Madison, one of Dred and Harriet Scott's two surviving grandsons. Yet the reporter included no quotes from the Scott descendants, instead interviewing Thomas C. Reynolds, a former secessionist governor of Missouri, who recalled the *Dred Scott* case but no specifics about the Scotts. Dred Scott, Harriet Scott, Eliza Scott, and John Madison, *St. Louis Daily Globe,* 1886. Image provided by 19th Century U.S. Newspapers, a Gale Digital Collection, a part of Cengage Learning.

observed, but he then said his recollections of the case were of the national attention, more than any specifics of the individuals involved.[39]

"What Became of Dred Scott?" the *Globe-Democrat* asked when Scott's portrait was given a place of honor at the 1904 World's Fair. And—despite the record present in the newspaper's own files—the reporter claimed Scott had lived past the Civil War. He quoted St. Louisans who recalled Dred as a cook during the St. Louis visit of the Prince of Wales in 1860. He even claimed—through senility? owing to racism-laced ventriloquism?—that James Milton Turner had said he had seen Scott in St. Louis in the 1870s.[40] Such stories held currency for white St. Louisans: in 1923 an "old-timer," Eugene H. Lahee, repeated the Prince of Wales anecdote and revealed Lahee's supposed encounter with Dred Scott as a bank janitor in 1868.[41] It is hard to know whether Lahee transferred the name of Dred Scott to any African American with a servile post, or whether African Americans were willingly playing on the prejudices of whites.

"I distinctly remember Dred Scott among the family servants," Julia Webster Blow wrote in 1907, calling him a "pensioner of the Blows until his death . . . never hunted nor sought after cruelly in his eventful life again."[42] Though Blow's words painted a sympathetic picture, her correspondent, Mary Louise Dalton, librarian of the Missouri Historical Society, summed it up differently: Scott was a "no-account nigger."[43] She told as much to her research patron, *Harper's* correspondent and amateur historian Frederick Trevor Hill. He then called Scott "a shiftless, incapable specimen" in his finished work.[44] Based more on racist prejudice than any recourse to fact, this characterization was repeated for decades.[45]

While the Scott family was being maligned, the power of the *Dred Scott* case in political rhetoric remained: In 1913, just after his defeat as a Bull Moose candidate, former president Theodore Roosevelt spoke of "the Dred Scott decisions of our own time; of decisions like the tenement-house cigar-factory decision, like the bakeshop decision, like the Knight Sugar Case, like the Workmen's Compensation Act decision." Citing Lincoln as his inspiration, Roosevelt said that "we mean to reverse [these cases], and we mean to do it peaceably."[46] The case was also wielded as a weapon of ridicule. In 1911, the University of Missouri yearbook, amid nicknames and witticisms, stated that John M. Slaughter, a junior in the College of Agriculture, "lives in constant fear of the Dred Scott Decision," a menacing if vague sobriquet (see fig. 2.10).[47] Even attempts to dignify the

John M. Slaughter
Grand View
Delta Theta Sigma, P.
  of H.
*❲Lives in constant fear
of the Dred Scott De-
cision. A little man who
expects to be a big
farmer.*

FIGURE 2.10. In the early twentieth century, the Scotts were forgotten, and the *Dred Scott* case was casually and abstractly referenced by defenders and detractors. Among the nicknames and witticisms, the claim that junior John M. Slaughter of the College of Agriculture "lives in constant fear of the Dred Scott Decision" is a menacing if vague testimonial to the times. 1911 *Savitar* (yearbook), University Archives, University of Missouri at Columbia

Scotts leapt free from the historical record. Walter B. Stevens, the dean of turn-of-last-century St. Louis historians, depicted Dred Scott as "the St. Louis slave who looked like an African king," though he gave no hint of his inspiration for such an idea.[48]

By the time of the publication of the *Dictionary of American Biography* in 1935, it was canonical that Dred Scott was "shiftless and unreliable, and therefore frequently unemployed and without means to support his family." The dictionary restored the correct date of his death, but the Dred Scott it presented was merely a placeholder for the actions of others—bought, sold, freedom filed for by others, court case fought by others. "The ignorant and illiterate Negro," Thomas S. Barclay pronounced there, "comprehended little of its significance, but signed his mark to the petition in the suit."[49] The memory of Dred and Harriet Scott had reached its nadir.

In the early twentieth century, the differences between Dred Scott and the *Dred Scott* case reached new extremes in the divided memory of whites and

African Americans. As Supreme Court justice George Sutherland proudly cited the *Dred Scott* case in a 1934 dissent that grounded originalism,[50] another perspective was also emerging. In 1937, Nathan B. Young Jr. published *Your St. Louis and Mine,* a compendium of African American history and culture in the city, in which he devoted two pages to Dred Scott and his descendants. Young had been born in Tuskegee, Alabama, in 1894, in the house next door to his father's mentor, Booker T. Washington; he graduated from Florida A&M in 1915 and Yale Law School in 1918, and moved to St. Louis in 1927 to serve as a lawyer in that segregated city.[51] Declaring that received history had "paid little attention to Dred Scott as a man and pictured him as a puppet, as a simpleton," Young instead argued that, better than his white contemporaries, Scott understood both the conditions of his slavery and the national import of his case.[52] Young openly challenged the white memories of slavery and Reconstruction.

In the wake of the New Deal and World War II, the struggle against segregation and for civil rights opened new connections between Dred and Harriet Scott and the *Dred Scott* case. Marcus A. Murphy, on trial as a communist in St. Louis in 1954, declared to the jury how he was proud that "I can at least speak to you as a human being." Repeating Taney's phrase, Murphy said it was "ninety-seven years ago" when "another Negro stood in federal court to hear . . . that he was not a human being and had no rights which a white man was bound to respect."[53] That year the *Brown v. Board of Education* decision repudiated formal segregation, and Rosa Parks refused to move from her bus seat. The time had come for Dred Scott's resurrection.

It was a genealogist, the Reverend Edward Dowling, S.J., who rediscovered Scott's grave site in time for the centennial of the *Dred Scott* case in 1957. Dowling spoke of a modest effort to mark the resting place. "We have in mind putting up only a simple monument," he told the newspapers. "Then if someone some day wants to put up a better monument it will at least be known where Dred Scott lies." Awareness of the Scott descendants was also renewed: the article contained a photograph of great-grandson John A. Madison with his wife and children. Madison was a postal worker studying for a law degree. He was preparing to argue cases in the "courts in which Dred Scott couldn't even sue."[54]

On March 6, 1957, Scott's descendants and Father Dowling joined the president of the St. Louis University Law School Student Bar Association to lay a wreath on the still unmarked grave, following ceremonies in the Old Courthouse (see fig. 2.11).[55] When the granddaughter of Taylor Blow came

FIGURE 2.11. Genealogist Father Edward Dowling, S.J., rediscovered Dred Scott's unmarked grave in time for the centennial of the *Dred Scott* case. "We have in mind putting up only a simple monument," he told reporters. "Then if someone some day wants to put up a better monument it will at least be known where Dred Scott lies." Father Dowling indicates Dred Scott's grave to John A. Madison, the Scotts' great-grandson, and his family. *St. Louis Globe-Democrat,* February 10, 1957. Courtesy of the St. Louis Globe-Democrat Archives of the St. Louis Mercantile Library at the University of Missouri–St. Louis

forward to pay for a gravestone, one commentator, Frank P. O'Hare, a socialist and local journalist, worried about the symbolism. "A hundred years has not erased the ideology of the slave owners," O'Hare charged, as forces still aligned to prevent "a monument for a slave to overtop the monument for the master."[56] Yet as O'Hare was writing, change was coming, with federal troops desegregating Little Rock High School. The efforts of Young, Dowling, and O'Hare reunited the historical particulars of Dred and Harriet Scott's actions with the conditions of slavery and the memory of the *Dred Scott* case.

In 1965, Nathan B. Young Jr. was appointed the first African American municipal court judge in St. Louis, and he linked his vocation with his avocation for the history of African American St. Louis. With his customary enthusiasm, in a 1979 speech Young called Dred Scott "undoubtedly the paramount figure in all American history and law!"[57] Young imagined Scott's life in a novel, *Dred the Revelator,* and in many poems.[58] And Young condemned Taney's decision as "suspect law—garbled history—and shoddy sociology," seeing it as a moment that horribly delayed the march of civil rights.[59] Young's efforts mixed history and myth to vividly and viscerally recall the person of Dred Scott.

By the time the Association for the Study of Afro-American Life and History placed the first historical marker on the Old Courthouse in 1977, indignant responses to the *Dred Scott* case had become more common. John A. Madison,

BREAKING the CHAINS
of
SLAVERY
DRED SCOTT
IN MEMORIAM
JUNE 24, 1977

Dr. John A Madison

FIGURE 2.12. The Scotts' great-grandson John A. Madison Jr. provided the invocation and designed the bold program illustration for the ceremony to commemorate the Scotts' efforts at the Old Courthouse, organized with the Association for the Study of Afro-American Life and History, the originators of Black History Month. "Breaking the Chains of Slavery," National Historic Marker Ceremony at the Old Courthouse, June 24, 1977. Courtesy of St. Louis University Archives, Nathan B. Young Collection, as well as Lynne M. Jackson and the Dred Scott Heritage Foundation

now juris doctor, provided the invocation, introduced his family, and created "Breaking the Chains of Slavery," the bold program illustration (see fig. 2.12).[60] The Scott relatives emphasized their ancestors' actions and their personal stories, stepping beyond the mere invocation of Dred Scott's name.

In the years since, such recoveries have continued. Harriet Scott received a cenotaph in 1999, reacknowledging her struggle alongside her husband and for her children.[61] In 2000, Dred and Harriet Scott's petitions for freedom were retrieved from storage and placed on display at the main branch of the St. Louis Public Library, their "X"s speaking across history and leading scholars toward hundreds of other freedom petitions.[62] In 2006, the true resting place of Harriet Scott was finally rediscovered, and a full-scale biography of this remarkable woman appeared in 2009.[63] A new plaque was affixed to the Old Courthouse, emphasizing the actions of the Scotts in their own legal proceedings and in precipitating the Civil War (see fig. 2.13).[64] In time for the 150th anniversary of the *Dred Scott* case, three novels about Dred Scott were published, two of which imagine the case from Scott's perspective and one from that of a young lawyer working on his case (see fig. 2.14).[65] They suggest a renewed effort to engage with the Scotts themselves and to think through their experience.

The Old Courthouse

On April 6, 1846, a slave named Dred Scott and his wife Harriet sued for their freedom in this courthouse. The Scotts had been taken by their owner to free jurisdictions and then returned to Missouri, a slave state. In 1857, Chief Justice Roger B. Taney of the U.S. Supreme Court announced the decision in the case of Dred Scott v. Sandford. He stated that Americans of African ancestry were not eligible to be citizens, based on the historical claim that they had no rights which the white man was bound to respect. Taney's opinion also declared that Congress could not prevent the spread of slavery into the Western territories. This decision fueled sectional conflict which led to the Civil War.

FIGURE 2.13. Not until 2006 was a new plaque placed at the Old Courthouse, displaying images of both Dred and Harriet Scott and emphasizing their efforts in their own legal proceedings as well as the importance of their claims within the *Dred Scott* case in precipitating the Civil War. Image courtesy of the National Park Service, Jefferson National Expansion Memorial

FIGURE 2.14. As the 150th anniversary of the *Dred Scott* case approached, the value of describing the case from Dred Scott's perspective inspired at least three writers of fiction, including Mary E. Neighbour, author of *Speak Right On*. These works demonstrate the renewed effort to engage with the Scotts themselves, and to think through their experience. Cover of *Speak Right On*, 2006, copyright © 2006 The Toby Press LLC

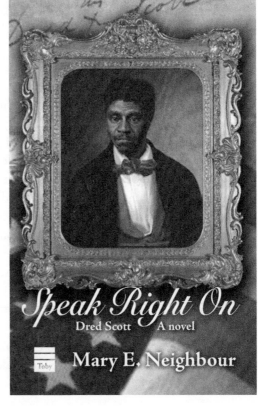

Speak Right On
Dred Scott   A novel

Mary E. Neighbour

Despite this recovery, the *Dred Scott* case has remained more a symbol to some. Fantastically, abortion opponents have equated *Roe v. Wade* with the *Dred Scott* case, imagining a world inside its injustices for their arguments.[66] In his 1996 dissent from *Planned Parenthood v. Casey*, Supreme Court justice Antonin Scalia invoked the 1859 portrait of Taney, reflecting on what he saw as its "expression of profound sadness and disillusionment . . . how the lustre of his great Chief Justiceship came to be eclipsed by *Dred Scott*," with danger to the Court and the nation in tow.[67] President George W. Bush also hinted at this interpretation in 2004, when he mentioned the *Dred Scott* case as an adequate test for his judicial nominees, not noting the irony of making the comment while in St. Louis for a presidential debate.[68]

Yet the damage done by such legal analogies is evident when the true historical context for the cases is not only recovered but considered as fundamental to a contemporary perspective on justice. Legal naming conventions encourage the separation of personhood from plaintiffs and defendants: referencing *Dred Scott v. Sandford*, or *Plessy v. Ferguson*, or *Korematsu v. United States*, lawyers rarely reference Dred and Harriet Scott, Homer A. Plessy, or Toyosaburo Korematsu. Yet, as this account of forgetting and recovering Dred and Harriet Scott demonstrates, the denigration of legal actors can do as much to sway our opinion of a case as the legal arguments made. True justice will come from recovering the heroic actions taken by those in painful, controversial cases and by judging their stinging defeats as an indictment of past American law and politics.

The cause of integrating the *Dred Scott* case to its context within the lives of Dred and Harriet Scott—and not the other way around—continues today, and the descendants of Dred and Harriet Scott remain its most prominent advocates. In 2007, Dred and Harriet Scott's great-great-granddaughter, Lynne Jackson Madison, founded the Dred Scott Heritage Foundation to promote anniversary events and to raise money for a life-size statue of Scott at the Old Courthouse, "as a memorial to the man and his cause," together. The foundation's events will provide a forum for evaluation of and reflection on the continuing impact of the Scott family, within and beyond their legal action.[69]

The *Dred Scott* case is known to every American lawyer and to practically every American student. But for too long the efforts and dreams of

Dred and Harriet Scott have been forgotten, discounted, or excluded, even as they ostensibly have been remembered. The search for their history—in conjunction as well as in contradistinction to the case—connects the traumas of slavery with the struggles for civil rights in the following century, and it places the system of legal precedent under scrutiny. Personal stories can strengthen our ability to grapple with the unfathomable legacies of slavery, with the unspoken contexts of American history lost amid legal formalisms. Dred Scott and his wife Harriet were and are more than just symbols. In the fight between the *Dred Scott* case and Dred and Harriet Scott, critical perspectives and historical recovery let their heroic acts of resistance finally win out.

Notes

This paper has benefited from the comments at the Washington University School of Law conference as well as from Sophia Lee, Gretchen Heefner, Jenifer Van Vleck, Theresa Runstedtler, Caroline Sherman, Helen Veit, and Katherine Foshko and from the support of the Gilder Lehrman Center for the Study of Slavery, Resistance, and Abolition.

1. "The Dred Scott Case," *New York Herald,* March 9, 1857, 1. The printed version of Taney's decision was revised and the language changed slightly: Walter Ehrlich, *They Have No Rights: Dred Scott's Struggle for Freedom* (Westport, Conn.: Greenwood Press, 1979), 137–43.

2. The newest and most accurate accounts are Ruth Ann Hager, *Dred and Harriet Scott: Their Family Story* (St. Louis: St. Louis County Library, 2010), and Lea VanderVelde, *Mrs. Dred Scott: A Life on Slavery's Frontier* (New York: Oxford University Press, 2009). For general problems in the history of slavery and American memory, see James Oliver Horton and Lois E. Horton, eds., *Slavery and Public History: The Tough Stuff of American Memory* (New York: New Press, 2006).

3. Don E. Fehrenbacher, *The Dred Scott Case, Its Significance in American Law and Politics* (New York: Oxford University Press, 1978), 572, 70, 72, 93; Ehrlich, *They Have No Rights,* 238n1.

4. Important recent exceptions include Lea VanderVelde and Sandhya Subramanian, "Mrs. Dred Scott," *Yale Law Journal* 106, no. 4 (1997): 1033–1122; and Barbara Bennett Woodhouse, "Dred Scott's Daughters: Nineteenth Century Urban Girls at the Intersection of Race and Patriarchy," *Buffalo Law Review* 48 (Fall 2000): 669–701.

5. Adam Arenson, "City of Manifest Destiny: St. Louis and the Cultural Civil War, 1848–1877" (Ph.D. diss., Yale University, 2008), chap. 5.

6. Adam Arenson, "Freeing Dred Scott: St. Louis Confronts an Icon of Slavery, 1857–2007," *Common-Place* 8, no. 3 (2008), http://www.common-place.org/vol-08/no-03/arenson/.

7. *New York Herald,* January 1, 1857; "Case of Dred Scott," *Boston Daily Adver-tiser,* January 2, 1857.

8. Donn Pratt to George R. Harrington, March 18, 1857, George R. Harrington Papers, Missouri Historical Society, St. Louis.

9. My analysis of this data is ongoing, relying on the list of emancipations regis-tered in the St. Louis Circuit Court, 1817–65, compiled in 2006 by Robert Moore Jr., National Park Service-Jefferson National Expansion Memorial, and Kristin Zapalac, Missouri Department of Natural Resources; and the list of freedom bonds from the Dexter P. Tiffany Collection compiled by Dennis Northcutt and Molly Kodner, Missouri Historical Society. Thanks to Bob Moore, Dennis Northcutt, and Molly Kodner for making these lists available.

10. March 18, 1857, and January 1, 1858, meetings, St. Louis University Histori-cal Records, Philalethic Society Minutes, 1850–63, St. Louis University Archives.

11. See Arenson, "City of Manifest Destiny," chap. 5.

12. For the sense of not being seen, Horton and Horton, eds., *Slavery and Pub-lic History;* Woodhouse, "Dred Scott's Daughters," 397.

13. "The Original Dred Scott a Resident of St. Louis—A Sketch of His History," *St. Louis [Daily Evening] News,* April 3, 1857. For similar estimations of appearance and age, "Visit to Dred Scott—His Family—Incidents of His Life—Decision of the Supreme Court," *Frank Leslie's Illustrated Newspaper,* IV, no. 82 (June 27, 1857).

14. Ehrlich, *They Have No Rights,* 180–81; Fehrenbacher, *Dred Scott Case,* 420–21, 473, 663n20. On the idea that Chaffee sought a ruling as a test deci-sion, see Albert P. Blaustein and Robert L. Zangrando, *Civil Rights and Afri-can Americans: A Documentary History* (Evanston, Ill.: Northwestern University Press, 1991), 147.

15. "General News," *Hartford Daily Courant,* May 28, 1857. For a different view, see Hager, *Dred and Harriet Scott,* 33–44.

16. "The Original Dred Scott a Resident of St. Louis."

17. One such traveler is Charles Elliott, "Correspondence. [Letter to Brother Haven]," *Zion's Herald and Wesleyan Journal* (July 25, 1857; printed September 23, 1857).

18. "Visit to Dred Scott."

19. Abraham Lincoln, "Speech at Springfield, June 27, 1857," in *The Collected Works of Abraham Lincoln,* ed. Roy P. Basler, 8 vols. (New Brunswick, N.J.: Rut-gers University Press, 1953–55), 2:405, 404, 401.

20. George Caleb Bingham to James Rollins, June 3, 1857, James Rollins Pa-pers, folder 39, Western Historical Manuscript Collections, Columbia, Mo.

21. Despite recording the letters and Bingham's politics, the connection be-tween the painting and the *Dred Scott* decision has not been made elsewhere.

For a brief discussion of the black dancing figures in relation to Mount and minstrelsy—but not politics—see Louis Gerteis, "Shaping the Authentic: St. Louis Theater Culture and the Construction of American Social Types, 1815–1860," in *St. Louis in the Century of Henry Shaw: A View beyond the Garden Wall*, ed. Eric Sandweiss (Columbia: University of Missouri Press, 2003), 212–15.

22. George Caleb Bingham, *The Jolly Flatboatmen*, 1846, The Manoogian Collection.

23. See brief mention of the influence in Jonathan Weinberg, "The Artist and the Politician—George Caleb Bingham," *Art in America* 88, no. 10 (2000): 138–45.

24. Thomas Hart Benton, *Historical and Legal Examination of That Part of the Decision of the Supreme Court of the United States in the Dred Scott Case, Which Declares the Unconstitutionality of the Missouri Compromise Act, and the Self-Extension of the Constitution to Territories, Carrying Slavery along with It* (New York: D. Appleton, 1857), 5.

25. David Thomas Konig, "Constitutional Law and the Legitimation of History: The Enduring Force of Roger Taney's 'opinion of the court,'" chapter 1 in this volume.

26. Cyprian Clamorgan, *The Colored Aristocracy of St. Louis* (St. Louis, 1858; repr., ed. Julie Winch, Columbia: University of Missouri Press, 1999), 47. Winch notes that no standard Taney biography corroborates Clamorgan's claim, but given his slaveholding lineage in Maryland and the nature of slave knowledge about parentage I find the claim plausible (69n16).

27. Elizabeth Rauh Bethel, *The Roots of African-American Identity: Memory and History in the Antebellum Free Communities* (New York: St. Martin's Press, 1997), 1–28. Thanks to Jill Lepore for this reference.

28. "Dred Scott," *New York Times*, September 21, 1858. See also "Dred Scott Gone to Final Judgment," repr. of *New York Herald* in *Liberator*, October 1, 1858.

29. *Daily National Intelligencer*, September 22, 1858.

30. Ehrlich, *They Have No Rights*, 183. For the exact date, see David Brown, "Dred Scott Centennial: Famous Slave Whose Case Split U.S. Lies in Unmarked Grave in Calvary Cemetery Here," *St. Louis Globe-Democrat*, February 10, 1957.

31. "Dred Scott: Life of the Famous Fugitive and Missouri Slave Litigant," *St. Louis Daily Globe*, January 10, 1886.

32. Hager, *Dred and Harriet Scott*, 64–66.

33. See especially David W. Blight, *Race and Reunion: The Civil War in American Memory* (Cambridge, Mass.: Belknap Press of Harvard University Press, 2001).

34. An earlier version of the research in this section appeared in Arenson, "Freeing Dred Scott."

35. Ehrlich, *They Have No Rights*, 183.

36. Irving Dilliard and James Milton Turner, "Dred Scott Eulogized by James Milton Turner: A Historical Observance of the Turner Centenary: 1840–1940,"

Journal of Negro History 26, no. 1 (1941): 9; passage quoted by Gary R. Kremer, *James Milton Turner and the Promise of America: The Public Life of a Post-Civil War Black Leader* (Columbia: University of Missouri Press, 1991), 1.

37. For more on the double burden on Harriet Robinson Scott, see Vander-Velde, "Mrs. Dred Scott."

38. "The Dred Scott Decision Explained," *San Francisco Daily Evening Bulletin,* October 17, 1883, 4.

39. "Dred Scott: Life of the Famous Fugitive and Missouri Slave Litigant."

40. A. W., "What Became of Dred Scott? The Question Answered by Investigation in St. Louis—How an International Celebrity Lived in a St. Louis Alley," *St. Louis Globe-Democrat,* October 9, 1904. Turner is quoted as saying Scott "was an ignorant old darky." The language suggests these are ventriloquisms rather than records of African American voices.

41. "Links Present with War Days: Resident of this City Knew Historic Figures," an interview with Eugene H. Lahee, July 22, 1923, clipping in the Dred Scott Collection, Missouri Historical Society.

42. Julia Webster Blow to Mary Louise Dalton, March 13, 1907, Dred Scott Collection, folder 5, Missouri Historical Society.

43. Mary Louise Dalton to Frederick Trevor Hill, February 11 and March 13, 1907, in ibid.

44. Frederick Trevor Hill, *Decisive Battles of the Law; Narrative Studies of Eight Legal Contests Affecting the History of the United States between the Years 1800 and 1886* (New York: Harper and Brothers, 1907), 116.

45. This chain of characterizations is traced in Fehrenbacher, *Dred Scott Case,* 571 and 714n7.

46. Theodore Roosevelt, "The Heirs of Abraham Lincoln," February 12, 1913. Online at http://teachingamericanhistory.org/library/index.asp?document=1140, accessed January 2007.

47. University of Missouri, *Savitar for 1911* (1912), 54. Online at http://www.virtuallymissouri.org/ accessed January 2007. It is amazing to note the items that can be found in the era of digitized texts and keyword searches, though one must always be cognizant of what might be missed by relying overmuch on such an approach.

48. Walter B. Stevens, "Lincoln and Missouri," *Missouri Historical Review* 10, no. 2 (1916): 64.

49. "Dred Scott," *Dictionary of American Biography* Base Set, American Council of Learned Societies, 1928–36, reproduced in *Biography Resource Center,* Thomson Gale, 2007, http://galenet.galegroup.com/servlet/BioRC. See discussion in Fehrenbacher, *Dred Scott Case,* 571 and 714n7.

50. Home Bldg. and Loan Ass'n v. Blaisdell, 290 U.S. 398, 450 (1934) (Sutherland, J., dissenting, quoting *Dred Scott*). Thanks to Austin Allen for this citation, from chapter 5 of this volume, "An Exaggerated Legacy, Dred Scott and Substantive Due Process."

51. Antonio Frederick Holland, *Nathan B. Young and the Struggle over Black Higher Education* (Columbia: University of Missouri Press, 2006).

52. [Nathan B. Young Jr.], "Who Was Dred Scott?" *Your St. Louis and Mine* (St. Louis: n.p., [1937]), 19, 41.

53. "Case of 5 Reds on Trial Here Likely to Go to Jury Tomorrow," *St. Louis Post-Dispatch,* May 27, 1954. Thanks to Bonnie Stepenoff for this citation, from her paper "St. Louis and the Sharecroppers" at the 2006 Western History Association annual meeting.

54. Brown, "Dred Scott Centennial."

55. "Wreath for Dred Scott's Grave" and "Dred Scott Case Celebrated Here," *St. Louis Post-Dispatch,* March 6, 1957. Nathan B. Young Jr. also spoke on this occasion at the St. Louis University School of Law.

56. Frank P. O'Hare to Irving [Dilliard], not sent, [February 13, 1957], Frank P. O'Hare Papers, Missouri Historical Society; Norman Kerr, Curate, St. David's Episcopal Church, Radnor, Pa., "Dred Scott Rests in Peace," Dred Scott Collection, folder 7, references Mrs. Charles C. Harrison Jr., of Villanova, Pa., the granddaughter of Taylor Blow. Despite what VanderVelde writes of her conversation with Kenneth Kaufman, the first grave marker seems to have been unveiled September 17, 1957, the ninety-ninth anniversary of Dred Scott's death. Yet the marker flush with the ground may have been placed in the 1920s, as she suggests: Ehrlich, *They Have No Rights,* 184; VanderVelde, "Mrs. Dred Scott," 1043n33.

57. Nathan B. Young Jr., "Speech for the Forty-One Fellows of the Danforth Foundation," January 30, 1979, 7.

58. Young, *Dred the Revelator* [the cover "1930s" date seems unlikely], and, for example, *Boots to the Levee,* Santopolis poems, 1960, Nathan B. Young, Jr., Collection, St. Louis University Archives.

59. Young, "The Missouri Compromise and the Dred Scott Case in the Anatomy of Civil Rights," Washington University lecture, March 15, 1971, in ibid., 14.

60. Association for the Study of Afro-American Life and History, Program for National Historic Marker ceremony, June 24, 1977, ibid.

61. "Lovejoy Society Will Set Stone for Wife at Grave of Dred Scott," *St. Louis Post-Dispatch,* November 4, 1999; Robert W. Tabscott, "Harriet Scott: A Woman Who Forged the Way," *St. Louis Post-Dispatch* editorial, November 25, 1999.

62. Tim O'Neil, "Dred Scott's Formal Petition for Freedom Will Go on Display; Old Courthouse Ceremony Will Highlight Papers That Detail Plight of Slave, Wife," *St. Louis Post-Dispatch,* February 8, 2000. For the broader recovery, see Freedom Suits in the St. Louis Circuit Court Records project, http://stlcourtrecords.wustl.edu/index.php.

63. Frankel, "Finding a St. Louis Legend"; Lea VanderVelde, *Mrs. Dred Scott: A Life on Slavery's Frontier* (New York: Oxford University Press, 2009).

64. O'Neil, "Dred Scott Case Is Remembered with New Plaque," *St. Louis Post-Dispatch,* December 1, 1999.

65. Shelia P. Moses and Bonnie Christensen, *I, Dred Scott: A Fictional Slave Narrative Based on the Life and Legal Precedent of Dred Scott* (New York: Margaret K. McElderry Books, 2005); Mary E. Neighbour, *Speak Right On: Dred Scott: A Novel* (New Milford, Conn.: Toby Press, 2006); Gregory J. Wallance, *Two Men before the Storm: Arba Crane's Recollection of Dred Scott and the Supreme Court Case That Started the Civil War* (Austin, Tex.: Greenleaf Book Group Press, 2006).

66. Timothy Noah, "Why Bush Opposes *Dred Scott:* It's Code for *Roe v. Wade,*" *Slate* Chatterbox, posted October 11, 2004, at 6:45 PM ET, http://www.slate.com/id/2108083/

67. Planned Parenthood of Southeastern Penn. v. Casey, 505 U.S. 833, 1002 (1992) (Scalia, J., concurring in part and dissenting in part). Thanks to Austin Allen for this citation. For a sense of Taney's eclipse, see James F. Simon, *Lincoln and Chief Justice Taney: Slavery, Secession, and the President's War Powers* (New York: Simon and Schuster, 2006).

68. Commission on Presidential Debates, second Bush-Kerry presidential debate transcript, October 8, 2004, http://www.debates.org/pages/trans2004c.html.

69. http://www.thedredscottfoundation.org/, accessed March 2007.

PART TWO

Historical Perspectives
The Legacy of Dred Scott

John Brown, Abraham Lincoln, *Dred Scott*, and the Problem of Constitutional Evil

Mark Graber

KENNETH STAMPP concluded the preface to his *And the War Came* by asking readers, "How many more generations of black men should have been forced to endure life in bondage in order to avoid its costly and violent end?"[1] Almost forty years later, Evan Carton concluded his *Patriotic Treason* by raising the same concerns. "There were opportunities to avert the war and opportunities to end it quickly that were not seized," he states, "but four million other Americans—along with millions more of their descendants for perhaps many years to come—would also have remained enslaved."[2] Their similar language masked fundamentally different purposes. Stampp was justifying Abraham Lincoln's decision in the spring of 1861 to go to war.[3] Carton was justifying John Brown's decision in 1859 to raid Harpers Ferry,[4] a decision repeatedly and vigorously condemned by both Lincoln and the Republican Party.[5]

From John Brown's perspective, Abraham Lincoln resembled the many Northern politicians who found more or less comfortable means for accommodating human bondage. Lincoln's consistent support for fugitive slave laws led Wendell Phillips to dub him "the Slave-Hound of Illinois."[6] The first Republican president's speeches before assuming that office offered little relief to those antebellum Americans most concerned with the plight of enslaved persons of color. Lincoln's constitutional attacks on the proslavery policies associated with *Dred Scott v. Sandford*[7] were consistently balanced with constitutional defenses of other proslavery policies.[8] The Republican platform of 1860, he admitted, would have almost no impact on the lives of those in bondage before the Civil War. The man who became known as the "Great Emancipator" "did not suppose that" after a congressional ban on slavery in all territories was implemented "ultimate extinction would occur in less than a hundred years at the least."[9] Some prominent abolitionists, uninspired by repeated Republican assertions about "the right of each state to order and control its own domestic institutions according to its own judgment exclusively,"[10] concluded that Lincoln and his political supporters offered little more of value than such Jacksonians as Stephen Douglas and Roger Taney to the vast majority of the enslaved. A Republican victory in 1860, Lydia Maria Child believed, would yield only "a miserable mush of concession, leaving the country in a worse state than it found it."[11]

This essay explores whether Abraham Lincoln from 1854 until 1861 successfully fashioned a viable middle ground between *Dred Scott*'s proslavery constitutionalism, as interpreted by Stephen Douglas, and John Brown's antislavery violence. The first section presents evidence that Lincoln and Brown were largely engaged in an argument over tactics. Both found violence and lawless conduct necessary to emancipate slaves, but Lincoln did so in ways that gained support from crucial border states. The second section presents evidence that Lincoln and Douglas were largely haggling over the price of union. Both assured Southerners that their policies would leave untouched the lives of most slaves for the foreseeable future, but Lincoln thought slaveholders not willing to move to the western territories would be willing to accept grudgingly a prohibition on slavery in those regions. The concluding paragraph briefly raises questions about whether any alternative existed to arguing tactics with Brown or haggling over price with Douglas. Lincoln allegedly teaches lessons about "the politics of the possible,"[12] but the precise nature of those lessons and possibilities are obscured by scholarly failures to acknowledge the proslavery compromises necessary in 1861 to preserve the Union peacefully or the justification of the violence actually responsible for the abolition of slavery.

Roger Taney/Stephen Douglas and John Brown may provide more realistic constitutional alternatives than Abraham Lincoln. The central question Americans faced during the late 1850s was how much slavery they were willing to accept to maintain national union. Taney and Douglas insisted that the price for Northerners was high, that a good deal of accommodation was necessary to preserve the Constitution of 1789. John Brown forthrightly insisted that all mainstream politicians proposed too dear a bargain for national union, that violence was the only means by which substantial numbers of slaves would be freed in the foreseeable future. By pretending that Lincoln's proposal to place slavery "in the course of ultimate extinction" over the course of a century or more might have both preserved union and justified the constitutional order, contemporary Americans fail to acknowledge just how much constitutional evil must be tolerated to maintain constitutions in divided societies and the necessity of violence as the only alternative for possibly advancing the good.

Arguing over Tactics: Abraham Lincoln as John Brown

While "he hoped to have God on his side," Abraham Lincoln insisted that he "must have Kentucky."[13] Concerned with maintaining Union support in the border states, the sixteenth president chastised more abolitionist Union officers who ordered emancipation in their military districts. "Liberating slaves of traitorous owners," Lincoln wrote in the late summer of 1861, might "ruin our rather fair prospect for Kentucky."[14] "I think to lose Kentucky is nearly the same as to lose the whole game," he later added to a correspondent who supported more aggressive emancipatory policies, for with "Kentucky gone, we can not hold Missouri, nor, as I think, Maryland."[15] Lincoln displayed the same concern with the border states during the first months of his administration. As Kenneth Stampp details, Lincoln upon taking office did not seek to avoid war but to find a means for forcing the Confederacy to fire the first shot. Doing so, he believed, would keep Kentucky and other states in the Union, thereby maximizing the Union chance of military success.[16]

Lincoln was less fastidious when considering the constitutional limitations on Civil War policies. As numerous commentators have detailed, the

Illinois Republican frequently made unprecedented assertions of executive power in support of the Union effort. These constitutionally questionable presidential actions included the suspension of habeas corpus, the imposition of martial law without congressional approval, the Emancipation Proclamation, the blockade, and unilateral press censorship.[17] Lincoln was particularly prone to toss constitutional restrictions and legality aside when taking actions designed to ensure that Kentucky and other border states would be "on his side." Lincoln administration officials arrested numerous Maryland legislators thought to have pro-Southern sentiments when preventing that state from adopting a secession ordinance. Some were held for more than a year without trials or even notice of the evidence against them.[18] Martial law and summary arrests played crucial roles when state elections were held in Maryland, Kentucky, and Missouri.[19] Federal troops frequently prevented voters opposed to the Civil War from casting ballots in other close elections. "Those merely suspected of hostilities to the Republican party," Richard Bensel documents, "were often physically ejected from the polling place."[20] Lincoln throughout the Civil War denied that he had ever acted illegally or unconstitutionally,[21] but he as vigorously insisted that illegal or unconstitutional action would have been justified in order to maintain the Union. "Are all the laws, but one, to go unexecuted, and the government itself go to pieces, lest that one be violated?" he famously asked.[22]

Many contemporary commentators endorse Lincoln's claim: "[E]ven in such a case, would not the official oath be broken, if the government should be overthrown, when it was believed that disregarding the single law, would tend to preserve it?"[23] Larry Alexander and Frederick Schauer assert that moral commitments may sometimes override legal commitments, and that both Lincoln's continued opposition to *Dred Scott* and his actions during the Civil War are rare instances where lawless executive action was justified. "If it was important for winning the Civil War that Lincoln suspend habeas corpus and infringe on other civil liberties," they write, "then the moral importance of winning the war was sufficient to justify his actions. Reaching this conclusion, however, does not mean that suspending habeas corpus was right. It just means that this wrong was outweighed by the greater wrong that would have occurred had the war been lost. Once we see that overridable obligations are still obligations, we need not say that Lincoln should have followed *Dred Scott,* all things considered, just because Lincoln had an overridable obligation to follow *Dred Scott* because of its source."[24] Richard Fallon similarly maintains that "the practical imperatives confronting the President" during the early years of the Civil War "morally justified his violation of constitutional law."[25]

Contemporary Americans who celebrate how Lincoln was able to provoke the Confederacy into firing the first shots of the Civil War and defend his unconstitutional exercises of executive power regard Lincoln and John Brown as engaged in an argument over tactics. Both recognized that violence was necessary to achieve their goals in the foreseeable future. Both recognized that this violence would not necessarily be entirely lawful. The difference between Brown and Lincoln had less to do with when lawless violence was justified than with the intelligent use of violence. Lincoln was successful because he recognized that the violence necessary to achieve his goals had to be employed in ways that maintained at least the passive support of the border states. Too confident that God was on his side, Brown forgot that he also needed Kentucky.

Brown and Lincoln might even have been part of an implicit conspiracy to bring about a violent emancipation. Carton probably exaggerates when he insists that the raid on Harpers Ferry "decisively tipped the balance of power and influence in the south in favor of the fire-eating secessionists, who had persuaded their constituents that, sooner or later, the Republican administration would allow or even encourage legions of John Browns to descend upon them."[26] Secession was overdetermined. Crucial events took place before and after John Brown's raid.[27] Nevertheless, John Brown almost certainly increased the probability that Southern states would secede upon Lincoln's election.[28] No secession in 1860 would have meant no Civil War in 1861, no Emancipation Proclamation in 1863, no use of African American troops in 1864 and 1865, and no post–Civil War Amendments during Reconstruction. Brown and Lincoln, from this perspective, engaged in a "bad cop/good cop" routine that provoked Southern secession while ensuring Union support sufficient to triumph in the subsequent hostilities.

If the distinction between Lincoln and Brown is something more than an argument (or implicit agreement) about tactics, the reason must lie in their different justifications for violence. Brown was fighting to free slaves. Lincoln at the beginning of the Civil War announced that combat was necessary solely for preserving national unity. "I would save the Union," he informed Horace Greeley in 1861.

> I would save it the shortest way under the Constitution. The sooner the national authority can be restored; the nearer the Union will be "the Union as it was." If there be those who would not save the Union, unless they could at the same time save slavery, I do not agree with them. If there be those who would not save the Union unless they could at the same time destroy slavery, I do not agree with them. My paramount object in this struggle is to save the Union, and is not either to save or to destroy slavery. If I could save the Union without freeing any slave I would do it, and if I could save it by freeing all the slaves I would do it; and if I could save it by freeing some and leaving others alone I would also do that. What I do about slavery, and the colored race, I do because I believe it helps to save the Union; and what I forbear, I forbear because I do not believe it would help to save the Union. I shall do less whenever I shall believe what I am doing hurts the cause, and I shall do more whenever I shall believe doing more helps the cause.[29]

This rhetoric might have been aimed solely at appeasing Kentucky, whose citizens in 1861 were unwilling to fight to free slaves but might be induced to fight to preserve union. If so, then the disagreement between Brown and Lincoln remains tactical, over when the public commitment to emancipation should have been declared. If Lincoln's actual goal was preserving the Union independent of any effect on human bondage, however, then such an effect to preserve "the Union as it was" might have best been accomplished by a public commitment to maintaining all Jacksonian policies on sectional issues. The conventional defense of Lincoln's lawless violence, in short, threatens to transform his argument over tactics with John Brown to mere haggling over price with Stephen Douglas and Roger Taney.

Haggling over Price: Lincoln as Stephen Douglas/Roger Taney

Abraham Lincoln during his debates with Stephen Douglas acknowledged only three differences between his position on slavery and that publicly championed by Douglas (and Chief Justice Roger Brooke Taney). First, Lincoln believed the national government had the power to prevent the westward expansion of slavery. He was "pledged to a belief in the right and duty of Congress to prohibit slavery in all the United States Territories."[30] Douglas maintained that elected officials were obligated to act consistently with the Supreme Court's ruling in *Dred Scott* that slaveholders had a constitutional right to bring their human property into all American territories.[31] Second, Lincoln repeatedly declared in public that slavery was evil. Slavery, he asserted during the sixth debate with Douglas, "is a moral, a social and a political wrong."[32] Douglas professed public indifference to whether persons voted "slavery up or down,"[33] although in private he declared human bondage to be "a curse beyond computation."[34] Third, Lincoln expressed concern that American expansion might fan sectional flames. While he was "not generally opposed to honest acquisition of territory," the Illinois Republican would consider whether "such acquisition would or would not a[g]gravate . . . the slavery question among ourselves."[35] Douglas disagreed. He contended, "[W]henever it becomes necessary, in our growth and progress to acquire more territory, . . . I am in favor of it, without reference to the question of slavery."[36]

Lincoln denied or blurred other possible differences between Douglas's positions and his on slavery, race, and sectional politics. During the second debate, Lincoln stated that he was opposed to the "unconditioned repeal of the fugitive slave law," would vote to admit additional slave states, and was not "pledged to the abolition of slavery in the District of Columbia" or "the abolition of the slave trade between the different states."[37] He repeatedly stated that federal power over slavery was limited to the territories. Lincoln had "no purpose, directly or indirectly, to interfere with the institution of slavery in the States where it exists."[38] When president-elect, he urged the repeal of the Northern personal liberty laws, which undermined enforcement of the Fugitive Slave Acts. Lincoln informed Thurlow Weed that "all opposition, real and apparant, to the fugitive slave [clause] of the constitution ought to be withdrawn.[39] He promised to forgo "strict legal right" and refrain from appointing "obnoxious strangers" to federal positions in the middle and lower South,[40] practically guaranteeing that federal postmasters in most slave states would not deliver abolitionist tracts. Lincoln bluntly stated that he "never ha[d] complained *especially* of the *Dred*

Scott decision because it held that a negro could not be a citizen"[41] and vigorously opposed black citizenship in Illinois.[42] The language Lincoln used when making these remarks permit the inference that he may have privately favored greater rights for persons of color and was waiting for a politically more opportune moment. Still, at no point before assuming the presidency did that more opportune moment occur. Instead, Lincoln maintained that the territories should be an "outlet for free white people everywhere,"[43] apparently sanctioning state laws prohibiting free black residents. Lincoln championed colonization for free persons of color until the last years of his life.[44] When president, he took far more conservative positions than most Republican congressmen on confiscation of slaves and the rights of former slaves during reconstruction.[45]

Lincoln's willingness to support constitutionally controversial proslavery policies casts doubt on whether he was as committed as some contemporary commentators to interpretive strategies aimed at making the constitution "the best it can be."[46] Prominent antislavery advocates made plausible constitutional arguments against federal power to pass fugitive slave laws.[47] Lincoln, as noted above, insisted that such laws were constitutional and urged free states to repeal personal liberty laws. Although the Supreme Court in *Gibbons v. Ogden* declared that the national government had the power to regulate "commerce which concerns more states than one,"[48] Lincoln publicly asserted that Congress had no power to ban the interstate slave trade and that he would not support prohibition even if bans were constitutionally permitted. These concessions cannot be explained entirely by Lincoln's personal constitutional beliefs or as tactics necessary to gain Electoral College majorities. Lincoln publicly claimed that the Fugitive Slave Act of 1850 did not provide constitutionally adequate safeguards for free persons of color.[49] While calls for repealing all federal slave laws were politically risky,[50] Lincoln would not have lost many Northern voters by insisting more emphatically on the protections for free citizens of color already on the books in many free states.[51] Personal liberty laws were fairly popular in the crucial Northern regions Republicans needed for control of the national government. Lincoln refrained from attacking some proslavery constitutional wrongs and exercising some constitutional antislavery powers in order to preserve union. "It will be much safer for all, both in official and private stations," he stated in discussing the rendition process for fugitive slaves, "to conform to, and abide by, all those acts which stand unrepealed."[52]

Many prominent constitutional commentators endorse Lincoln's commitment to tempering constitutional justice with expediency. Alexander Bickel regarded Lincoln's moderation as the model for constitutional statesmanship. "Principled government by the consent of the governed," Bickel claimed Lincoln taught American citizens,

> often means the definition of principled goals, and the practice of the art of the possible in striving to attain them. The hard fact of an existing evil institution such as slavery and the hard practical difficulties that stood in the way of its sudden abolition justified myriad compromises short of abandoning the goal. The goal itself—the principle—made sense only as an absolute, and as such it was to be maintained. As such it had its vast educational value, as such it exerted its crucial influence on the tendency of prudential policy. But expedient compromises remained necessary also, chiefly because a radically principled solution would collide with widespread prejudices, which no government resting on consent could disregard, any more than it could sacrifice its goals to them.[53]

Harry Jaffa similarly praises Lincoln for "never attempt[ing] to propose what was more than one step ahead of the great body of political public opinion." Lincoln correctly realized, Jaffa claims, that the best political actors can achieve is "the highest degree of equality for which general consent [can] be obtained."[54]

To the extent Lincoln was seeking this "highest degree of equality for which general consent can be obtained," he may be best characterized as doing little more than haggling with his political rivals over the constitutional accommodations necessary for preventing secession. Taney, Douglas, and Lincoln each justified their preferred policies as the measures most likely to preserve union. The Southern Jacksonians on the Supreme Court who determined that slavery could not be banned in the territories insisted that "the peace and harmony of the country required" their decision.[55] Douglas maintained that "neither can the Union be preserved or the Democratic party maintained upon any other basis" than his interpretation of *Dred Scott* as consistent with popular sovereignty. Lincoln disagreed with the means by which Taney and Douglas would secure union, but some speeches suggest agreement with their end. Lincoln claimed slave states would not secede should antislavery forces drive a harder bargain.[56] He assured followers that he had "many assurances . . . from the South that in no probable event will there be any very formidable effort to break up the Union."[57] The combination of federal support for slavery in the states and federal bans on slavery in the territories, he insisted, would better guarantee "the peace of society" than the Northern or Southern Jacksonian alternatives.[58] Events proved Lincoln wrong. If "general consent" is understood as the consensus necessary to secure "the peace of society," then Douglas was the proper "one step ahead of the great body of public opinion" when successfully opposing the Lecompton constitution, which would have made Kansas a slave state. Lincoln's demand for bans on slavery in the territories was the "radically principled solution" Bickel would have constitutional actors forswear. The price Lincoln asked citizens to pay for maintaining the Union was particularly imprudent because much evidence suggests that the Republican program in 1861 was not much more likely than the Jacksonian alternatives to achieve the antislavery end of placing human bondage "in a course of ultimate extinction."[59]

Persons committed to securing the liberty of many actually enslaved persons before the Civil War had little reason to prefer Lincoln's position on human bondage in the territories to that of Douglas or even Taney. The number of slaveholders willing to move west during the 1850s was insufficient to gain a popular proslavery majority in any territory. Douglas and his Jacksonian political allies stood firm when Southerners sought to secure statehood on the basis of a fraudulent proslavery majority. Kansas was the only territory where slaveholders even put up a fight. The number of slaves in other territories before the Civil War was negligible. When Lincoln was elected president, many political actors had concluded that *Dred Scott* resolved the constitutional status of "an imaginary Negro in an impossible place."[60] The Southern failure to colonize the West explains why Lincoln expressed no objections to leaving slavery alone in the New Mexico territories[61] and why the Republican Congress waited for more than a year before passing a largely symbolic ban.[62] Future political or economic developments, of course, might have eventually made the West more hospitable to the South's peculiar institution. Whether slavery had reached its natural limit remains a subject for intense scholarly debate.[63] Nevertheless, given the circumstances on the ground in 1861, a Republican ban on territorial slavery would be better characterized as ratifying the status quo than as a means for hurrying the demise of human bondage.

Whether presidential assertions that slavery was wrong would have had a significant impact on human bondage is doubtful. Lincoln maintained that for the first "eighty years" of American constitutional life, "the public mind did rest in the belief that [slavery] was in the course of ultimate extinction."[64] Before Douglas proposed the Kansas-Nebraska Act, Lincoln claimed to find nothing objectionable about his Jacksonian rival's positions on slavery.[65] When the public philosophy in the United States committed Americans to what Lincoln believed were sufficiently antislavery principles, however, the number of slaves and slave states in the United States increased dramatically, as did the political power of slaveholders.[66] Presidents George Washington, John Adams, Thomas Jefferson, James Madison, James Monroe, and John Quincy Adams each asserted that slavery was wrong.[67] During their administrations, Americans determined that Congress had no power to emancipate slaves in existing states and began the process of national expansion that was thought to privilege slave states.[68] Perhaps Lincoln would have done better. Nevertheless, the evidence suggests that, in the absence of strong antislavery policies, human bondage flourished in a regime whose leaders did little more than call the institution wrong.[69]

Contemporary reproductive politics cast further doubt on whether the combination of calling some behavior wrong and placing relatively weak limits on that behavior are likely to cause dramatic changes in the incidence of that behavior. American presidents and both major political parties for the past thirty years have either condemned abortion or asserted that public policy should be directed at reducing the number of abortions. The Republican Party Platform in 2004 declared that "the unborn child has a fundamental individual right to life which cannot be infringed."[70] "Abortion," the Democratic Party Platform of 2004 stated, "should be safe, legal, and rare."[71] The Supreme Court during this time period, while prohibiting state bans on abortion,[72] has sustained laws requiring parental notification,[73] imposing waiting periods and "informed" consent,[74] refusing to fund even medically necessary abortions,[75] and prohibiting certain means of performing abortions.[76] The influence of antiabortion rhetoric and policies on the number of abortions has been quite weak. The abortion rate in the United States has declined only modestly since 1980 and much of that decline is explained by similar declines in the number of unwanted pregnancies. Significantly, the rate of decline appears to have no relationship to which party controls the national government. The decline in the number of abortions slowed during the Bush administration in the years for which there is good data.[77] Calling abortion "wrong" has seemingly had no impact on public opinion.[78] A Gallup Poll taken in May 2007 found unchanged from 1982 the percentages of Americans who believe abortion should always be legal or sometimes be legal. Yearly fluctuations have occurred, but there are no long-term changes in the percentages of Americans who regard themselves as pro-choice. Given the strong support for reproductive liberty in such states as New York and California, states where the gubernatorial candidates from both parties take pro-choice stands, even a Supreme Court decision overruling *Roe v. Wade* is unlikely to place abortion in a course of ultimate extinction. Assuming the Republican Party's analogous antislavery rhetoric and policies would have approximately the same impact as contemporary antiabortion rhetoric and policies, few persons of color at the turn of the twentieth century would have had much reason for praising Lincoln. We might expect only that the number of slaves would have been reduced by 15 percent, that most of that reduction would have been unrelated to any official antislavery policy, that the rate of decrease would be slowing down, and that public opinion would be about as evenly divided on slavery issues as was the case when Lincoln was first elected to the presidency.

Lincoln and Douglas were doing something more than haggling over the price of union when their conversation during the debates briefly turned to expansion. Douglas was committed to making the United States an "ocean-going republic."[79] His call for unlimited acquisition of new territories throughout the Western hemisphere promised new lands for both free- and slave-state settlers. Lincoln condemned the likely "grab for the territory of poor Mexico" followed by an "invasion of the rich lands of South America, then the adjoining islands"[80] should Douglas become president. Harry Jaffa is surely correct to praise Republican politicians who recognized that "only a national commitment to confine slavery . . . would put an end to the drive for foreign conquest and domination."[81] Radical abolitionists who ignored Lincoln's position on expansion[82] grossly underestimated the different impacts Republican and Democratic administrations were likely to have on the immediate future of human bondage.

While Lincoln's opposition to acquiring new territories for slaveholders obviously distinguished his position from that of both Douglas and Brown, both the nature and moral adequacy of this middle ground are problematic. Lincoln placed far more emphasis on preventing slavery's expansion westward than its spread southward. He attacked the Kansas-Nebraska Act at every opportunity, but he never publicly condemned efforts to annex Cuba.[83] Several speeches suggest that Lincoln might have tolerated Southern expansion in return for opening up more territory for free-state settlers. The Compromise of 1850 was a legitimate bargain, he insisted, because "the North gained two measures and the South three."[84] A new party was hardly necessary to prevent further expansion. The Whig Party had historically been opposed to extending the borders of the United States.[85] John Bell, the Constitutional Union Party's candidate in 1860, led those fights against territorial expansion.[86] Finally and most important, a Republican policy limited to preventing Southern expansion was unlikely to have any immediate impact on the lives of those already enslaved. As Lincoln informed his friend Alexander Stephens, "there is no cause for [Southern] fears" that "a Republican administration would, directly, or indirectly, interfere with their slaves, or with them, about their slaves."[87]

Lincoln might have been employing a deeper strategy for emancipating most slaves in the foreseeable future. He may have intended that his combination of strong antislavery rhetoric and tepid antislavery proposals provoke Southern secession while retaining enough support in the crucial border states to make a Union victory highly probable. That victory, in turn, laid the groundwork for the Thirteenth Amendment. While Lincoln publicly doubted whether slave states would secede should Republicans be elected, he always insisted secession was treason and would be put down militarily. "The Union," he declared, "won't be dissolved. We don't want to dissolve it, and if you attempt it, we won't let you. With the purse and sword, the army and navy and treasury in our hands and at our command, you couldn't do it. . . . All this talk about the dissolution of the

Union is humbug—nothing but folly. We 'WON'T' dissolve the Union, and you 'SHAN'T.'"[88] Alternatively, Lincoln may have been prepared to announce bolder antislavery policies, perhaps after being reelected with increased support from the border states in 1864. A high tariff designed to raise the revenue necessary to buy most slaves from their owners in the middle South would either immediately emancipate slaves in that region or result in a broader emancipation after Southern secession and Union success in the resulting Civil War.

These strategies acquit Lincoln of the charge that he was merely haggling over price with Douglas and Taney by portraying him as arguing over tactics with Brown. Lincoln's tactics, as I asserted in section 1, were aimed at ensuring that Kentucky was on his side when violence broke out. If with Kentucky on his side, Lincoln as Stephen Douglas could peacefully implement aggressive antislavery policies, so much the better. On this account, however, Lincoln recognized that possibility as unlikely. Once the border states were committed to placing slavery on a course of fairly immediate extinction, Lincoln as John Brown intended to begin an antislavery program that would leave slaveholders with only the option of surrendering their slaves before or after most slaveholders were slaughtered by Union military forces.

Skipping the Middleman

Abraham Lincoln is consistently presented as occupying the happy ground between John Brown and Stephen Douglas. Unlike Brown, Lincoln was committed to freeing slaves peacefully within the law. Unlike Douglas, Lincoln was committed to placing slavery "in a course of ultimate extinction." The problem with this position is that Americans in 1861 did not have the option of adopting peaceful means that would place slavery on a course of ultimate extinction. Lincoln's program might have stopped the expansion of slavery, but he offered almost nothing of value to persons enslaved before the Civil War. If the question is, as Kenneth Stampp insists, "how many more generations of black men should have been forced to endure life in bondage in order to avoid its costly and violent end," perhaps we ought to focus more on the differences between Stephen Douglas and John Brown, cutting out the middleman.

Notes

1. Kenneth M. Stampp, *And the War Came: The North and the Secession Crisis, 1860–1861* (Baton Rouge: Louisiana State University Press, 1970), xvii.

2. Evan Carton, *Patriotic Treason: John Brown and the Soul of America* (New York: Free Press, 2006), 338–40.

3. See Stampp, *And the War Came,* 285–86.

4. See Carton, *Patriotic Treason,* 337.

5. Abraham Lincoln, "Address at Cooper Institute, New York City," in *The Collected Works of Abraham Lincoln,* ed. Roy P. Basler, 8 vols. (New Brunswick, N.J.: Rutgers University Press, 1953–55), 3:538; "Republican Party Platform of 1860," The American Presidency Project, http://www.presidency.ucsb.edu/ws/index.php?pid=29620. See William W. Freehling, *The Road to Disunion,* vol. 2, *Secessionists Triumphant, 1854–1861* (New York: Oxford University Press, 2007), 220.

6. Irving H. Bartlett, *Wendell Phillips, Brahmin Radical* (Boston: Beacon Press, 1961), 222.

7. Dred Scott v. John F. A. Sandford, 60 U.S. (19 How.) 393 (1857).

8. See the section titled "Haggling over Price: Lincoln as Stephen Douglas/Roger Taney," *infra.*

9. Lincoln, "Fourth Debate with Stephen A. Douglas, at Charleston, Illinois," in Basler, *Collected Works,* 3:181.

10. Lincoln, "First Inaugural Address," ibid., 263.

11. Carton, *Patriotic Treason,* 278 (quoting Lydia Maria Child).

12. Sean Wilentz, "Homegrown Terrorist," *New Republic,* October 24, 2005.

13. James M. McPherson, *Battle Cry of Freedom: The Civil War Era* (New York: Oxford University Press, 1988), 284.

14. Lincoln, "To John C. Fremont," in Basler, *Collected Works,* 4:507.

15. Lincoln, "To Orville H. Browning," ibid., 533.

16. See Stampp, *And the War Came,* 285.

17. For an excellent discussion of this issues, see Daniel Farber, *Lincoln's Constitution* (Chicago: University of Chicago Press, 2003).

18. See McPherson, *Battle Cry of Freedom,* 289–90; Mark E. Neely Jr., *The Fate of Liberty: Abraham Lincoln and Civil Liberties* (New York: Oxford University Press, 1991), 14–18.

19. Forrest McDonald, *States' Rights and the Union: Imperium in Imperio, 1776–1876* (Lawrence: University Press of Kansas, 2000), 201.

20. Richard Franklin Bensel, *The American Ballot Box in the Mid-nineteenth Century* (New York: Cambridge University Press, 2004), 217. See McDonald, *States' Rights and the Union,* 201.

21. Lincoln, "Message to Congress in Special Session," in Basler, *Collected Works,* 4:430–31.

22. Ibid., 430.

23. Ibid.

24. Larry Alexander and Frederick Schauer, "On Extrajudicial Constitutional Interpretation," *Harvard Law Review* 110, no. 7 (1997): 1383.

25. Richard H. Fallon Jr., "Executive Power and the Political Constitution," *Utah Law Review* 2007, no. 1 (2007): 21.

26. Carton, *Patriotic Treason*, 338–39.

27. See especially Freehling, *Secessionists Triumphant.*

28. Ibid., 205–21.

29. Lincoln, "To Horace Greeley," in Basler, *Collected Works*, 5:388–89

30. Lincoln, "Mr. Lincoln's Speech, Second Debate with Stephen A. Douglas at Freeport, Illinois," ibid., 3:40. Lincoln sometimes suggested that Congress had the power, but not the constitutional obligation, to ban slavery in the territories. He regarded the Missouri Compromise, which divided the West into slave and free territories, as a "sacred compact." In his First Inaugural, he declared: "*May* Congress prohibit slavery in the territories? The Constitution does not expressly say. *Must* Congress protect slavery in the territories? The Constitution does not expressly say." Ibid., 4:267 (emphasis in original).

31. Stephen Douglas, "Mr. Douglas's Speech, Third Debate with Stephen A. Douglas at Jonesboro, Illinois," ibid., 3:112.

32. Lincoln, "Mr. Lincoln's Speech, Sixth Debate with Douglas at Quincy, Illinois," ibid., 254.

33. Douglas, "Mr. Douglas's Reply, Fifth Debate with Stephen A. Douglas, at Galesburg, Illinois," ibid., 241.

34. See Robert W. Johannsen, "Stephen A. Douglas and the South," *Journal of Southern History* 33, no. 1 (1967): 32.

35. Lincoln, "Mr. Lincoln's Speech, Second Debate with Stephen A. Douglas, at Freeport, Illinois," in Basler, *Collected Works*, 3:41.

36. Douglas, "Mr. Douglas's Speech, Second Debate with Stephen A. Douglas, at Freeport, Illinois," ibid., 54.

37. Lincoln, "Mr. Lincoln's Speech, Second Debate with Stephen A. Douglas at Freeport, Illinois," ibid., 40.

38. Lincoln, "First Inaugural Address," ibid., 4:263.

39. Lincoln, "To Thurlow Weed," ibid., 154.

40. Lincoln, "First Inaugural Address," ibid., 266.

41. Lincoln, "Mr. Lincoln's Reply, Seventh Debate with Stephen A. Douglas," ibid., 3:298–99.

42. Lincoln, "Mr. Lincoln's Rejoinder, Fourth Debate with Stephen A. Douglas, at Charleston, Illinois," ibid., 179.

43. Lincoln, "Mr. Lincoln's Reply, Seventh Debate with Stephen A. Douglas," ibid., 312.

44. Lincoln, "Annual Message to Congress," ibid., 5:530.

45. See Daniel W. Hamilton, *The Limits of Sovereignty: Property Confiscation in the Union and the Confederacy during the Civil War* (Chicago: University of

Chicago Press, 2007), 74–78; Eric Foner, *Reconstruction: America's Unfinished Revolution, 1863–1877* (New York: Harper and Row, 1988), 61–62.

46. See Sotirios Barber and James E. Fleming, *Constitutional Interpretation: The Basic Questions* (New York: Oxford University Press, 2007), xiii; Ronald Dworkin, *Law's Empire* (Cambridge, Mass.: Harvard University Press, 1986), 379.

47. Salmon Portland Chase, *Speech of Salmon P. Chase in the Case of the Colored Woman, Matilda* (Cincinnati: Pugh and Dodd, Printers, 1837), 17–27; Salmon Portland Chase, *Reclamation of Fugitives from Service* (Cincinnati: B. P. Donogh, 1847), 75, 96–106.

48. Gibbons v. Ogden, 22 U.S. (9 Wheat.) 1, 194 (1824).

49. Lincoln, "First Inaugural Address," in Basler, *Collected Works,* 4:264.

50. See William C. Harris, *Lincoln's Rise to the Presidency* (Lawrence: University Press of Kansas, 2007), 205.

51. See Thomas D. Morris, *Free Men All: The Personal Liberty Laws of the North, 1780–1861* (Baltimore: Johns Hopkins University Press, 1974), 199.

52. Lincoln, "First Inaugural Address," in Basler, *Collected Works,* 4:264.

53. Alexander M. Bickel, *The Least Dangerous Branch: The Supreme Court at the Bar of Politics* (Indianapolis: Bobbs-Merrill, 1962), 68.

54. Harry V. Jaffa, *Crisis of the House Divided: An Interpretation of the Issues in the Lincoln-Douglas Debate* (Garden City, N.Y.: Doubleday, 1959), 386, 377.

55. Scott, 60 U.S. at 493. See Philip Auchampaugh, "James Buchanan, the Court, and the *Dred Scott* Case," *Tennessee Historical Magazine* 9 (1929): 236; Freehling, *Secessionists Triumphant,* 109–22.

56. Robert W. Johannsen, "Stephen A. Douglas, 'Harper's Magazine,' and Popular Sovereignty," *Mississippi Valley Historical Review* 45, no. 4 (1959): 609 (quoting Douglas).

57. Lincoln, "To John Fry," in Basler, *Collected Works,* 4:95.

58. Lincoln, "Speech at Leavenworth, Kansas," ibid., 3:501.

59. Lincoln, "Mr. Lincoln's Reply, First Debate with Stephen A. Douglas at Ottawa, Illinois," ibid., 18.

60. James G. Blaine, *Twenty Years of Congress: From Lincoln to Garfield* (Norwich, Conn.: Henry Bill Publishing Company, 1884), 1:272.

61. Lincoln, "To William H. Seward," ibid., 183.

62. 12 Stat. 432 (1862).

63. See, e.g., Chas. W. Ramsdell, "The Natural Limits of Slavery Expansion," *Mississippi Valley Historical Review* 16, no. 2 (1929): 151–71; Michael A. Morrison, *Slavery and the American West: The Eclipse of Manifest Destiny and the Coming of the Civil War* (Chapel Hill: University of North Carolina Press, 1997), 112–13.

64. Lincoln, "Mr. Lincoln's Reply, First Debate with Stephen A. Douglas at Ottawa, Illinois," in Basler, *Collected Works,* 3:18.

65. Lincoln, "Fragment: Last Speech of Campaign at Springfield, Illinois," ibid., 334. See Harris, *Lincoln's Rise to the Presidency,* 145.

66. See Don E. Fehrenbacher, *The Slaveholding Republic: An Account of the United States Government's Relations to Slavery*, ed. Ward M. McAfee (New York: Oxford University Press, 2001).

67. W. B. Allen, ed., *George Washington: A Collection* (Indianapolis: Liberty Classics, 1988), 319; Charles Francis Adams, ed., *The Works of John Adams, Second President of the United States*, vol. 9 (Boston: Little, Brown, 1854), 480; Merrill D. Peterson, ed., *The Portable Thomas Jefferson* (New York: Penguin Books, 1975), 185–86; Charles F. Hobson and Robert A. Rutland, eds., *The Papers of James Madison*, vol. 12 (Charlottesville: University Press of Virginia, 1979), 437; Arthur Scherr, "Governor James Monroe and the Southampton Slave Resistance of 1799," *Historian* 61, no. 3 (1999): 577; Charles Francis Adams, ed., *Memoirs of John Quincy Adams, Comprising Portions of His Diary From 1795 to 1848*, vol. 5 (Freeport, N.Y.: Books for Libraries Press, 1969), 9–10.

68. See Mark A. Graber, *Dred Scott and the Problem of Constitutional Evil* (New York: Cambridge University Press, 2006), 115–26.

69. For 1789 to 1821, see George Van Cleve, *A Slaveholder's Union: Slavery's Relation to American Politics and Law, 1770–1821* (Chicago: University of Chicago Press, forthcoming).

70. "2004 Republican Party Platform," The American Presidency Project, http://www.presidency.ucsb.edu/ws/index.php?pid=25850.

71. "Democratic Party Platform of 2004," The American Presidency Project, http://www.presidency.ucsb.edu/ws/index.php?pid=29613.

72. See Roe v. Wade, 410 U.S. 113 (1973); Planned Parenthood of Southeastern Penn. v. Casey, 505 U.S. 833 (1992).

73. See Ayotte v. Planned Parenthood of N. New England, 546 U.S. 320 (2006).

74. See Planned Parenthood v. Casey, 505 U.S. 833.

75. Maher v. Roe, 432 U.S. 464 (1977); Harris v. McCrae, 448 U.S. 297 (1980).

76. Gonzales v. Carhart, 550 U.S. 124 (2007).

77. See Lawrence B. Finer and Stanley K. Henshaw, "Estimates of U.S. Abortion Incidence, 2001–2003," Guttmacher Institute, August 3, 2006, http://www.guttmacher.org/pubs/2006/08/03/ab_incidence.pdf.

78. The data discussed below can be found at "Abortion and Birth Control," The Polling Report, http://www.pollingreport.com/abortion.htm.

79. *Congressional Globe,* 28th Cong., 2d sess., appendix, 68.

80. Lincoln, "Fifth Debate with Stephen A. Douglas, at Galesburg, Illinois," in Basler, *Collected Works,* 3:235.

81. See Jaffa, *Crisis of the House Divided,* 405.

82. See Harris, *Lincoln's Rise to the Presidency,* 215.

83. See Lincoln, "To Lyman Trumbull," in Basler, *Collected Works,* 3:356 ("I do not perceive that there is any feeling here about Cuba; and so I think, you can safely venture to act upon your own judgment upon any phase of it which may be presented").

84. Lincoln, "Speech at Bloomington, Illinois," ibid., 2:238.

85. See Robert E. May, *The Southern Dream of a Caribbean Empire, 1854–1861* (Baton Rouge: Louisiana State University Press, 1973), 194–205.

86. See Graber, *Dred Scott and the Problem of Constitutional Evil,* 240–41.

87. Lincoln, "To Alexander H. Stephens," in Basler, *Collected Works,* 4:160.

88. Lincoln, "Speech at Galena, Illinois," ibid., 2:355.

FOUR

The Legacy of the *Dred Scott* Case

The Uncertain Course of Emancipation in Missouri

Louis Gerteis

IN CHIEF Justice Roger B. Taney's *Dred Scott* decision, a defense of slavery became the essential condition of constitutional government and national unity in the United States. Republicans uniformly denounced the decision and held to their founding principle that the municipal limits of slave law confined the institution to existing slave states. As unconditional Unionists, Republicans also supported the use of military force by the federal government to defeat efforts to create a separate, proslavery nation. But, the *Dred Scott* case also focused on the issue of citizenship rights. Here, Republicans sharply divided. As the editors of this volume point out in their introduction, Republicans broadly shared the view that at the national level slavery was "a curse that had blighted the past and would corrupt the future." But conservative Unionists clung to slavery in their own states and opposed extending citizenship rights to African Americans. On the issue of slavery's constitutional status, then, the legacy of the *Dred Scott* case was clear: Republicans agreed that Taney's assertion of proslavery nationalism died with the Confederacy. And, with some reluctance, and many misgivings, conservative Unionists eventually accepted emancipation: slavery, too, died with the Confederacy.

In the area of citizenship rights, however, the *Dred Scott* case left a dual legacy. On the one hand, Taney's insistence that African Americans could never be citizens of the United States created the conditions for the passage of the Fourteenth Amendment. On the other hand, persistent hostility to citizenship rights for African Americans represented a competing legacy. Conservative Unionists could not hold back the tide of wartime emancipation or block the passage of the Thirteenth, Fourteenth, and Fifteenth amendments. But, as the uncertain course of emancipation in Missouri revealed, the strength of conservative Unionist hostility to citizenship rights for African Americans remained strong. During the late nineteenth century, this hostility fused with the ideology of the Lost Cause to shape the national narrative of the Civil War and sectional reunion.[1]

Leading the conservative Unionists in Missouri were Hamilton Gamble, Edward Bates, and Francis P. "Frank" Blair Jr. Gamble, who served as wartime governor of Missouri, had cast the dissenting vote in the *Dred Scott* decision of the Missouri Supreme Court. On the court's three-man panel, Gamble argued that established precedent made Scott free by virtue of his residence in a free state. Nevertheless, Gamble defended slavery in Missouri during his tenure as governor. With similar views, Gamble's brother-in-law and Lincoln's attorney general, Edward Bates, opposed the proslavery implications of the *Dred Scott* case. In the wake of the U.S. Supreme Court decision, Bates dismissed most of Taney's labored decision as obiter dictum. At the same time, however, he explained to the Missouri delegation to the 1860 Republican national convention (as it prepared to support him for the presidential nomination) that he agreed with Taney regarding citizenship rights. Taney had correctly concluded that Dred Scott, "a Negro of African descent, not necessarily a slave, could not be a citizen of Missouri, and therefore, could not sue in the Federal Court."[2]

For Frank Blair, as well, opposition to Taney's decision and staunch Unionist views implied neither a moral hostility toward slavery nor sympathy for equal rights. As editor of the *St. Louis Democrat,* Blair expressed the views of one of the country's most influential political families. His father, Francis P. Blair, had presided over the first Republican national convention in 1856. His brother, Montgomery Blair, defended Dred Scott before the

U.S. Supreme Court and became Lincoln's choice for postmaster general. Frank Blair argued to whoever would listen—and Lincoln listened during the first year of the Civil War—that emancipation must be accompanied by colonization of all African Americans to Central America. An independent nation of African Americans on the Isthmus of the Americas would promote U.S. interests in securing a transportation link between the Atlantic and Pacific oceans. Emancipation, racial separation, and American nationalism advanced in tandem.[3]

Lincoln's border state policy lent support to Missouri's conservative Unionists. In the loyal slave states, Lincoln urged gradual, compensated emancipation. At the outset of the war, Lincoln adopted Blair's colonization plan as well. In his August 1862 meeting with African American leaders in the White House, Lincoln urged them to support Blair's program of colonization. As Congress moved toward emancipation in the District of Columbia and provided for the freedom of slaves owned by rebellious masters in the Second Confiscation Act, Lincoln grew deeply troubled. Convinced that Congress did not possess the constitutional authority to abolish slavery in the states, Lincoln began to carefully craft his own Emancipation Proclamation. In his preliminary Emancipation Proclamation, Lincoln exercised his powers as commander in chief and took executive control of the emancipation process. As he did so, however, he continued to insulate loyal slaveholders from the immediate impact of wartime emancipation.[4]

Citizenship remained the central issue for Missouri Unionists as the war progressed and first Congress and then President Lincoln adopted emancipation policies. Missouri's political leaders were willing to discuss gradual, compensated emancipation and, with it, an extended period of apprenticeship. But the widening wartime discussion of emancipation clearly alarmed them, and they defended Unionist slaveholders whenever they could.

When the Unionist Democrat from Missouri, John B. Henderson, took the Senate floor on March 27, 1862, he cautiously joined a discussion of federal appropriations to support gradual emancipation in the loyal slave states. Henderson was cautious, he said, because he continued to believe that agitation of the issue of slavery had led to the present troubles. It was for this reason that he had earlier opposed the measure providing for emancipation in the District of Columbia. He thought any discussion of slavery "ill-timed and unwise" when unity was paramount in the struggle against the rebellion.

Now, as the emancipation discussion focused on the loyal slave states, including Missouri, Henderson feared that further discussion of slavery would agitate senators from Delaware and Kentucky. Henderson joined his Northern colleagues to fight against secessionists who would make slavery the cornerstone of government. But he did not agree with those Northerners who argued that slavery was the fundamental cause of the Civil War.

Henderson supported the offer of compensation because it approached the troublesome issue of slavery in a practical manner, not as a moral issue. Amid the uncertainties of war, compensation and gradual emancipation offered loyal slaveholders a reasoned proposal: "It comes not in the spirit of arrogance, demanding conformity with the views of others, but with humility acknowledging if slavery be an evil it is a sin for which we are all responsible, and for the removal of which we are willing to come with practical benevolence."[5]

A few days later, Frank Blair rose to the House floor to defend Lincoln from those who argued that, until the president embraced emancipation as a war measure, the administration lacked a clear war policy. Blair had been elected to Congress in 1860 and served until July 1862, when he resigned to accept a military commission. Blair extolled the virtues of Lincoln's border state policy. He reminded his colleagues that the president had clearly stated in his annual message that the integrity of the Union was his paramount interest and that, as president, he struggled purposefully to ensure that the conflict "shall not degenerate into a violent and remorseless revolutionary struggle." It was "fallacious," said Blair, to speak of the conflict as a slaveholders' rebellion. If the war had been caused by slaveholders, then it might be "a complete remedy to extirpate the institution." But such was not the case. The war, Blair insisted, reflected the "abhorrence" of the non-slaveholding majority of Southern whites to "emancipation and amalgamation and their fear of 'negro equality.'" Under these circumstances, a Republican emancipation policy would confirm them in their rebellion. Far from bringing a swift end to the rebellion, emancipation would strengthen and extend it. Emancipation as a war measure would "make rebels of the whole of the non-slaveholders of the South," warned Blair, and simultaneously "weaken the sympathy of a large number of the working men of the North, who are not ready to see their brethren in the South put on an equality with manumitted negroes."

In Blair's view, the great genius of Lincoln's border state policy was its intention "to disarm the jealousy of race." It was this jealousy that animated the rebellion. The colonization scheme, a plan that Blair had designed and that the president now embraced, provided an alternative to the racial subordination sustained by slavery. In Blair's analysis, the leaders of the rebellion had convinced the mass of whites in the South (who owned no slaves) that a defense of slavery provided them with their only protection against Northern-imposed emancipation and amalgamation. With colonization paired with compensation for loyal slaveholders, the president calmed the fears of Southern whites and protected the property interests of loyal men. Blair looked forward to the day "when the flag of the Union shall float over no slave, and our country shall be absolutely the land of the free." But, the fight now was for the country and "not for the emancipation of the African race."

Blair's views on race had been shaped by his father's Jacksonian-era antiabolitionist appeal to Northern workingmen. To the abolitionists' claim that equal rights should be extended to blacks, Francis P. Blair responded angrily as editor of the pro-Jackson *Washington Globe*. To do so, argued the elder Blair, would degrade the white workingman to the level of the black man and, by promoting amalgamation, render that degradation permanent. When, for example, abolitionists opposed the Dorrite demand in Rhode Island for universal white manhood suffrage because it excluded blacks from the polls, Blair struck back. Abolitionists knew, Blair insisted, that barriers of class secured them from social degradation and racial amalgamation. By seeking equality for blacks, they intended "to put the poor white man on a level with the negro." Abolitionists "know full well that their firesides will never be polluted by the degrading admixture of colored offspring," Blair continued. "*Practical* abolitionism" would not touch them: "the *odor* of abolitionism will never taint the atmosphere of their silk-curtained chambers and carpeted saloons." The practical effects of abolitionism were aimed at the workingmen:

> *They* [the abolitionists] theorize; but *practical* abolitionism is
> not for them, but the people—the poor white man of the free
> States. It is with *his* wife and *his* daughter that amalgamation
> approaches; and to degrade him politically and socially, by
> any and all means, has ever been the policy of that proud and

unfeeling aristocracy, which sees its elevation in the poor white man's degradation. Why should he have a privilege a negro has not? He is no better, they say. Let, therefore, his tainted offspring receive the last eternal seal of inferiority, which abolitionism and amalgamation can alone affix.[6]

Although the politics of race had changed as the Blairs joined the Republican Party's opposition to the Slave Power, their hostility to equal rights for African Americans remained paramount. Frank Blair updated his father's Jacksonian-era racist appeal and made it the rationale for Lincoln's border state policy. It was a central tenet of Blair's argument that it was not slavery as a property interest that enabled secessionist politicians to unite the South: "It was the *negro question* and not the *slavery question* which made the rebellion." Many slave owners did not support the secessionist party. The "sensitiveness that enabled southern politicians to unite the South by playing on the slavery chord" arose from "that morbid condition inseparable from the presence of diverse races in the same community." The only solution was a separation of the races.

Blair acknowledged that some would object to the practicality of colonization: "[M]any assume that Mr. Lincoln's programme of conciliation by separation of the races is inadequate because African Americans are so numerous." Blair admitted that in the Jacksonian era the American colony of Liberia failed to attract large numbers of African Americans, but he insisted that colonization in Central America under the American flag made all the difference. Under Lincoln's colonization plan, American blacks would find a true home, not "banishment." The success of Lincoln's policy would bring an end to the rebellion by removing the problem of race: "[T]he idea of the separation of the race[s] is a complete antidote" to the current rebellion.

Arguments of practicality actually worked in favor of colonization, Blair insisted. It would be impossible to emancipate the slaves of the South "and maintain them in the condition of freedmen upon the soil of those States" without the continued presence of an immense occupying army "equal to that which is required to set them free." African Americans could not be sustained in freedom any other way. Without the continuous use of force, no law could be imposed which "is against the sense of the people of a community." Blair warned that whites in the North would not support a war for emancipation without colonization. "How long," Blair asked, "would it be endured by the northern people that a war should be waged upon the people of their own race at the South to make the blacks their equals?" Linking emancipation to colonization disarmed the jealousy of race, removed the sentiments sustaining the rebellion, and united the mass of whites in the North and South.[7]

By the time Lincoln issued the preliminary Emancipation Proclamation in September 1862, he had come to the conclusion that conditions of war would sweep away slavery in the lower South. Reluctantly and with considerable worry, Lincoln also came to the conclusion that able-bodied black men must be enlisted in the Union army. In the final Proclamation of January 1, 1863, Lincoln directed that such enlistments take place, although he suggested that black troops should be limited to garrison duty. It was an "unstated corollary" of this decision, in the view of historian David Donald, that Lincoln broke with Blair and abandoned his earlier embrace of colonization. "Henceforth," wrote Donald, "Lincoln recognized that blacks were to make their future as citizens of the United States."[8]

Historians generally agree with Donald's assessment and regard Lincoln's conversion on this point as the major turning point in the social history of the war.[9] But many Missouri Republicans had not been similarly converted. Frank Blair, as a commander in the field, Montgomery Blair and Edward Bates, as increasingly alienated and embittered members of Lincoln's cabinet, and Hamilton Gamble, as Missouri's provisional governor—all continued to support slavery and to regard citizenship for African Americans as, at best, a distant possibility.

Under these circumstances, the wartime path to freedom in Missouri was littered with obstacles. Most slaveholders in the state remained nominally loyal to the federal government and to Gamble's provisional state government. As long as Gamble remained in power, Lincoln supported the property rights of loyal slaveholders in Missouri. But as Lincoln moved gradually toward emancipation as a war aim, the legal edifice of slavery in Missouri began to crack.

Lincoln famously revoked General John C. Frémont's 1861 emancipation order in Missouri and directed the general to enforce the newly passed Confiscation Act that directed federal military officers to confiscate slaves owned by disloyal masters. These confiscated slaves were officially denominated "contraband of war" because they were property whose labor materially aided the rebellion. "Contraband" became a term popularly applied to Southern blacks who made their way to Union military encampments and to Union-controlled cities like St. Louis seeking freedom.[10]

As Congress moved beyond emancipation in the District of Columbia and proposed compensated emancipation in the loyal slave states, it also began debate on what would become the Second Confiscation Act. That act provided for the emancipation of slaves of masters in rebellion against the United States. Missouri's representatives resisted the measure. Elijah Hise Norton, a Platte County Democrat, warned against an expansion of federal powers. Not only was emancipation a bad idea, he argued, but confiscation itself was unconstitutional. Rebels could be punished for treason in the manner defined in the Constitution (Article 3, Section 3), but Congress had no power to "confiscate or forfeit property for a longer period than the life of the owner."[11] Representative John S. Phelps echoed Norton's argument. A Democrat later appointed military governor of Arkansas by Lincoln, Phelps insisted that Congress did not have the power to confiscate a man's estate beyond the duration of his life. Phelps acknowledged that "this rebellion has grown into a civil war more formidable than anyone expected." Nevertheless, he insisted, the "rules of civilized warfare" applied. He agreed with Blair's argument, made in his speech of April 11, 1862, that slaveholders were not driving the rebellion. "What is to become of the slaves freed by this bill?" Phelps asked as passage of the Second Confiscation Act moved forward. The Southern states would certainly expel emancipated slaves, and Northern states were not willing to admit them.[12]

The prospect that emancipation would advance without provisions for racial separation increased measurably with the emergence of the Second Confiscation Act. Frank Blair followed Representative Phelps to the House floor to press once more his conviction that emancipation must be accompanied with colonization. Blair disagreed with Phelps about the applicability of international law to the Civil War in America. "The punishment which this government shall inflict upon its own rebellious citizens," Blair insisted, "is regulated by its own discretion." Blair would not hesitate to punish rebels by confiscating their slaves, but, he asked (as had Phelps), what would be the fate of freedmen? Most assuredly the Southern states would act as quickly as they could to banish freedmen from their borders. And Congress could not forbid such legislation without also dictating to the Northern states regarding immigration. Blair proposed an amendment to the Second Confiscation Act that linked emancipation to colonization in Central America. To those who argued that the freedmen would not want to colonize, Blair replied, "if they are fit for freedom they will go." African Americans were "designed" to find their freedom "in the tropics under our supervision."

As Blair spoke, the Pennsylvania Quaker William Morris Davis gravely shook his head. Davis interjected that he did not believe that "any class or nation of men would leave the land of their birth of their own free will and accord." Blair responded that the United States had been peopled by immigrants from Europe. More broadly, Blair insisted that "the Almighty" had created the black race for the tropics and the white man for the temperate regions. To restore the races to their proper geographical zones "is to conform to nature."[13]

Lincoln's decision to enroll black troops hastened slavery's end, but in Missouri it was the election of November 1864—following Hamilton Gamble's death in January 1864—that created the political conditions for abolition in the state. In that election, Radicals took control of the state's politics, and Blair (a military commander in the field) lost political influence in Missouri.

Eligible to vote in the 1864 election were men willing to swear allegiance to the constitutions of the United States and Missouri and to promise not to take up arms against the government of either. Loyal Missourians voted under extremely unsettled conditions. Sterling Price's raid in October 1864 left St. Louis untouched, but much of the rest of the state remained in anxious and uncertain circumstances.[14]

In Missouri's governor's race, Thomas C. Fletcher, a prominent St. Louis Republican and a respected military leader, easily defeated his Democratic rival. Fletcher moved directly from a field command to the governor's mansion. Born in Jefferson County, southwest of St. Louis, he moved to the city in 1856 as a land agent for the Pacific Railroad. He quickly rose to prominence in politics and helped to build the city's Republican Party. Early in the war, Fletcher recruited the Thirty-first Missouri Volunteers and led that regiment into battle as a colonel. Wounded and captured north of Vicksburg in December 1862, he languished for five months in Richmond's notorious Libby Prison before being exchanged in May 1863. He rejoined his regiment in time to witness the surrender of Vicksburg. Later, at Chattanooga, he led his regiment in the legendary fight at Lookout Mountain. He then joined William Tecumseh Sherman's Atlanta campaign. In 1864 illness brought him back to St. Louis. While he recuperated, Missouri's federal commander, William Rosecrans, called on him to take command of two volunteer regiments and engage Price's invading army. Fletcher's men inflicted heavy damage on the Confederates at the Battle of Pilot Knob in September 1864. Promoted to brigadier general, he rejoined Sherman and participated in the destructive federal March to the Sea. While still in the field, Fletcher learned that Missouri Republicans had nominated him for governor.[15]

Fletcher took office on January 2, 1865. Four days later the newly elected members of the state constitutional convention began meeting in St. Louis at the Mercantile Library. The delegates quickly decided to amend the constitution to end slavery. On January 11, only four delegates voted against the measure. The convention paused in its deliberations as the St. Louis Unitarian minister William Greenleaf Eliot led the delegates in prayer: "Thanks be to God for this day that light has now come out of darkness." Fletcher then declared the newly passed emancipation ordinance to be the law of the state. On Saturday, January 14, one of the St. Louis delegates to the constitutional convention, George K. Budd, read Fletcher's emancipation proclamation at a public meeting in the city. Missouri's federal commander, General Grenville Dodge, ordered a sixty-gun salute. "The sonorous voices of the great guns," reported the *Daily Democrat*, "sent their reverberations far and near, telling people for miles around that Missouri was free." The celebration continued into the evening. The *Democrat* reported that "for two or three hours the whole length of Fourth Street from Franklin Avenue to Walnut, was crowded with people of both sexes and all colors." In churches throughout the city, African Americans gathered, as an observer explained, to sing "songs of deliverance and Thanksgiving."[16]

The day of festivities ended with a display of fireworks and with the friends of emancipation illuminating public and private buildings throughout the city. According to the *Democrat*, Fourth Street was "the center of attraction." Rockets were fired from the cupola of the courthouse and all of the windows of the Planters House Hotel were illuminated and decorated with transparencies. All along Fourth Street businesses were "handsomely lit up" with "illuminated mottoes." A few weeks later, in February 1865, the Missouri General Assembly ratified the newly passed Thirteenth Amendment to the U.S. Constitution. That amendment would be fully ratified by the states on December 18, 1865.[17]

Lincoln's determination to embrace emancipation and abandon colonization left Blair isolated and embittered. The ratification of the Civil War–era amendments—the Thirteenth Amendment ending slavery, the Fourteenth Amendment extending citizenship rights and equal protection of the law to the freedmen, and the Fifteenth Amendment extending voting rights to black men—all came after Lincoln's death and after Blair had lost power to Radicals in Missouri. In time, the Liberal Republican movement reunited Blair with his Radical cousin, B. Gratz Brown. Despite his earlier support for emancipation, Brown came to see the Radical regime in Missouri, and Reconstruction generally, as a source of corruption. Brown shared Blair's hostility toward the extension of federal power into the states to protect the rights of freedmen.[18]

On this point, Blair had been prescient. It did, indeed, require a sizable military presence in the former slave states to protect the civil rights of former slaves. As Blair predicted, majority rule could undermine civil rights and the laws Congress passed to sustain them. As the Democratic Party's vice presidential candidate in 1868, Blair saw Grant elected in a landslide, but he also saw what he had earlier called the "slavery chord" transformed into the race chord as a powerful weapon in the Democratic Party's "New Departure." B. Gratz Brown accepted the Democratic Party's nomination as its vice presidential candidate in 1872 and the family reunion was complete. Grant won reelection easily, but hostility toward Radical Reconstruction had grown sufficiently to doom it to extinction. Blair died in 1875, before President Rutherford B. Hayes began to dismantle the remaining Reconstruction regimes in the former Confederacy.[19] But Blair enjoyed one last opportunity to denounce the course taken by the Republican Party and to predict what proved to be the outcome of those policies.

Blair's election to the Senate in 1870 (replacing Charles Daniel Drake, a Radical) offered him an opportunity to address once more the issue of African American citizenship. Blair took pleasure in the fact that Democrats had won control of the state legislature in Indiana in the fall elections of 1870. A joint resolution from the Indiana legislature withdrawing its assent to the ratification of the Fifteenth Amendment provided Blair with the occasion to take the floor and denounce Radical policies. The Fifteenth Amendment had been duly ratified on March 30, 1870, and the Indiana resolution had only symbolic significance. But Blair seized on it to denounce the haste with which Republican legislators, including those from Missouri, ratified the Fifteenth Amendment despite popular referenda that strongly opposed black suffrage. Blair continued his denunciation of the Reconstruction Acts and test oaths as destructive of constitutional liberties.

Blair introduced his final assault on equal rights with the observation that Radical Republican leader Oliver P. Morton, senator from Indiana, had declined an appointment by President Grant to serve as minister to Great Britain. With Democrats in control of the Indiana legislature, Morton did not want to vacate his Senate seat. As Blair railed against equal rights, Morton asked whether his colleague from Missouri "regards the fifteenth amendment as having been adopted, and as now being a part of the fundamental law of the land." "I should think," replied Blair, drawing laughter from the Senate floor, "the gentleman ought to have got my opinion of the fifteenth amendment by this time." In Missouri, Blair continued, the amendment had been ratified "in legal form" but "by the most infamous perfidy." Grant had carried Missouri in 1868 with a majority of twenty-five thousand votes. In the same election, voters rejected black suffrage by a majority of thirty thousand votes—and the state's electorate had been greatly reduced by the Radical test oath. Morton again interrupted to ask that Blair offer an "explicit" answer to his question. "The question was," Morton repeated, "whether he regards the adoption of the amendment as complete and the amendment as being now a part of the law of the land?" Blair responded: "I do regard it as complete. I do regard it as a part of the law of the land." But the Reconstruction Acts that empowered the army to enforce the Fifteenth Amendment were not constitutional in Blair's view and were not part of the law of the land. A president properly disposed to uphold the Constitution had only "to withdraw the army from the South, where it is employed in driving voters from the polls and carrying the elections against the majority of the legal voters in those States, and the people will resume their rightful authority."[20]

Union victory brought a definitive end to Taney's proslavery nationalism. Slavery and the Slave Power had been expunged from the body politic. But the more complex issue of extending citizenship rights to former slaves proved to be more elusive. Ending Reconstruction meant ending enforcement of the Fifteenth Amendment and, to a considerable extent, the Fourteenth Amendment as well. As Daniel Hamilton points out in his essay in this volume, the Supreme Court also imposed a narrow interpretation of the Thirteenth Amendment.

Blair proved to be correct on two points: the full protection of citizenship rights for freed slaves required a sizable presence of federal authority in the states; and that presence could be withdrawn at the direction of the president. The rise of the segregated South would not have surprised or offended Blair. What he could not foresee, however, was that in a Second Reconstruction in the 1950s and 1960s, the positive legacy of the *Dred Scott* case reemerged. As Adam Arenson notes in his essay in this volume, during the Second Reconstruction Dred Scott reemerged from the invisibility that had befallen him and slaves generally. Eventually, what Frank Blair had viewed as the excesses of Radical Reconstruction provided the foundation for lasting change.

Notes

1. On the ideology of the Lost Cause, see David W. Blight, *Race and Reunion: The Civil War in American Memory* (Cambridge, Mass.: Harvard University Press, 2001), 128–92.

2. Howard K. Beale, ed., *The Diary of Edward Bates, 1859–1866* (Washington, D.C.: Government Printing Office, 1933), 111–13. See also Marvin R. Cain, *Lincoln's Attorney General: Edward Bates of Missouri* (Columbia: University of Missouri Press, 1965), 101–4. On Gamble's career, see Dennis K. Boman, *Lincoln's Resolute Unionist: Hamilton Gamble, Dred Scott Dissenter and Missouri's Civil War Governor* (Baton Rouge: Louisiana State University Press, 2006), 65–92.

3. Francis P. Blair Jr., *The Destiny of the Races of This Continent: An Address Delivered before the Mercantile Library Association of Boston, Massachusetts. On the 26th of January, 1859* (Washington, D.C.: Buell and Blanchard, 1859). See also William E. Parrish, *Frank Blair: Lincoln's Conservative* (Columbia: University of Missouri Press, 1998), 138–39. On the significance of the Blair family in the formation of the Republican Party, see Eric Foner, *Free Soil, Free Labor, Free Men: The Ideology of the Republican Party before the Civil War* (New York: Oxford University Press, 1970), 63–64, 178–79, 268–80; Richard H. Sewell, *Ballots for Freedom:*

Antislavery Politics in the United States, 1837–1860 (New York: Oxford University Press, 1976), 116–17.

4. David Herbert Donald, *Lincoln* (New York: Simon and Schuster, 1996), 365–66.

5. Speech of John B. Henderson, *Congressional Globe,* 37th Cong., 2d sess., 1390–93 (March 27, 1862).

6. *Washington Globe,* June 6, 1842. See also Harry L. Watson, *Liberty and Power: The Politics of Jacksonian America* (New York: Farrar, Straus and Giroux, 1990), 242–43.

7. Frank Blair, "Emancipation in the District," *Congressional Globe,* 37th Cong., 2d sess., 1631–33 (April 11, 1862).

8. Donald, *Lincoln,* 430.

9. On Lincoln's emancipation decision, see James M. McPherson, *Abraham Lincoln and the Second American Revolution* (New York: Oxford University Press, 1990), particularly 65–91; and Mark E. Neely Jr., *The Last Best Hope of Earth: Abraham Lincoln and the Promise of America* (Cambridge, Mass.: Harvard University Press, 1993), 95–122. On the role that African Americans played in securing their emancipation, see Ira Berlin et al., *Free at Last: A Documentary History of Slavery, Freedom, and the Civil War* (New York: New Press, 1992), 435–539; and Steven Hahn, *A Nation under Our Feet: Black Political Struggles in the Rural South from Slavery to the Great Migration* (Cambridge, Mass.: Harvard University Press, 2003), 62–115.

10. For a general history of wartime emancipation, see James M. McPherson, *Ordeal by Fire: The Civil War and Reconstruction,* 2d ed. (New York: McGraw-Hill, 1992), 316–17, 377–84, 425–35.

11. Speech of E. H. Norton, *Congressional Globe,* 37th Cong., 2d sess., 1826–28 (April 24, 1862); *Biographical Directory of the United States Congress,* available online at http://bioguide.congress.gov/biosearch/biosearch.asp. On the failure of efforts to secure widespread confiscation, see Daniel W. Hamilton, *The Limits of Sovereignty: Property Confiscation in the Union and the Confederacy during the Civil War* (Chicago: University of Chicago Press, 2007), 169–71.

12. Speech of John Phelps, *Congressional Globe,* 37th Cong., 2d sess., 2294–98 (May 22, 1862).

13. "Speech of Hon. F. P. Blair, Jr., of Missouri, in the House of Representatives," *Congressional Globe,* 37th Cong., 2d sess., appendix, 171–73 (May 23, 1862); *Biographical Directory of the United States Congress.*

14. On Price's Missouri raid, see Albert Castel, *General Sterling Price and the Civil War in the West* (Baton Rouge: Louisiana State University Press, 1968), 208–37; and Robert E. Shalhope, *Sterling Price: Portrait of a Southerner* (Columbia: University of Missouri Press, 1971), 263–80.

15. William E. Parrish, *Missouri under Radical Rule* (Columbia: University of Missouri Press, 1965), 11–14; Louis S. Gerteis, *Civil War St. Louis* (Lawrence: University Press of Kansas, 2001), 307–11.

16. The January 14 celebration of emancipation is described in the *Missouri Democrat,* December 15, 1865.

17. St. Louisans continued to celebrate emancipation on January 11. The *Democrat* reported, sometimes in considerable detail, January 11 celebrations through 1872. Each year, often in bad weather, members of black benevolent societies and Sunday schools paraded through the streets accompanied by bands. In the evening, celebrants gathered in Turner's Hall to listen to speeches. See, for example, *Missouri Democrat,* January 11, 1875.

18. Norma L. Peterson, *Freedom and Franchise: The Political Career of B. Gratz Brown* (Columbia: University of Missouri Press, 1965), 173–75, 214–15.

19. On the ending of Reconstruction, see C. Vann Woodward, *Reunion and Reaction: The Compromise of 1877 and the End of Reconstruction* (Boston: Little, Brown, 1951), 216–46; and Heather Cox Richardson, *The Death of Reconstruction: Race, Labor, and Politics in the Post–Civil War North, 1865–1901* (Cambridge, Mass.: Harvard University Press, 2001), particularly 183–224.

20. "Fifteenth Amendment Speech of Hon. F. P. Blair of Missouri, in the United States Senate, February 15, 1871," *Congressional Globe,* 41st Cong., 3d sess., appendix, 114–17 (February 15, 1871).

FIVE

An Exaggerated Legacy

Dred Scott *and Substantive Due Process*

Austin Allen

SCHOLARS FREQUENTLY cite Chief Justice Roger B. Taney's majority opinion in *Dred Scott v. Sandford* (1857) as the birthplace of substantive due process, one of the most controversial concepts in American constitutional law.[1] This concept holds that the Constitution's Fifth and Fourteenth amendments' due process clauses guarantee that certain fundamental rights will not be abridged under almost any circumstances. The theory has essentially no grounding in the Constitution's text, and the specific rights it protects have varied widely over time.[2] Proponents contend, however, that properly applied substantive due process provides a powerful mechanism to balance state interests against individual rights.[3] Critics disagree. For them, the lack of a textual foundation offers reason enough to abandon the theory. If not, then the correlation between substantive due process's rather arbitrary protection of rights and what critics see as an abuse of judicial power should do so. Some of the most controversial cases in the Court's history have employed substantive due process to subordinate the will of democratic majorities to the opinions of a few unelected judges. Classic examples include *Roe v. Wade*'s elevation of privacy rights over antiabortion laws and *Lochner v. New York*'s protection of contractual rights in the face of worker-protection laws.[4] *Dred Scott,* which held that Congress possessed no authority to stop slavery's expansion into the federal territories, claims a special status on this list. The 1857 decision is one of the few Supreme Court rulings to be repudiated by a constitutional amendment, and it played a role in the coming of a civil war.

These features have made *Dred Scott* a particularly useful case for critics of substantive due process, because the decision's legacy permits them to portray the concept as one that has been devoid of legitimacy from its inception. Such arguments generally reduce the decision to a single passage in Taney's sprawling opinion: "an act of Congress which deprives a citizen of the United States of his liberty or property, merely because he came himself or brought his property into a particular Territory of the United States, and who had committed no offence against the laws, could hardly be dignified with the name of due process of law."[5]

There was in 1857 no term for the concept Taney employed here, but modern lawyers have no difficulty labeling it substantive due process. Indeed, they have associated that reasoning with this decision since the early twentieth century, when Edward S. Corwin portrayed *Dred Scott* as a forerunner to *Lochner.*[6] But in the 1990s, commentators seeking to undermine *Roe v. Wade*—most notably Robert Bork and Justice Antonin Scalia—put forward influential assertions that the controversy generated by *Dred Scott* stemmed precisely from Taney's invocation of substantive due process. Steven G. Calabresi recently employed this tactic by asserting that one of the Fourteenth Amendment's primary objectives involved overturning "the Supreme Court's activist, substantive due process decision in *Dred Scott*" to counter an argument in favor of broad powers of judicial review under the amendment. This interpretation, he insisted, led to decisions like *Lochner* and *Roe* and ran counter to the Fourteenth Amendment's original intent, which "sought to overrule *Dred Scott,* not to authorize future *Dred Scott*s!"[7]

This essay rejects such interpretations of *Dred Scott.* It argues that the use of the decision by Bork, Scalia, Calabresi, and others fails to undermine the concept of substantive due process. Although it remains agnostic as to the concept's legitimacy, this essay contends that these currently influential readings of *Dred Scott* rest on a number of misleading assumptions about the nature of Taney's opinion, the scope of judicial power in American society, and the decision's similarities with twentieth-century substantive due process rulings. None of those assumptions can withstand historical scrutiny. After examining the relationship between *Dred Scott* and substantive due process as it was understood in the early twentieth century and noting how those accounts differ from those developed in the 1990s by Bork, Scalia, and others, this essay will argue that *Dred Scott* cannot bear the explanatory weight that critics of substantive due process ascribe to it.

On one level, Bork, Scalia, and others assert nothing new when they portray *Dred Scott* as a substantive due process decision. Legal scholars established *Dred Scott*'s relationship to that concept in the early twentieth century, as they struggled to explain the Supreme Court's aggressive review of state economic regulation exemplified by *Lochner v. New York. Lochner* held that state efforts to regulate the hours worked in a bakery arbitrarily violated an individual right to contract protected by the Fourteenth Amendment's due process clause.[8] According to Justice Oliver Wendell Holmes Jr.'s influential dissenting opinion in the case, the Court ruled in that way primarily because a majority of its members found the state policy disagreeable.[9] *Dred Scott* became fused to the developing concept of substantive due process in this period as a consequence of the scholarly effort to uncover *Lochner*'s antecedents, but this fusion carried none of the influence that contemporary invocations of the link regularly assert.

Edward S. Corwin first exposed the doctrinal connection between *Lochner* and *Dred Scott* in the early twentieth century. He contended, in an argument that James W. Ely has recently shown to have been wrong, that *Lochner*-style reasoning had little foundation in American constitutional law before 1860.[10] Early nineteenth-century courts, Corwin wrote, heavily emphasized the protection of vested property rights and recognized "that legislative power . . . is not absolute, but is constrained both by its own nature and by the principles of republican government, natural law, and the social compact."[11] At the beginning of the nineteenth century, judges usually rested their contentions on statements of general principles, but by the mid-nineteenth century judges increasingly enforced the limits of legislative power by resorting to "due process" or "law of the land" clauses contained in state constitutions. "Law of the land" clauses performed most of the work in these cases primarily because judges considered "due process of law" clauses to refer specifically to matters of procedure, not substance.[12]

Corwin identified two major exceptions to this trend: *Wynehamer v. People* and *Dred Scott*. *Wynehamer* involved an 1855 New York antiliquor law that criminalized the possession of small quantities of alcohol and provided for the confiscation of any subsequently found in the state. The Court ruled that the law violated the state constitution's law of the land and due process clauses because it arbitrarily deprived owners of property they had lawfully enjoyed the day before.[13] Corwin understood *Wynehamer* as a significant departure in due process jurisprudence. By shifting the emphasis on the clause's language from the phrase "without due process of law" to "deprived of life, liberty, or property," the Court found a way to insert extraconstitutional principles into the written document.[14]

Numerous state courts rebuffed this reading. Only Indiana struck down a statute similar to New York's.[15] *Wynehamer*, Corwin concluded, "found no place in the constitutional law that was generally recognized throughout the United States in the year 1856."[16] The ruling had neither been anticipated nor subsequently adopted, and the profession scorned it. "All that was needed apparently to dispose of the doctrine at once and for all time was another such Pyrrhic victory."[17] And that turned out to be *Dred Scott*. In a separate essay, Corwin argued that Taney's use of the Fifth Amendment sought "to engraft the doctrine of 'vested rights' upon the national constitution."[18] He did so, Corwin asserted (despite finding "no hint of the matter in the briefs"), by drawing inspiration from *Wynehamer*.[19] Although he offered a relatively close reading of both opinions, Corwin never paused to consider whether *Wynehamer* and *Dred Scott* were distinguishable.[20] He simply asserted a connection between the two and permitted *Dred Scott's* reputation to provide the "Pyrrhic victory" that would cast a shadow over what would eventually become known as substantive due process.

By the 1930s, the link between *Dred Scott* and substantive due process had established itself in the law review literature. This connection appeared initially in matter-of-fact references in footnotes.[21] A few years later the link appeared in the text of law review articles criticizing substantive readings of the due process clause as extraconstitutional mechanisms for striking down laws that "offended . . . judges' innermost convictions,"[22] or for "perpetuating the *laissez faire* system of economics,"[23] or for use as "a weapon . . . in periods of crisis and under the pressure of intense conviction."[24] Each of these references owed a debt to Corwin. Although they did not cite his work directly, these scholars embraced his argument that substantive readings of due process clauses constituted a response to social movements to which the judges were hostile. Their efforts also elaborated the linkages between antebellum cases like *Wynehamer* and *Dred Scott* and more recent ones like *Lochner*.[25]

What is striking about these arguments, however, was their relative lack of influence compared to their prominence at the end of the twentieth century. With the exception of occasional references in debates over whether the Fourteenth Amendment's framers contemplated a substantive reading of the due process clause, few legal commentators made much of the link.[26] Courts at the time paid no attention. Early twentieth-century judges, when they cited *Dred Scott* at all, did so to emphasize that the Constitution's meaning never changed.[27] In 1905, Justice David J. Brewer, while he was applying aspects of the federal tax code against the agents of a state, favorably quoted Taney's statement that the Constitution "speaks not only in the same words, but with the same meaning and intent with which it spoke when it came from the hands of its framers."[28] Texas's Supreme Court cited the same page a few years later while it upheld a statute enabling (white) women to vote in state primaries.[29] And Justice George Sutherland invoked the passage in his protests against the Supreme Court's embrace of New Deal legislation in the 1930s.[30] Sutherland's complaint may provide a hint as to why judges made so little of the connection between *Dred Scott* and substantive due process that commentators perceived. The Court's embracing of the New Deal entailed a flat rejection of *Lochner* and its reading of the due process clause.[31] By the time legal commentators were pointing to a link between *Dred Scott* and the doctrine of substantive due process, the doctrine itself seemed all but dead.

Court rulings in the 1960s and 1970s, notably *Roe v. Wade*, changed all of that.[32] Substantive due process returned, although the doctrine now protected privacy rights rather than economic ones. Recent discussions of the link between that doctrine and *Dred Scott* have developed primarily in the context of the debate over *Roe,* a decision that Robert Bork and Justice Antonin Scalia effectively portrayed in the early 1990s as a direct descendant of the Court's infamous 1857 ruling. Bork's book, *The Tempting of America,* portrayed substantive due process as a central component in the politicization (and thus corruption) of constitutional law, and he called for a return to a jurisprudence of original intent as a salvation.[33] Throughout the argument, Bork worked to connect the corrupting doctrine to *Dred Scott.* Scalia invoked the link two years later in his dissent against the Court's upholding of *Roe* in *Planned Parenthood of Southeastern Pennsylvania v. Casey.*[34] Like Bork, Scalia argued that only a resort to originalism would save the Court from its errors. In the process, they drew from *Dred Scott* a series of implications that reduced rulings with which they disagreed to pure politics and that justified a complete rejection of the Court's substantive due process rulings.

Bork made the most explicit case for *Dred Scott*'s status as a direct antecedent to *Roe.* He characterized *Dred Scott* "as the worst in our history until the twentieth century provided rivals for that title."[35] Taney's reading of the Fifth Amendment—the only part of that lengthy decision to occupy Bork's attention—"is as blatant a distortion of the original understanding of the Constitution as one can find."[36] Within a few pages, Bork identified *Dred Scott* as the "very ugly common ancestor" of both *Lochner* and *Roe* because they each rest on the same constitutional theory:[37] "[O]nce it's conceded that a judge may give the due process clause substantive content, *Dred Scott, Lochner,* and *Roe* are equally valid concepts of constitutional law. You may or may not like the judge's politics or his morality, but you have conceded, so far as the Constitution is concerned, the legitimacy of his imposing that politics and morality upon you. Lenin is supposed to have written: 'Who says A must say B.' In that he was logically correct. Who says *Roe* must say *Lochner* and *Scott.*"[38]

Scalia extended this argument in his *Casey* dissent, where he insisted that the Court's abortion decisions rested on nothing more than "a collection of adjectives that simply decorate a value judgment and conceal a political choice."[39] He then quoted Justice Benjamin Curtis's criticism of the Court's ruling in *Dred Scott:* "When a strict interpretation . . . is abandoned . . . , we have no longer a Constitution; we are under the government of individual men, who . . . have power to declare what the Constitution is, according to their own views of what it ought to mean."[40] The Court's use of substantive due process, Scalia continued, stripped the Court of legitimacy because it drew on the same discredited logic employed in *Lochner* and in *Dred Scott,* which, the justice added, quoting an assertion by David Currie, was "very possibly the first application of substantive due process in the Supreme Court."[41]

Such erroneous rulings generated social division. Bork quipped that "there is something wrong . . . with a judicial power that can produce a decision it takes a civil war to overturn."[42] Scalia focused on a portrait of Taney painted two years after *Dred Scott:* "There seems to be on his face . . . [a] profound sadness and disillusionment. . . I expect that two years earlier he, too, had thought himself 'calling the contending sides of national controversy to end their national division by accepting a common mandate rooted in the Constitution.'"[43] Courts possessed neither the power nor the mandate to handle issues such as abortion and enslavement. They only make matters worse: "By foreclosing all democratic outlet for the deep passions this issue arouses . . . , the Court merely prolongs and intensifies the anguish."[44]

Bork and Scalia used *Dred Scott* to develop a criticism of substantive due process that has become influential among other judges, who have taken the argument further and called for a complete rejection of the doctrine. Judge Emilio Garza provided the most thorough example of this line of thought in 1997 when he concurred in a Fifth Circuit ruling finding a Louisiana parental consent law to be in conflict with the Fourteenth Amendment's due process clause.[45] In a separate opinion, Garza restated the Bork-Scalia position. The 1857 Court resorted to substantive due process and removed "one of the most contentious and personal of political issues out of the national debate," hoping thereby to unify a divided country.[46] The effort failed, and "*Dred Scott* tore the nation apart."[47] Late twentieth-century abortion rulings, which relied on the same reasoning, had a similarly disturbing influence. "The last twenty years have seen political protest over the Court's abortion jurisprudence unmatched by any other political issue of our day. Protest marches, clinic bombings, and fatal shootings have punctuated the debate."[48] Upholding decisions with such results, Garza continued, will bring nothing positive. Moreover, the Court's most "celebrated . . . constitutional moments" came about in decisions like

Brown v. Board of Education and *West Coast Hotel v. Parrish,* both of which rejected earlier rulings (*Plessy v. Ferguson* and *Lochner,* respectively) that "were . . . defensible on *stare decisis* grounds."[49] The time had come "for our Supreme Court to write the analog to *West Coast Hotel*" and remove "itself from the substantive due process morass of abortion cases."[50]

Four years later, the Alabama Supreme Court moved in that direction by overruling its own precedent dealing with the granting of waivers to the state's parental consent requirement for minors seeking abortions.[51] Alabama law permits trial courts to grant waivers if a minor can demonstrate that she is well informed and mature enough to make the decision on her own.[52] In this case, the trial judge had overlooked testimony that the minor in question had sought information from a variety of sources, including adult family friends and several nurses at different providers, and focused on her lack of contact with an actual physician. (She had tried to reach physicians but never got past the nurses.[53]) The judge denied the waiver, arguing that the minor, "a beautiful young girl with a bright future," did "not need to have a butcher get a hold of her."[54] Breaking with precedent, the Alabama Supreme Court then treated the lower court's ruling as if it were equivalent to a jury verdict. In response to the dissenters' cry of judicial activism, Chief Justice Roy Moore invoked *Dred Scott.* In a concurring opinion that decried the legitimacy of *Roe* and its progenitor, *Griswold v. Connecticut,* Moore contended that the doctrine of substantive due process demanded his court's response in this situation. *Griswold* and *Roe* stood in the tradition of *Dred Scott.* "This ruling was patently incorrect, and many citizens of this Country still suffer the legacy of such a poorly reasoned United States Supreme Court opinion."[55] Consequently, his court had the responsibility to limit the impact of these contemporary *Dred Scotts.*

Over the past few years, these judges have developed a powerful narrative as part of their effort to challenge the Court's substantive due process rulings. By connecting the Court's abortion rulings to a decision like *Dred Scott,* which contemporary constitutional theory assumes as an axiom to be incorrect and which legal scholars revile for a variety of very good reasons, Bork, Scalia, and others have placed advocates of substantive due process on the defensive and cast themselves as ones who would bring the constitutional order back to proper principles.[56] Decisions like *Roe,* or even broad interpretations of constitutional provisions (as Calabresi asserted), stand in the tradition of *Dred Scott* and therefore deserve only condemnation. Rejecting such decisions, by this account, would allow the Court to relive the great moments it achieved in *West Coast Hotel* and *Brown* when it repudiated other doctrines found to be in conflict with the Constitution.

This is a nice story, and one can understand the appeal of a narrative that ascribes to critics of substantive due process such a heroic role. Even so, this account, when subjected to historical analysis, is deeply problematic. Every reference to *Dred Scott* in this narrative is either misleading or simply wrong. The errors begin with the characterization of the decision as nothing more than an example of judicial activism resting on newly invented legal theory. The errors continue in the narrative's overstatement of judicial power in the descriptions of the consequences that followed *Dred Scott* and in the discussions of the Court's relation to the democratic process. If one takes Taney's argument seriously, in fact, *Dred Scott* simply cannot carry the explanatory load that this judicial narrative asks it bear.

Bork, Scalia, and their followers characterize *Dred Scott* as a blatant departure from the framers' original intent and argue that only a resort to a jurisprudence of originalism will stave off future instances of politically motivated judicial activism. Legal commentators, most notably Christopher Eisgruber and Jamin Raskin, have subjected this argument to withering criticism, and the issue need not be belabored here.[57] Three points ought to be made in passing, however. First, as Eisgruber and Raskin point out, Taney self-consciously employed what would later be termed an originalist framework throughout *Dred Scott*.[58] Although, as Mark Graber has noted, commentators cannot write the decision off as *only* an originalist opinion, the commitment to remain faithful to the framers' intent runs throughout Taney's argument.[59] Early twentieth-century judges—and this is the second point—certainly noted that aspect of the opinion.[60] Finally, Taney's discussion of the Fifth Amendment's limitation on Congress's power to block slavery's expansion took place in a historically grounded analysis of the possible meanings of the needful rules clause and other relevant constitutional provisions at the time of ratification.[61] Scholars may debate whether Taney ruled correctly on this point, but there should be little disagreement that the methods Taney employed closely resembled those that we would now term originalist.

The Bork-Scalia narrative also overstates the disruptive power of the judiciary, because the storyline assumes a causal relationship between *Dred Scott* and the outbreak of Civil War.[62] Scalia therefore spends a page or so describing Taney brooding in a portrait. Garza writes about *Dred Scott* tearing the nation apart. And Bork states that the decision required a war to overturn it. The implication of this argument is straightforward: poor judicial reasoning leads to potentially cataclysmic social outcomes (although generally not open warfare). Connecting *Dred Scott* to the Civil War also tends to magnify the stakes of constitutional interpretation. In Garza's formulation, if a judge interprets correctly, then society gets "regular debate, lobbying, and legislation at the state level."[63] If not, then society faces "protest marches, clinic bombings, . . . fatal shootings," and perhaps worse.[64] That instability, in the final analysis, stems directly from the Court's poorly reasoned intervention in issues with which it has no business.

Using *Dred Scott* in this manner is deeply misleading. Although none of them would deny that the decision constituted a significant link in the chain of events that led to the Civil War, *Dred Scott*'s leading scholars would not draw a direct connection between the two events. Don E. Fehrenbacher in his book on the decision argued that a later event—an effort to bring Kansas into the Union as slave state against the wishes of the majority of its population—set into motion the forces that would ultimately lead to secession and Civil War.[65] Mark Graber recently made a similar point.[66] Indeed, *Dred Scott*'s major contribution to the coming of Civil War rests primarily in the decision's usefulness as propaganda for Republican partisans intent on convincing Northern voters that they were threatened by a "Slave Power Conspiracy."[67] Little of this process had to do with constitutional interpretation. Republican strategists, as David Potter pointed out long ago, consciously decided to criticize the ruling by attacking the composition of the Court (southerners held five of its nine seats) rather than by confronting the decision's substance.[68] Indeed, the first comprehensive analysis of the opinion itself did not appear until the 1970s, when Fehrenbacher powerfully pronounced the Court to be wrong on all the major points of the decision. New scholarship may force a revision of that view. Recent studies have argued that the Court's ruling in *Dred Scott* was at least plausible.[69] Even so, the interpretive positions and substantive rulings of the Court in 1857 had essentially no direct connection to the chain of events leading to the Civil

War. The instability that resulted from *Dred Scott* came from factors larger than the Court, and the ensuing conflict was emphatically not a product of legal doctrines like substantive due process.

In fact, *Dred Scott* really ought not to be regarded as a substantive due process decision. Recent writing, and not just that of Bork and Scalia, simply asserts the connection rather than explaining it. Those assertions ultimately trace back to Corwin's work at the beginning of the twentieth century. Corwin, of course, did more than assert a connection between *Dred Scott* and substantive readings of the due process clauses, but his interpretation rested heavily on the temporal proximity of that ruling to the one in *Wynehamer v. People,* and he portrayed the rulings as two sides of the same coin.[70] Yet *Wynehamer* and *Dred Scott* differ significantly, primarily as a consequence of the institutional context in which each emerged. *Wynehamer* involved a state court's effort to enforce limits against a state legislature's novel application of the police power.[71] Without question, this ruling anticipated the Supreme Court's reasoning in *Lochner,* and its substance supports the argument developed by Corwin that such uses of the due process clause, which he believed to be aberrant, came about because nineteenth-century judges sought to protect vested property rights.[72]

Dred Scott does not fit well into this explanatory framework, although many judges and commentators assume that it does. In the 1950s, for example, Richard V. Carpenter argued that Taney's invocation of the Fifth Amendment due process clause developed out of a "prominent feature of the Supreme Court's thinking during this period[:] . . . its deep concern for the unalienable, fundamental, and sacred rights of individuals."[73] Justice David Souter put forth a similar argument a few years ago in a concurring opinion in *Washington v. Glucksberg.*[74] The assumption that the Court had a significant interest in the protection of individual rights (property or otherwise), however, fundamentally mischaracterizes the priorities of the antebellum Supreme Court or, at least, the Taney Court. Very few Taney Court decisions exhibited such a concern. Court members generally considered the protection of individual liberties to be a matter for the states, and they sometimes allowed state governments to run roughshod over individual liberties.[75] Thus in 1837, the Court permitted a state legislature to destroy the value of a preexisting toll bridge by chartering a new bridge that would operate free of charge at a location just a few yards away from the older structure.[76] On a like note, the Court refused to intervene in the 1840s when litigants presented it with the opportunity to choose between two competing constitutions for Rhode Island. The Court declined, and in so doing it effectively sanctioned the preexisting one, which disenfranchised a majority of the state's inhabitants.[77]

Those outcomes stemmed from what the Taney Court perceived as its fundamental priority: the policing of jurisdictional boundaries within the federal system. The Constitution created a complex institutional arrangement in which a federal government of enumerated (and, for the Taney Court, starkly limited) powers presided over a growing assortment of nearly autonomous state governments that possessed authority to regulate most aspects of social life under the police power. The central challenge for the Court in the mid-nineteenth century lay in determining where the power of the states ended and where that of the federal government began. So the justices spent much of their time making the lines clear and bright.[78]

Taney's use of the Fifth Amendment's due process clause therefore emerged in this context. Indeed, his entire discussion of the Missouri Compromise's constitutionality centered on the way in which the enumerated character of federal power shaped Congress's authority over the territories.[79] Although he conceded that Congress had a great deal of discretion over the governance of the territories, Taney insisted that the protections contained in the Bill of Rights placed absolute limits on the way in which Congress could regulate the territories.[80] The federal government simply had no authority to bar the expansion of slavery into the territories so long as various American legal regimes continued to define some human beings as property.[81] This argument differed markedly from the reasoning in cases like *Wynehamer* and *Lochner*. In those decisions, courts confronted legislatures that employed legitimately held police powers in ways that made judges uncomfortable, and they used due process clauses to balance their concern for individual rights against a generally legitimate regulatory authority. Taney, in contrast, faced a situation where Congress arguably assumed a power that it simply did not possess under the Constitution. The protection for slaveholders' property rights that his opinion created was merely incidental to the larger structural limitations that shaped federal power.[82] Whatever Taney was doing here, he was not anticipating substantive due process as it is currently understood.

Glib comparisons of *Dred Scott* to twentieth-century decisions like *Lochner* and *Roe* therefore cannot withstand close scrutiny. Arguments that Taney's opinion represented an example of unbridled activism falter upon Taney's determined attempt to discern the framers' intent. Efforts to associate the negative consequences of *Dred Scott* with modern substantive due process cases overstate the power Courts hold and only work by pulling the case out of its antebellum context. Finally, the reasoning in *Dred Scott* differs significantly from that of modern substantive due process cases and does so to such a degree that they are not truly comparable. Judges and legal commentators would be better served in this instance by resisting the temptation to cite *Dred Scott* once again.

Such citations contribute very little toward an understanding of either *Dred Scott* or of substantive due process. That case and that doctrine resulted from radically different sets of rules that render them incomparable. Although analyses of *Dred Scott* remain important to discussions of judicial supremacy and issues of equality, the ruling is basically irrelevant for discussions of substantive due process. Taney's development of the concept was at best, as Fehrenbacher noted, "tentative and sketchy."[83] Since the 1990s, however, judges and commentators have moved beyond merely noting that *Dred Scott* shared similarities with controversial twentieth-century decisions like *Lochner* to arguing that, because *Dred Scott* was an "activist, substantive due process decision" (to borrow Calabresi's phrase), certain consequences must follow.[84] The links to the Supreme Court's controversial 1857 decision therefore point to a need to construe the Fourteenth Amendment narrowly and to overturn particular cases. Very few of these arguments draw any support from the historical record, and scholars should think carefully before invoking *Dred Scott*. Restraint on this issue will hardly undermine critical accounts of Supreme Court doctrine. References to *Lochner* already perform the same work as citations to *Dred Scott*, and they have the advantage of invoking a dubious Court ruling (although perhaps not one as well known to nonlawyers) that did in fact employ substantive due process. Allowing *Dred Scott* to fade into insignificance in this context would not seriously affect legal argument, but it would demonstrate fidelity to the historical record and decouple *Dred Scott* from a legacy that it did not truly bequeath to American law.

Notes

1. Dred Scott v. John F. A. Sandford, 60 U.S. (19 How.) 393 (1857).

2. John Harrison, "Substantive Due Process and the Constitutional Text," *Virginia Law Review* 83, no. 3 (1997): 493–558.

3. See Justice David Souter's discussion of the concept in his concurring opinion in Washington v. Glucksberg, 521 U.S. 702, 755–73 (1997).

4. Roe v. Wade, 410 U.S. 113 (1973); Lochner v. New York, 198 U.S. 45 (1905).

5. Scott, 60 U.S. at 450.

6. Edward S. Corwin, "The Doctrine of Due Process of Law before the Civil War," *Harvard Law Review* 24, no. 5 (1911): 366–85 [hereinafter cited as Corwin, "Doctrine of Due Process, pt. 1"]; Edward S. Corwin, "The Doctrine of Due Process of Law before the Civil War (continued)," *Harvard Law Review* 24, no. 6 (1911): 460–79 [hereinafter cited as Corwin, "Doctrine of Due Process, pt. 2"]; Edward S. Corwin, "The Dred Scott Decision, in the Light of Contemporary Legal Doctrines," *American Historical Review* 17, no. 1 (1911): 52–69.

7. Steven G. Calabresi, "The Originalist and Normative Case against Judicial Activism: A Reply to Professor Randy Barnett," *Michigan Law Review* 103, no. 1 (2005): 1093.

8. U.S. Const., amend. 14, § 1.

9. Lochner, 198 U.S. at 75 (Holmes, J., dissenting).

10. James W. Ely Jr., "The Oxymoron Reconsidered: Myth and Reality in the Origins of Substantive Due Process," *Constitutional Commentary* 16, no. 2 (1999): 315–45 (arguing that Corwin's interest in undermining *Lochner* led him to downplay evidence that did not fit his thesis).

11. Corwin, "Doctrine of Due Process, pt. 1," 376.

12. Ibid., 380–85; Corwin, "Doctrine of Due Process, pt. 2," 463–64.

13. Wynehamer v. People, 13 N.Y. 378, 393; N.Y. Const. of 1846, art. 1, §§ 1, 6.

14. Corwin, "Doctrine of Due Process, pt. 2," 467–68.

15. Beebe v. State, 6 Ind. 501 (1855).

16. Corwin, "Doctrine of Due Process, pt. 2," 474–75.

17. Ibid., 475.

18. Corwin, "Dred Scott Decision," 62–63.

19. Ibid., 64–65 (quotation on 64).

20. See text at notes 79–82; Austin Allen, *Origins of the* Dred Scott *Case: Jacksonian Jurisprudence and the Supreme Court, 1837–1857* (Athens: University of Georgia Press, 2006), 191–92.

21. For example, see Walter Nelles, "Towards Legal Understanding: II," *Columbia Law Review* 34, no. 6 (1934): 1057n59.

22. Edwin Borchard, "The Supreme Court and Private Rights," *Yale Law Journal* 47, no. 7 (1938): 1062.

23. Louis B. Boudin, "Truth and Fiction about the Fourteenth Amendment," *New York University Law Quarterly Review* 16, no. 1 (1938): 80.

24. Howard Jay Graham, "Justice Field and the Fourteenth Amendment," *Yale Law Journal* 52, no. 4 (1943): 859.

25. Boudin, "Truth and Fiction about the Fourteenth Amendment," 80–81; Borchard, "Supreme Court and Private Rights," 1062–65.

26. See Boudin, "Truth and Fiction about the Fourteenth Amendment," 74n36; Howard Jay Graham, "The Conspiracy Theory of the Fourteenth Amendment," *Yale Law Journal* 47, no. 3 (1938): 393–402.

27. See Girard v. Diefendorf, 54 Idaho 467, 474–75 (1934); Tapley v. Futrell, 187 Ark. 844, 850 (1933); Des Moines Joint Stock Land Bank v. Nordholm, 217 Iowa 1319, 1386 (1933) (Clausen, J., dissenting); State ex rel. Diederichs v. State Highway Comm'n, 89 Mont. 205, 210 (1931); State ex rel. Richards v. Moorer, 152 S.C. 455, 562 (1929); Ex parte Rhodes, 202 Ala. 68, 77 (1918); State ex rel. West v. Butler, 70 Fla. 102, 134–35 (1915); Booten v. Pinson, 77 W. Va. 412, 435–36 (1915); Borino v. Gen'l Registrars of Voters, 86 Conn. 622, 627–28 (1913).

28. South Carolina v. U.S., 199 U.S. 437, 449 (1905) (quoting Scott, 60 U.S. at 426).

29. Koy v. Schneider, 110 Tex. 369, 378 (Tex. 1920).

30. Home Bldg. and Loan Ass'n v. Blaisdell, 290 U.S. 398, 450 (1934).

31. See West Coast Hotel v. Parrish, 300 U.S. 379 (1937).

32. Griswold v. Connecticut, 381 U.S. 479 (1965).

33. Robert H. Bork, *The Tempting of America: The Political Seduction of the Law* (New York: Free Press, 1990).

34. Planned Parenthood of Southeastern Pennsylvania v. Casey, 505 U.S. 833 (1992).

35. Bork, *Tempting of America,* 28.

36. Ibid., 29. All of the references to *Dred Scott* in *Tempting of America* take place in discussions of substantive due process. See the references cited in the index (417).

37. Ibid., 32.

38. Ibid.

39. Planned Parenthood v. Casey, 505 U.S. at 784.

40. Ibid., 985 (quoting *Scott,* 60 U.S. at 621) (ellipses added).

41. Ibid., 998 (quoting David Currie, *The Constitution in the Supreme Court: The First Hundred Years* [Chicago: University of Chicago Press, 1985], 271).

42. Bork, *Tempting of America,* 34.

43. Planned Parenthood v. Casey, 505 U.S. at 1002 (quoting joint opinion of O'Connor, Kennedy, and Souter, JJ., ibid., 866).

44. Ibid., 1002.

45. Causeway Medical Suite v. Ieyoub, 109 F. 3d 1096 (5th Cir. La. 1997).

46. Ibid., 1123.

47. Ibid.

48. Ibid.

49. Ibid. Brown v. Bd. of Educ., 347 U.S. 483 (1954); West Coast Hotel, 300 U.S. 379; Lochner, 198 U.S. 45; Plessy v. Ferguson, 163 U.S. 537 (1896).

50. Causeway Medical Suite, 109 F. 3d at 1123.

51. Ex parte Anonymous, 803 So. 2d 542 (Ala. 2001).

52. Ala. Code 1975 § 26–21–4.

53. Justice Douglas I. Johnstone, dissenting, provides extensive quotations of the proceedings. See Anonymous, 803 So. 2d at 560–64.

54. Ibid., 561.

55. Ibid., 548–49; Griswold v. Connecticut, 381 U.S. 479 (1965).

56. On *Dred Scott* and constitutional theory, see Mark A. Graber, *Dred Scott and the Problem of Constitutional Evil* (New York: Cambridge University Press, 2006), 15–18. On the various reasons for reviling it, see Austin Allen, "Rethinking *Dred Scott:* New Context for an Old Case," *Chicago-Kent Law Review* 82, no. 3 (2007): 141–43.

57. Christopher L. Eisgruber, "*Dred* Again: Originalism's Forgotten Past," *Constitutional Commentary* 10, no. 1 (1993): 37–66; Jamin B. Raskin, "*Roe v. Wade* and the *Dred Scott* Decision: Justice Scalia's Peculiar Analogy in *Planned Parenthood v. Casey,*" *American University Journal of Gender and Law* 1, no. 1 (1993): 61–85.

58. Eisgruber, "*Dred* Again," 46; Raskin, "*Roe v. Wade* and the *Dred Scott* Decision," 68.

59. Graber, *Dred Scott and the Problem of Constitutional Evil,* 15–89.

60. See text at notes 26–30.

61. U.S. Const. art. 4, § 3; Scott, 60 U.S. at 432–42, 447–52.

62. The connection between *Dred Scott* and the Civil War is not limited just to this narrative; legal scholars frequently note it. For examples, see Louise Weinberg, "*Dred Scott* and the Crisis of 1860," *Chicago-Kent Law Review* 82, no. 3 (2007): 97–140; Ely, "Oxymoron Reconsidered," 318; Jenna Bednar and William N. Eskridge Jr. "Steadying the Court's 'Unsteady Path': A Theory of Judicial Enforcement of Federalism," *Southern California Law Review* 68, no. 6 (1995): 1480; Lino A. Graglia, "Interpreting the Constitution: Posner on Bork," *Stanford Law Review* 44, no. 5 (1992): 1036.

63. Causeway Medical Suite, 109 F. 3d at 1123.

64. Ibid.

65. Don E. Fehrenbacher, *The Dred Scott Case: Its Significance in American Law and Politics* (New York: Oxford University Press, 1978), 449–84.

66. Graber, *Dred Scott and the Problem of Constitutional Evil,* 44–45.

67. Allen, "Rethinking *Dred Scott,*" 149–50.

68. David M. Potter, *The Impending Crisis, 1848–1861,* ed. Don E. Fehrenbacher (New York: Harper Torchbooks, 1976), 283–84.

69. See Allen, *Origins of the* Dred Scott *Case;* Graber, *Dred Scott and the Problem of Constitutional Evil;* Paul Finkelman, "Was *Dred Scott* Correctly Decided? An 'Expert Report' for the Defendant," *Lewis and Clark Law Review* 12, no. 4 (2008): 1219–52.

70. Corwin, "Doctrine of Due Process, pt. 2," 475; Corwin, "Dred Scott Decision," 64–65.

71. Allen, *Origins of the* Dred Scott *Case,* 191–92.

72. Corwin, "Doctrine of Due Process, pt. 2," 463–64. But see Ely, "Oxymoron Reconsidered," 327–42 (arguing that *Wynehamer* was not aberrant).

73. Richard V. Carpenter, "Substantive Due Process at Issue: A Resume," *UCLA Law Review* 5, no. 5 (1958): 62.

74. Washington v. Glucksberg, 521 U.S. at 757–60.

75. Allen, *Origins of the* Dred Scott *Case,* 19.

76. Proprietors of Charles River Bridge v. Proprietors of Warren Bridge, 36 U.S. 420 (1837); Allen, *Origins of the* Dred Scott *Case,* 102–7.

77. Luther v. Borden, 48 U.S. (7 How.) 1 (1849); Allen, *Origins of the* Dred Scott *Case,* 19–21.

78. Allen, *Origins of the* Dred Scott *Case,* 26–27.

79. Ibid., 186–94.

80. Scott, 60 U.S. at 449–52.

81. Christopher Eisgruber has correctly noted that the definition of human beings as slaves is crucial to understanding Taney's argument ("*Dred* Again," 53–56).

82. Allen, *Origins of the* Dred Scott *Case,* 191–92.

83. Fehrenbacher, *Dred Scott Case,* 384.

84. Calabresi, "Originalist and Normative Case against Judicial Activism," 1093.

SIX

Emancipation and Contract Law

Litigating Human Property after the Civil War

Daniel W. Hamilton

IN 1859, in *United States v. Amy,* Chief Justice Roger Taney was asked to rule on a claim by a Virginia slave owner that it was a violation of the Fifth Amendment to send his slave to prison.[1] Amy had allegedly stolen a letter from the post office and was prosecuted under an 1825 federal law that provided that "if any person shall steal a letter from the mail, the offender shall be imprisoned not less than two and not more than ten years."[2] At trial, Amy had no defense attorney of her own; instead her owner was represented by one John Howard. Howard asserted, first, that a slave was not a "person" for the purposes of the act and, second, that the criminal statute was unconstitutional if applied to Amy on the grounds that during the term of her imprisonment her master would be deprived of private property put to public use without just compensation.[3] District court judge James Halyburton stopped the trial on the grounds that these were novel issues and announced that Taney was riding circuit, was soon expected in the jurisdiction, and could address these questions.

The question of the status of slave property under the Fifth Amendment was suddenly timely. The issue had recently been litigated by the

Supreme Court in the *Dred Scott* case, where Taney seemed to declare that slaves were definitively a kind of property protected by the amendment.[4] For decades the federal government, and particularly federal courts, had in multiple ways protected slavery.[5] Yet slaves were conspicuously never explicitly categorized as property in the Constitution, and not until *Dred Scott* had the Supreme Court so openly asserted that slaves were property for purposes of the Fifth Amendment. In antebellum congressional debates over emancipation in Washington, D.C., Senator John C. Calhoun argued that slavery was a type of property protected by the Fifth Amendment. Yet while "Calhoun himself acknowledged that his interpretation of the due process clause as a bulwark of slavery lacked broad support in the Senate" his view was "judicially confirmed two decades later in the Dred Scott decision."[6]

With this recent precedent in place, Taney was asked to consider the extent to which Amy's constitutional status as property undermined her status as a legal person, and also whether her status as property required the state to pay her owner compensation if she was imprisoned. Justice Taney, sitting in circuit court, declared: "It is true that a slave is property of the master, and it is equally true that he is not a citizen." Yet, in the eyes of the law, "he is a person," and in "expounding the law we must not lose sight of the twofold character that belongs to the slave. He is a person and also property."[7] Taney asserted that the claim for just compensation "cannot upon any fair interpretation, apply to the case of a slave who is punished in his own person. Although the punishment may incidentally affect the property of another to whom he belongs."[8]

United States v. Amy was hardly a victory for Amy, but it does illustrate, first, some of the unintended consequences of the *Dred Scott* case for Taney and, second, that not even Taney was willing to disrupt the law's long-standing ambivalent treatment of human property. The status of Amy as property was in crucial ways quite clear. Most immediately, she could be bought or sold at auction at anytime; she could be mortgaged and seized by creditors if her owner defaulted; and she could be leased to someone else without her consent. Yet her status as property was not total. She did have some legal personality in the eyes of the law. As Ariela Gross has demonstrated, there was a complex and uneasy relationship in the antebellum era between treating slaves primarily as people or primarily as property in the eyes of the law.[9] This ambivalence remained part of the law even after slaves were freed, and human property was continually recognized by the courts for decades after emancipation.

It is customary to treat the adoption of the Thirteenth Amendment in 1865 as a decisive moment when slavery and human property were forever abolished in American law and the Constitution.[10] Of course it cannot be denied that the Thirteenth Amendment freed millions of people still in bondage and prohibited the reinstitution of chattel slavery.[11] It is certainly the case that one of the signal changes of the Civil War, and one of the major shifts in the history of American property law, was the legal removal of millions of people from established categories of property, without compensation. Yet the long debate over the legal protection of human property did not end the instant the amendment took effect, and the legacy of slave property survived emancipation, in surprising and important ways.

In particular, the debate over the place of human property in American law and the Constitution came to the fore in cases contesting the status of contracts for the sale of slaves made before emancipation. In these cases, courts were asked to reconcile competing commitments both to the protection of property and contract and also to some measure of racial equality in the Thirteenth and Fourteenth amendments. At the heart of this litigation was the extent to which contracts with slave property as consideration could be enforced under those amendments, and whether state constitutional provisions voiding these contracts violated the contracts clause of the Constitution. States seeking to enforce a broad conception of emancipation clashed with a Supreme Court unwilling to demolish all legal vestiges of human property. The Supreme Court was called upon to determine the extent to which the recognition of human property had been eradicated from the private law.

The emancipation of four million slaves without compensation during the Civil War emancipation is what the property scholar Carol Rose calls one of the three examples of revolutionary property expropriation in American history.[12] Indeed it is fair to say that the federal emancipation of millions of slaves was the biggest act of property confiscation in the history of the United States, and one of the biggest in the history of the world. Before the war, slaves were, after decades of settled law and precedent, a type of property recognized by the Constitution and the Congress. William Lloyd Garrison had burned the Constitution as a "covenant with death," and before the war abolitionism was confined to a small number of vocal activists whose views were at odds with seventy-five years of legal precedent and constitutional interpretation recognizing and protecting slave property.[13] The Thirty-sixth Congress, in the original Thirteenth Amendment passed in January 1860, was willing to make explicit what had been recognized as implicit and to add to the Constitution a clause prohibiting the federal government from ever interfering with slavery in states where it existed.

The capital investment in slave property before the Civil War was astonishing. The economic historian Claudia Goldin estimates "the capital value of all slaves in 1860 to have been 2.7 billion 1860 dollars."[14] Given the value of slave property and decades of settled constitutional and state law protecting slave property, it was, before the Civil War, ideologically and legally inconceivable for the Congress to effectively seize from private owners one of the single biggest economic assets in the United States without compensation.[15]

By 1865 this is exactly what happened, and slavery was abolished altogether without compensation in the Thirteenth Amendment. Yet the move to uncompensated emancipation was halting and at first incomplete. In April 1862, Congress abolished slavery in Washington, D.C. Importantly, though, slave owners in Washington had been compensated, signaling quite clearly that slaves were still in the eyes of a majority of the Congress a form of property requiring compensation when seized. Congress authorized emancipation in the federal territory of Washington, D.C., providing for compensation to slaveholders of up to $2,000 per slave. Ultimately, Congress paid out some $993,000 to slave owners to emancipate roughly 3,100 slaves at an average of $300 per slave.[16]

The text of the Thirteenth Amendment does not explicitly prohibit compensation by states of the federal government to former slave owners. Taking advantage of this ambiguity, Georgia and West Virginia moved to compensate slave owners for the emancipation of their slaves, and Georgia made it part of its 1865 state constitution that ratification of the Thirteenth Amendment in that state "is not intended to operate as a relinquishment, waiver, or estoppel of such claim for compensation of loss sustained by reason of the emancipation of his slaves."[17]

Ultimately, amid signs that states were still pursuing compensation for emancipation, and that Congress might yet pursue it, particularly under a

Democratic administration, Congress moved to include in the Fourteenth Amendment an explicit ban on compensation for emancipation by states and the federal government. Section 4 of the Fourteenth Amendment reads: "[N]either the United States nor any State shall assume or pay any debt or obligation incurred in aid of insurrection or rebellion against the United States, or any claim for the loss or emancipation of any slave; but all such debts, obligations and claims shall be held illegal and void."[18]

Even then, with the text of the Constitution clear, the battle over compensation for slave property turned to the courts, specifically the question of what to do about contracts for the sale of slaves entered into before emancipation in which slaves formed the consideration, or installment contracts for the sale of slaves in which the installment payments were still due.[19] The constitutional questions surrounding these contracts were considered in several state and federal cases, the most significant of which were ultimately heard by the Supreme Court, *Osborn v. Nicholson*[20] and *White v. Hart,* a companion case challenging a similar provision barring the enforcement of slave contracts in the Georgia constitution.[21] *Osborn* was first heard in federal district court in Arkansas in 1869.[22] The facts of the case were straightforward. In March 1861 the defendant, A. G. Nicholson, signed over a promissory note and a bill of sale to Henry Osborn. The bill of sale read: "For the consideration of $1,300 I hereby transfer all the right, title, and interest I have to a negro boy named Albert, aged about twenty-three years. I warrant said negro to be sound in body and mind, and a slave for life; and I also warrant the title to said boy clear and perfect."[23] The note was due on December 26, 1861, at an annual interest rate interest rate of 10 percent. Before Osborn could collect, three important intervening events took place. First, Albert was liberated by the U.S. Army in January 1862. Second, the Thirteenth Amendment was adopted in 1865. Third, the Arkansas state constitution, in a period when the legislature was under Republican control, was amended in 1868 to bar the enforcement of slave contracts, or contracts in which slaves formed the consideration.[24]

Article 15 of the amended Arkansas constitution provided that "all contracts for the sale or purchase of slaves are null and void, and no court of this state shall take cognizance of any suit founded on such contracts, nor shall any amount be collected on any such judgment."[25] Arkansas was not alone in amending its constitution in this way, and there were similar constitutional provisions enacted by Reconstruction legislatures in Georgia and Louisiana.[26]

Nicholson, claiming protection under the Arkansas and U.S. constitutions, refused to pay, and Osborn sued, demanding payment for the sale of Albert. Osborn's claim was straightforward: as of the date of the contract Albert was property recognized by the U.S. Constitution and the state of Arkansas, and the Thirteenth Amendment did not strip Osborn of this vested contract right. Any attempt to strip him of this right in article 15 of the Arkansas constitution, he claimed, was a violation of the contracts clause of the U.S. Constitution, and any state constitutional provision that undermined the contracts clause must be declared null.[27]

At the district court, Judge Henry Clay Caldwell, appointed by Abraham Lincoln in 1864, denied the plaintiff's claim on several grounds. Caldwell first asserted that the Thirteenth Amendment had acted as a broad repealing statute, one issued in the U.S. Constitution, "the highest power known in our form of government." The Thirteenth Amendment had "effected the repeal to annihilate slavery and all its incidents, and all rights and obligations growing out of it."[28] After destroying slavery, Caldwell asked, "would it not be a strange anomaly if there existed in the constitution a principle that would coerce the states to open their courts to the slave-dealer and let him recover the fruits of his barbarous traffic."[29]

The court here was making a constitutional argument on the breadth of the Constitution's destruction of slave property. Albert's status as property, and more radically the claim that he ever had been property, was utterly destroyed by the Thirteenth Amendment. For the court, that amendment was "based on the broad principle that there shall be no further recognition by the national government or the states of the idea that there could lawfully be property in man." This principle, said Caldwell, "cuts its way through all vested rights and obligation of contracts based on slave codes." Ranging outside of contract law, the court held that the amendment "operates with full force on claims and demands of every character originating in the idea that human beings were property."[30]

Caldwell here was asserting a conception of the Thirteenth Amendment that stripped slavery, and the legal recognition of human property, root and branch out of the American constitutional order. Osborn's contract claim was unconstitutional in that it undermined this interpretation. The court declared, "The fundamental ground on which emancipation proceeded was that the right of the slave to his freedom was paramount to the claim of his master to treat him as property." As a consequence, "no vested right of property could arise out of a relation thus created."[31]

To illustrate his point, Caldwell moved from theoretical to concrete arguments. The contract for the sale of Albert had a warranty that the deal was contingent on the condition that Albert was of "sound body and mind." If this was indeed a valid contract, could the defendant Nicholson claim a defense on the grounds that Albert was not of sound mind or body, that the warranty was not met? If so, could Albert, by now a free man and a U.S. citizen, be summoned into court to have his mental and physical fitness tested? For Caldwell this "would be giving full force and effect to one of the most obnoxious features of the slave code," and the Constitution's destruction of slavery in the Thirteenth Amendment by necessary implication prohibited "free citizens to be thus degraded in the interest of slavery and slave traders."[32]

The judge argued also that enforcing a slave contract was unconstitutional on the grounds that it violated Section 4 of the Fourteenth Amendment. This provision clearly prohibited federal and state government from compensating slave owners for emancipation. But did Section 4 reach private contracts for slave sales entered into before the Fourteenth Amendment was ratified? The district court ruled that they did. It was clear, he wrote, that in emancipating the slaves, the Constitution "takes from A slaves he purchased from B." At some point, that is, A had purchased his slaves from B. It was acknowledged by all that A could not as a slave buyer demand compensation by the state or federal government for the loss of his slaves, just as no one who had bought slaves could demand compensation for the loss of their slave property under Section 4 of the Fourteenth Amendment.

Yet in this case, Caldwell analogized, "B claims from A the price of these slaves."[33] That is, here a slave seller was claiming he was owed compensation for the sale of slaves. To find a constitutional obligation under the contracts clause to pay compensation to a slave seller "would do violence to the whole spirit of the constitution." Such a ruling would effectively provide compensation for slavery based on a nonsensical distinction that the Constitution prohibited compensation to slave buyers who bought slaves before the Thirteenth Amendment but guaranteed compensation to slave sellers who sold their slaves before ratification of the amendment in December 1865.[34] Instead, he asserted, Section 4 of the Fourteenth Amendment should be understood as a general ban on compensation for slaves emancipated by the Thirteenth Amendment. In the two amendments, "A living force and vitality was imparted to the words of the declaration of independence 'that all men are created equal'" and also to the due process clause of the Fifth Amendment." In this light, the effect of the amendments "cannot be limited to the mere severance of the legal relation of master and slave. They are far reaching in their results."[35]

On a more strictly doctrinal level, Caldwell held that once slavery had been stripped from state and federal law by the Constitution, there was no longer any basis to sue to enforce the contract and no remedy available. Caldwell took the position that slavery was supported only by positive law, with no basis in natural or common law. Thus once a state's law had been changed to prohibit slavery, as was the case in Arkansas, and banned by the U.S. Constitution, a plaintiff had no remedy in common law or the Constitution. Caldwell quoted the dissent of Justice Benjamin Curtis in *Dred Scott*, asserting that "slavery being contrary to natural right is created only by municipal law."[36] Thus, for Caldwell, it was only by virtue of the slave law of the state of Arkansas, "that the plaintiff ever could have maintained an action in any court on this contract."[37]

The court also made customary, but still powerful, arguments that did not rest on these broad interpretations of the Reconstruction amendments. First, Caldwell made a federalism-based argument that slavery was always primarily subject to state regulation, and the federal courts were bound to recognize the terms of the amended Arkansas constitution on the issue of slavery. He wrote: "[T]his state in the exercise of her undoubted rights over the institution of slavery, and all its incidents, has by its constitution abolished the institution." Given the state's plenary power over slavery, "this is the end of the plaintiff's case."[38] Second, he asserted a version of the contract doctrine of "unclean hands," holding that he was not bound to enforce a contract "against good morals, or against religion, or against public right, nor contracts opposed to our national policy or national institutions."[39]

Importantly, these arguments ultimately lost. *Osborn v. Nicholson* was soon reversed by the Supreme Court.[40] The Court ruled that the provision of the Arkansas constitution barring the enforcement of slave contracts violated the contracts clause of the U.S. Constitution and was therefore void. Justice Noah Swayne wrote for the majority that the contract was valid when it was made and so could be enforced in every state at any time. For the Supreme Court, the legal issue was clear: "[W]hatever we think of the institution of slavery, viewed in the light of religion, morals, humanity, or a sound political economy,—as the obligation here in question was valid when executed, sitting as a court of justice, we have no choice but to give it effect." Swayne went to lengths to deplore the institution of slavery but nevertheless "that when the 13th amendment was adopted the right of the plaintiff in this action had become legally and completely vested."[41] For Swayne this vested right was identical to any other, whether acquired by contract, deed, will, or marriage. Its basis in slave property was identical to a contract based on any other kind of property.

Here Swayne was making an argument that the Thirteenth Amendment should operate as an ordinary statute, and be applied only prospectively. This was "a principle of universal jurisprudence" and was "necessary to the repose and welfare of all communities." The idea of retroactively voiding contracts—contracts legal when made—was for Swayne a ruling that "would shake the social fabric to its foundations and let in a flood-tide of intolerable evils" and would constitute a deprivation of due process. There was "nothing in the language of the amendment which in the slightest degree warrants the inference that those who framed or those who adopted it intended that such should be the effect."[42]

The majority opinion prompted a strong dissent by Chief Justice Salmon Chase, both in this case and in the companion case of *White v. Hart*.[43] Chase in his dissent supported most of the claims advanced by the district court. In particular Chase endorsed the argument that slavery was supported only by positive law, with no basis in natural or common law, and that "if not perpetuated it dies" and "the common law is restored to original principles of liberty."[44] For Chase, as for Caldwell, slave contracts, whenever entered into, were void in that they were no longer supported by positive law. These contracts were "annulled by the thirteenth amendment which abolished slavery" and in abolishing slavery had destroyed all positive law that supported slavery, including contracts with slaves as consideration. Chase similarly endorsed the district court's claim that the

Fourteenth Amendment prohibited compensation for the loss of slave property, whether in public or private law.[45]

Chase was of course writing in dissent. What divided the district court and the Supreme Court was a fundamentally different interpretation of the meaning of the Thirteenth and Fourteenth amendments. For the district court, the Thirteenth Amendment stood for "the broad principle that there shall be no further recognition by the national government or the states of the idea that there could lawfully be property in man." Application of this broad principle meant that upholding slave contracts, whenever formed, would be equivalent to upholding the idea of human property. The dissent did not argue that the slave contract was invalid when it was formed. Instead it took the position that a slave contract, however valid when made, was made invalid by a new constitutional ideal that made enforcement of the contract unconstitutional and which subordinated any claim for enforcement.

The Supreme Court majority took a much less expansive view of the scope of the Thirteenth Amendment. The timing was all, and the timing was clear: the amendment banned the enforcement of slave contracts the day after ratification, while leaving untouched those signed the day before. Property was simply property, whether slave or otherwise, in the eyes of the law, and the Court asserted, "[W]e cannot regard it as different in its legal efficacy from any other unexecuted contract to pay money made upon sufficient consideration." For Swayne, the conception of the Thirteenth Amendment advanced by the district courts and the dissent undermined basic constitutional protections and even worse. The prospect of retroactively voiding contracts legal when made, whatever the underlying consideration, was "forbidden by the fundamental principles of the social compact."[46]

For both courts, as their language makes clear, the stakes were high, though the majority took pains to minimize the implications of its decision for freed slaves. Swayne asserted in his opinion that "neither the rights nor the interests of those of the colored race lately in bondage are affected by the conclusions we have reached." At first glance, this seems obvious. That is, these cases turned on disputes between two litigants, in all likelihood white litigants, over who was or was not owed money. The cases attempted to allocate the burden between a slave buyer and a slave seller, and the rights of African Americans were not, at least at first glance, immediately implicated. So what was in fact at stake in these opinions?

Potential answers come from renewed historical attention to the arguments made and actions taken by the losing side, or the arguments made by lower courts and in constitutional amendments enacted by several state legislatures. This is not to suggest that the losing side was in some absolute sense right on the merits, only that their arguments were a significant part of the ongoing debate over the reach of the Thirteenth and Fourteenth amendments and the meaning of emancipation. The debate over the meaning of these amendments is of course at the heart of the legal and constitutional history of Reconstruction, and the enforcement of slave contracts was an important, but still little noticed, part of that debate.

The Supreme Court transformed these disputes into routine contracts cases, rejecting, and in large part ignoring, the central claim of the district courts, namely that upholding these contracts amounted to ongoing legal recognition of slaves as a kind of property for which sellers were due compensation. Once the losing arguments are examined, however, we see in high relief a tension between an expansive view of emancipation in the Thirteenth Amendment, one barring compensation of any kind for a seller of slaves, and a more narrow conception that maintained a kind of vested property right in slaves, even as the Constitution destroyed the institution of slavery.

Attention to the full debate shows the Supreme Court consciously rejecting a robust conception of emancipation, and in their rulings in effect stripping from state and federal constitutions the power to create an alternate hierarchy of legal and constitutional rights, one in which the destruction of all vestiges of human property took precedence over strict construction of contracts and vested rights. This losing alternative view is a path not taken, a motif that, as in the *Civil Rights Cases* and the *Slaughterhouse Cases,* drives much of the history of Reconstruction.[47] We cannot know how this power might have translated into other private law disputes and other constitutional battles.[48]

What is clear is that cases like *White v. Hart* and *Osborn v. Nicholson* should be understood as in sync with the *Slaughterhouse Cases* and the *Civil Rights Cases,* even though they are less well known. Just as the *Slaughterhouse Cases* stripped the privileges and immunities clause of much of its potential power, and the *Civil Rights Cases* restricted congressional attempts to achieve greater equality, so cases like *Osborn v. Nicholson* put in place a narrow conception of emancipation, a conception that had been rejected by several state legislatures and several state and federal courts. Indeed in some respects *Osborn* is the more fundamental case in that it turns, not on the elaboration of legal rights and remedies alone, as in the *Slaughterhouse* and *Civil Rights Cases,* but on the actual status of African Americans as property, and the question of whether human property itself was or was not still protected by the Constitution decades after the Civil War.

This debate of course had more immediate concrete importance as well. That state legislatures, with new input from African American lawmakers, enacted constitutional amendments in Arkansas, Louisiana, and Georgia banning the enforcement of slave contracts shows that, contrary to Swayne's assertion in *Osborn,* the "rights and interests" of African Americans were affected by the Supreme Court's decision to strike them down, or at least that several state legislatures and district courts thought they were.

It is not difficult to see why. Once these constitutional provisions were struck down, the Court was allowing for some measure of compensation for the sale of slaves many years after the Civil War. If from one perspective these cases simply shifted the burden between white litigants, from another they amounted to a decisive rejection of the idea that anyone could make a claim for compensation for slave property after emancipation. Absent such a ban, the end of slavery, or at least the end of recognition of human property, was less definitive and less fixed in the Constitution.

For the majority in *Osborn,* the ruling was driven by timing. The determination of which slave contracts were valid and which were not was driven almost entirely by when they were made. This attention to the precise moment when vested rights attached and when they did not made for a set of surprising cases in which former slaves asked the Court to make precise determinations of the end of slavery in order to make demands for compensation for labor taken by their former masters. The effective use of this novel legal argument was especially well illustrated in the Supreme Court case *Worthington v. Mason.*[49] Martha Mason was born a slave in Arkansas and was the property of Elisha and Edward Worthington. She also was the daughter of Edward Worthington, a claim conceded at trial. The Worthingtons had taken Marsha to Oberlin, Ohio, during the Civil War, and there she went to school. At this point, according to the district court, "the Constitution and the laws of Ohio immediately dissolved the relation of master and slave previously existing." The plaintiff "thereby became a free woman, and could never thereafter lawfully be claimed or held by Colonel Worthington as his slave." Marsha was, however, put to labor upon their return to Arkansas, apparently until Elisha Worthington died. At that point, Marsha sued the estate, claiming she was owed compensation for labor done after her legal status as a slave was dissolved. The jury found for Marsha and rendered a verdict of $12,000. The case came before the Supreme Court on a narrow factual question of the legality of the charge to the jury, and in 1879 Justice Samuel Miller upheld the verdict without much comment.[50]

Here the ruling in *Dred Scott* was turned on its head. Marsha not only obtained her freedom by moving to a free state, but she was also owed back wages. In these cases it fell to the court to pinpoint exactly when freedom began, for at that point one could claim compensation. A consequence of a constitutional regime in which a contract based on slavery was legal so long as slavery was legal was that legal rights and remedies attached or failed to attach depending on the determination of the precise moment that slavery was abolished. Different courts chose different points for the precise endpoint of slavery, but whatever the endpoint, this allowed former slaves to come into court relying on a bright line as part of a claim that their right to compensation attached at that same instant.

Emancipation is frequently presented as the wholesale triumph at the time of the Civil War of the conception that slaves are people, defined as people because they were no longer defined as property. This constitutional transformation from property to person is too frequently understood as a near inevitable consequence of the war, embodied perhaps in the Emancipation Proclamation and certainly in the Thirteenth Amendment. Emancipation is thus presented as an epiphany, a decisive legal break. This analysis has advantages. First, it is conceptually clear. Second, the dramatic eradication of human property in a decisive constitutional moment fits within a compelling and popular narrative of the Civil War, in which the Civil War is understood as a crusade against slavery, a decisive moment when the nation came to recognize its original sin and recommit itself to its founding ideals.

This analysis, of course, is not untrue. It envisions a legal and constitutional scenario, however, in which slaves are recognized as property in the Constitution the day before ratification of the Thirteenth Amendment and as people the day after. That view, while appealing, can too easily blind us to the staying power of a conception of human property that had been a fixture of American law for centuries.

A legal category of human property survived the Civil War and survived even emancipation. The sudden move to complete and uncompensated emancipation in the Thirteenth Amendment took effect even as the centuries-old legal recognition of slave property persisted in the private law. Emancipation was experienced simultaneously as an instance of property confiscation and as the constitutional eradication of the recognition of human property. This contradiction forced courts, legal scholars, and freed slaves into debate over the meaning and scope of emancipation and the Civil War, and it brought to the fore conflicting ideological commitments. In cases that pitted the common law of contract against an expansive conception of freedom and the nascent constitutional promise of racial equality, the Supreme Court took a stance that recognized emancipation while, at the same time, leaving the vestiges of human property intact.

Notes

I thank David Konig, Paul Finkelman, Chris Bracey, and all the participants in the symposium "The Dred Scott Case and Its Legacy," held at Washington University in St. Louis. Thanks also for the valuable comments received at faculty workshops at the University of Texas Law School, Vanderbilt Law School, the Chicago-Kent College of Law as well as from students in the Kent Legal Scholars program.

1. U.S. v. Amy, 24 F. Cas. 792 (C.C.Va. 1859).

2. Ibid., 809.

3. U.S. Const., amend. 5. The Fifth Amendment provides, in relevant part: "No person shall . . . be deprived of life, liberty or property without due process of law; nor shall private property be taken for public use, without just compensation."

4. Dred Scott v. John F. A. Sandford, 60 U.S. (19 How.) 393 (1857).

5. See Paul Finkelman, "The Centrality of Slavery in American Legal Development," in *Slavery and the Law,* ed. Paul Finkelman (Madison, Wis.: Madison House, 1997), 4–26; Don E. Fehrenbacher, *The Slaveholding Republic,* ed. Ward E. McAfee (New York: Oxford University Press, 2001).

6. Fehrenbacher, *Slaveholding Republic,* 80.

7. U.S. v. Amy, 24 F. Cas. at 809–10.

8. Ibid., 810.

9. Ariela J. Gross, *Double Character: Slavery and Freedom in the Antebellum Southern Courtroom* (Princeton, N.J.: Princeton University Press, 2000).

10. U.S. Const., amend. 13, provides, "Neither slavery nor involuntary servitude, except as a punishment for crime whereof the party shall have been duly convicted, shall exist within the United States, or any place subject to their jurisdiction."

11. For an excellent account on the drafting and passage of the Thirteenth Amendment, see Michael Vorenberg, *Final Freedom: The Civil War, the Abolition of Slavery, and the Thirteenth Amendment* (Cambridge: Cambridge University Press, 2001).

12. Carol M. Rose, "Property and Expropriation: Themes and Variations in American Law," *Utah Law Review* 2000, no. 1 (2000): 1, 24. For Rose, the other two are the confiscation of loyalist property during the American Revolution and the expropriation of land from Native Americans.

13. In the 1850s the antislavery movement had split into a militant faction, led by William Lloyd Garrison and Wendell Phillips, and a moderate faction, associated in the Congress with Charles Sumner, John Hale, and Benjamin Wade. The second faction had enjoyed increasing influence with the rise of the Republican Party. Before the war, their goals were organized in large part around preventing the expansion of slavery. The Garrisonians had been increasingly marginalized and frustrated with the massive legal and constitutional apparatus in place protecting slavery. With the outbreak of war, the Garrisonians gained influence as the whole of the movement shifted left. See William E. Gienapp, *The Origins of the Republican Party, 1852–1856* (New York: Oxford University Press, 1987); and James M. McPherson, *The Struggle for Equality: Abolitionists and the Negro in the Civil War and Reconstruction* (Princeton, N.J.: Princeton University Press, 1964).

14. Claudia Dale Goldin, "The Economics of Emancipation," *Journal of Economic History* 33, no. 1 (1973): 66–85, 74.

15. See Daniel W. Hamilton, *The Limits of Sovereignty: Property Confiscation in the Union and the Confederacy during the Civil War* (Chicago: University of Chicago Press, 2007), 9–11.

16. "An Act for the Release of certain Persons held to Service or labor in the District of Columbia," 12 Stat. 376 (April 16, 1862). Page Milburn, "The Emancipation of the Slaves in the District of Columbia," *Records of the Columbia Historical Society* 16 (1913): 96–119.

17. Georgia const. of 1865, art. 1, § 20.

18. U.S. Const., amend. 14, § 4.

19. For detailed accounts of the operation of contractual slave sales in the antebellum era, see Jenny Bourne Wahl, *The Bondsman's Burden: An Economic Analysis of the Common Law of Southern Slavery* (Cambridge: Cambridge University Press, 1998); Thomas D. Russell, "Slave Auctions on the Courthouse Steps: Court Sales of Slaves in Antebellum South Carolina," in *Slavery and the Law*, ed. Finkelman, 329–64.

20. Osborn v. Nicholson, 80 U.S. (13 Wall.) 654 (1872) (Chase, C.J., dissenting).

21. White v. Hart, 80 U.S. (13 Wall.) 646 (1872).

22. Osborn v. Nicholson, 18 F. Cas. 846 (C.C.E.D. Ark. 1870).

23. Osborn, 80 U.S.

24. Arkansas const. of 1868, art. 15, § 14.

25. Ibid.

26. Georgia const. of 1868, art. 5, § 17; Louisiana const. of 1868.

27. U.S. Const. art 1, § 10 (the contracts clause), provides that "no state shall . . . pass any . . . law impairing the obligation of contracts."

28. Osborn, 18 F. Cas. at 851.

29. Ibid., 854.

30. Ibid., 856.

31. Ibid., 855.

32. Ibid., 854–55.

33. Ibid., 855.

34. Ibid.

35. Ibid.

36. Ibid., 846.

37. Ibid., 850.

38. Ibid., 853.

39. Ibid., 850.

40. Osborn, 80 U.S. at 654.

41. Ibid., 662.

42. Ibid.

43. White v. Hart, 80 U.S. at 646.

44. Osborn, 80 U.S. at 663.

45. Ibid., 664.

46. Ibid., 662.

47. The Slaughterhouse Cases, 83 U.S. 36 (1873); The Civil Rights Cases, 109 U.S. 3 (1883).

48. Michael Les Benedict finds in Chase's dissent in *Osborn* "a tantalizing hint" of a kind of powerful constitutional argument that might have been available to the federal judiciary before the Civil War, particularly Chase's assertion that slavery was "without support except in positive law." "Review of Don E. Fehrenbacher, *The Slaveholding Republic: An Account of the United States Government's Relations to Slavery*," H-Law, H-Net Reviews, March 2002, http://www.h-net.org/reviews/showrev.cgi?path=73411015347997. For a similarly nuanced and persuasive analysis of how the possibilities for legal and constitutional change during Reconstruction were circumscribed by a reliance on traditional common law reasoning, see Michael Vorenberg, "Imagining a Different Reconstruction Constitution," *Civil War History* 51, no. 4 (2005): 416, 421.

49. Worthington v. Mason, 101 U.S. 149 (1879).

50. Ibid., 149–50.

PART THREE

Contemporary Perspectives

PART THREE

Contemporary Perspectives

SEVEN

Dred Scott, Human Dignity, and the Quest for a Culture of Equality

Christopher Alan Bracey

MUCH HAS been said and written about the *Dred Scott* decision over the past 150 years. We are all familiar with the basic holding of the case—the U.S. Supreme Court's declaration that black persons descended from slaves, whether free or not, could never become citizens of the United States, and thus could not maintain a lawsuit in federal court. We know that, in reaching this conclusion, the Court not only affirmed Dred Scott's legal status as a slave, but went much further—declaring not only that Dred Scott (and by extension all blacks) had no rights that white men were bound to respect, but concluding that blacks were justifiably reduced to slavery for the benefit of white society.[1]

Chief Justice Roger Taney's majority opinion embodied much of the vulgar racist attitudes held by many whites in the middle of the nineteenth century. He declared the natural inferiority of blacks to be an axiom or essential truth "fixed and universal in the civilized portion of the white race," a truth that no man or person could reasonably dispute.[2] Put differently, anyone who sought to challenge this prevailing view of the inherent inferiority of blacks was either unreasonable (and thus the argument could be rejected on the merits, as it were), or less than a person—less than a man, as was the case of the slave Dred Scott, and thus deemed unworthy of being heard in the first instance.

For the white supporters of the Scotts, the Court's decision signaled a rejection of an *idea*—the notion that blacks could be equal citizens. It was an abstract intellectual and moral defeat. For Dred and Harriet Scott, and all similarly situated African Americans, however, Taney's pronouncement constituted not only a rejection of the idea of equality but also a dramatic affirmation of some of the most palpable and devastating modes of racial oppression this world has ever seen.

In this chapter, I want to use this tragic and indisputably retrograde episode of American legal history as a launching pad to talk about a topic of progressive, transhistorical significance. I want to suggest that this historic legal dispute over the meaning of U.S. citizenship for African Americans can be more powerfully understood as part of a much larger quest for human dignity and cultural equality—an epic and, in many ways, incomplete struggle to better the lives of everyday people.

Citizenship and Community: The Importance of Framing the Issue

Lawyers and legal commentators appreciate the importance of framing the issue. In many instances, the framing of the issue not only identifies the stakes of the dispute but can also prefigure the outcome. Recall that Taney framed the issue in *Dred Scott v. Sandford,* not in antiseptic terms of legal status, but in a mix of legal and sociocultural humanistic terms. The central issue, in his view, was whether "a negro, whose ancestors were imported to this country, and sold as slaves, [can] become *a member of the political community* formed and brought into existence by the Constitution of the United States."[3]

Taney's framing of the issue of citizenship with explicit reference to "community" has particularly powerful implications. Humans are necessarily communal in nature. We are social beings. We define ourselves and often thrive in our relations to one another. Our existence relies on mutual dependency with other people. In short, our social and communal interactions are arguably the key features that designate and distinguish us as fully human.

But if the language of community triggers the image of social sanctuary, it is equally effective at delineating boundaries. Communities typically have criteria of membership, and it is this feature of community—the power of inclusion and exclusion—that animates Taney's concept of citizenship and his understanding that the framers of the Constitution, "by common consent, had [excluded the Negro race] from civilized Governments and the *family of nations,* and doomed [him] to slavery."[4]

The question of citizenship, in Taney's view, was (and perhaps still is) at bottom a question of humanity. When we acknowledge citizenship or bestow it on an individual, we embrace that individual as a full member of our political family. We are, at the deepest levels, acknowledging and affirming that individual's essential humanity. We are telling that person that he or she is one of us—our political, social, and cultural equal.

When viewed from this perspective, the *Dred Scott* decision is a particularly tragic moment both in American legal and cultural history because it represents such an emphatic rejection of the idea of black humanity. Dred, Harriet, Eliza, and Lizzie Scott, as well as most, if not all, other blacks, did not simply lack equivalent legal status as whites. In the eyes of the highest court in the land, they were judged to possess a deeper, sociocultural failing. Blacks, according to the Supreme Court, were social and cultural pariahs, unworthy of basic human interaction and certainly not worthy of inclusion in the political community or family of nations. Put differently, the Court's legal determination that blacks were not worthy of citizenship was simultaneously a denial of their essential human dignity.

Racism as Dignity Expropriation

The *Dred Scott* decision as cultural moment, of course, was not a significant departure from what had come before it. As we all know, the founding of the American Republic embodied a formal commitment to the liberal ideals of freedom, equality, and democracy for all. Yet this formal commitment took shape against the backdrop of devastating modes of racial oppression. Thus, American culture from the outset embodied both the triumph of liberal ideals and an unflinching commitment to the principles and practices of racial subordination, exploitation, pain, and death.

The *Dred Scott* decision does provide, however, a particularly poignant example of the way in which racism and racial inequality work to undermine human dignity. Indeed, it perhaps best exemplifies the manner in which racial oppression—in all its various forms—is at its core a dignity-expropriative enterprise. By this I mean that racial repression is perhaps best understood as a thoroughgoing attempt to deny basic dignity and equal humanity of others because of their race. Moreover, this theme of dignity expropriation not only underlies the *Dred Scott* decision—it is the touchstone of all forms of racial oppression, past and present. Dignity expropriation is at the heart of the historic practices of slavery, Indian removal, and Eurocentric immigration and naturalization policy. It also drives modern modes of racial oppression, such as employment discrimination, racial profiling in law enforcement, housing discrimination, discriminatory lending practices, and the like.

One should keep in mind that there are symbolic implications as well as distinctly materialist implications of racial repression. That is, dignity expropriation through racial repression is both symbolically stigmatizing—marking someone as an outsider, an "other"—*and* economically debilitating. The denial of dignity has concrete materialist consequences. The lived experience of the Scotts and generations of black families reveals that dignity expropriation through racial repression leads not only to the denial of equal citizenship but also to denial of access to education, employment, and the full range of wealth-generating and life-sustaining activities as well.

On Dignity Expropriation and Culture

As we mark the sesquicentennial of the *Dred Scott* case, there is little doubt that the fundamental ideals of freedom, justice, and equality that were denied to the Scotts are now enjoyed as a matter of course by millions of African Americans. But it is also true, despite the radical expansion and transformation of these liberal ideals and significant progress in American race relations, that racism, racial inequality, and the corresponding denial of basic human dignity remain naturalized elements within the American cultural landscape. In this way, a little bit of *Dred Scott* remains with us.

So, the essential question is this: How exactly does one go about eradicating the culture of racial inequality? This culture of dignity expropriation that confounded Dred Scott, those before him, and continues to confound us today? Our culture of racial inequality influences our private attitudes and beliefs, informs our public policy and sense of justice, and shapes our institutions and social practices. It teaches us to expect and, to some extent, accept the sorry state of affairs produced by decades of efforts to deprive blacks of their dignity—the reality of racial disparities in virtually every index of socioeconomic well-being. How are we to remedy a culture that for nearly half a millennium has worked the magic of blunting our collective sense of outrage over the profoundly uncivil and unequal treatment of racial minorities in America?

The most obvious response—both in Dred Scott's time and in ours—is to promote a culture of *racial equality and racial inclusiveness.* But how exactly does one do that? In my view, the key to accomplishing this may lie in placing greater emphasis on the issue of paramount importance to Dred Scott and to black Americans past and present: the acknowledgment and deep affirmance of equal dignity and equal humanity of all races, enforceable by law.

The basic argument I want to advance is that dignity is (and always has been) a central area of concern in the struggle for racial justice, and for good reason. The reason, as I alluded to earlier, is that racial oppression is, at bottom, a dignity-expropriative enterprise. Early proponents of racial justice were well aware of this connection (although they perhaps did not describe it in this way). The Reconstruction amendments, of course, directly repudiated Taney's declaration in *Dred Scott* that blacks could not be citizens because they were widely regarded by whites as "being of an inferior order, and altogether unfit to associate with the white race."[5] Indeed, as others routinely point out, the repudiation of Taney via the Fourteenth Amendment was done in a manner that would grant Congress, in the words of one commentator, substantial enforcement power "to enact certain laws designed to affirm that blacks were equal citizens, worthy of respect and dignity."[6]

The dignitary interests attended to by the Reconstruction amendments were openly acknowledged and affirmed in the Court's first interpretation of those amendments in the *Slaughterhouse Cases.*[7] Justice Samuel Miller, writing for the majority, stated unequivocally that the Reconstruction amendments should be interpreted in light of their overriding purpose:

"the freedom of the slave race, the security and firm establishment of that freedom, and the protection of the newly-made freeman and citizen from the oppressions of those who had formerly exercised unlimited dominion over him."[8] The Court reiterated this sentiment eight years later in *Strauder v. West Virginia*. Justice William Strong, in striking down a West Virginia statute that systematically excluded black jurors from participation in trials, addressed the twin dignitary concerns of self-worth and social value with surprising candor:

> The very fact that colored people are singled out and expressly denied by a statute all right to participate in the administration of the law, as jurors, because of their color, though they are citizens and may be in other respects fully qualified, is practically a brand upon them, affixed by law, an assertion of their inferiority, and a stimulant to the race prejudice which is an impediment to securing individuals of the race that equal justice which the law aims to secure to all others.[9]

Despite these episodic acknowledgments of the interests of dignity, the early twentieth century would become infamous as a period of radical expansion of segregation and racial repression.

Although the latter half of the twentieth century would provide an important resurgence of human dignity as a concept in American law and culture,[10] we appear to be in the midst of a downcycle in the concept of dignity once again. Today, dignity is currently undervalued or underappreciated in law and culture. In my view, the evasion of the interests of dignity today represents a crucial failing because it deprives us of a coherent and comprehensive moral vision or theory of racial justice. Law and culture that overlook the dignity-expropriative aspects of racial oppression are fundamentally nonresponsive to the core feature of racial inequality. This may explain why contemporary race jurisprudence (civil rights and constitutional law cases dealing with race matters) remains fundamentally unsatisfying: whatever it is doing, it is not doing the work of cultural remediation, of replacing prevailing attitudes of complacency and indifference to racial disparities with a culture fundamentally committed to racial equality.

Normatively anchoring race jurisprudence to a robust conception of dignity may prove useful in remediating this culture of racial inequality because taking dignity seriously demands deep, contextual scrutiny of the lived experiences of both the oppressors and the oppressed. Importantly, it opens up the possibilities of substantive racial justice because it reaches beyond mere formal equality and asks what sort of preconditions must be established for the creation of a truly racially egalitarian culture.

Dignity Defined

What does it mean to invoke dignity as the normative anchor for race jurisprudence? Dignity, of course, is a term that is notoriously difficult to capture. Writers and thinkers across the ages have not used the term consistently—indeed, dignity has been used to signal a host of different and, sometimes, competing values (e.g., social rank versus inherent worth).[11]

For purposes of this chapter, I want to offer yet another working definition of dignity, one that is understood in both personal and communal terms. Personal dignity operates at the individual level and is perhaps best understood as a sense of perspective on self-worth. To have perspective on self-worth is to appreciate oneself sufficiently that one would withstand pressures to lower one's self-esteem. Perspective on self-worth explains how African Americans emerged from slavery, Jim Crow, and the agonistic mid-twentieth-century movement for civil rights with a sense of dignity intact. One might refer to dignity of this type as first-order dignity.

In contrast, communal dignity operates at the level of community. At the communal level, inclusion is the essence of dignity. To treat another with dignity is to consider another presumptively worthy of integration into community membership. Communal dignity, in this sense, is universal and undifferentiated respect for social value. It is universal in that dignity inheres in every member of the community. It is undifferentiated in that the forms of social respect extended are equal among all community members. One might refer to dignity at the communal level as second-order dignity.

Why Dignity Matters

The acknowledgment and affirmation of both first- and second-order dignity matters tremendously. It matters because there is, I believe, an important relationship between dignity and substantive racial justice. By substantive racial justice, I mean policies, initiatives, and norms that are self-consciously employed to promote and achieve real, progressive changes in the material conditions of subordinated racial minorities. Antidiscrimination law and other policies that promote formal equality and equal opportunity are certainly crucial elements to the racial justice equation. But substantive racial justice goes further insofar as it places greater emphasis on material and redistributive approaches directed at concrete manifestations of deep-seated subordination, such as chronic disparities in wealth, health, employment, and education.

Sincere attention to concerns about dignity—respect for equal humanity and social value—provides a mechanism to open up the possibilities of substantive racial justice. This is because an emphasis on dignity forces us to historicize, contextualize, and deepen the discussion. One cannot acknowledge another's equal humanity without first interrogating the nature of that person's humanity as well as one's own. One cannot affirm another's presumptive social value or worthiness of inclusion into one's community without first interrogating the conditions of one's community that make inclusion possible.

Acknowledgment and affirmation of dignity, from this perspective, are neither passive nor stress-free. Rather, the acknowledgment and affirmation of dignity entail an active engagement with life's harshest truths. A crucial aspect of those harsh truths is that slavery, segregation, and modern forms of so-called societal discrimination involve extensive efforts to degrade, dishonor, isolate, and ostracize. We see the consequences of this reflected in enduring racial stereotypes and chronic disparities in health, wealth, and society. Importantly, these disparities are not mere by-products of these efforts—they are the intended consequence of these regimes.

We can imagine that an emphasis on formal equality alone contemplates the formal inclusion of racial minorities in an ever-expanding circle of people who may deserve respect but leaves the center of that circle unexamined. Formal equality extended without reference to dignity leaves unaddressed the question of what allows white Americans to see racial minorities as their presumptive inferiors and unworthy compatriots in the first place.

By contrast, an emphasis on dignity asks what conditions must be established among the ranks of the whites so that whites might self-consciously and deliberately seek to overcome the difficulties of expanding the company of equals to include members of socially disfavored or oppressed groups. And this has profound materialist implications because communal perceptions of dignity inform a great deal of our social interactions, including relations that provide the means for securing and accumulating material stability and wealth.[12]

In other words, an emphasis on dignity brings materialist considerations to the fore, especially those that bear a close relationship to the ability of subordinated racial minorities to "realize" freedom. Thus, an emphasis on dignity has the effect of focusing attention on the preconditions to political and social equality as well as economic inclusion and materialist empowerment.

What Has Happened to Dignity?

If dignity is the linchpin to political and social equality as well as economic and materialist empowerment, why does it not figure more prominently in jurisprudence about race? It turns out that dignity has figured prominently in jurisprudence about race, but it has also undergone a series of life cycles and, more recently, some transformations.

The law of slavery was an all-out assault on the dignity of blacks. Not surprisingly, dignity figured prominently in the Reconstruction amendments and the early judicial interpretation of those amendments. That moment subsides, perhaps most dramatically, in *Plessy v. Ferguson* but then returns to full glory on the road to *Brown v. Board of Education,* only to retreat once again.

The reasons for the serial abandonment of the material agenda of civil rights litigation are varied and complex. Some commentators argue that the rise of domestic, anticommunist repression put the NAACP and labor activists on the defensive and, arguably, forced a retreat from labor-related cases specifically and a materialist civil rights agenda more generally.[13] Others point to politics within the NAACP and the institutional privileging of middle-class interests at the expense of the interests of poor and working-class blacks.[14] Certainly, larger shifts in the constitutional landscape—such as the decline of Lochnerian substantive due process and the ascendancy of a narrow equal protection doctrine—left little doctrinal space in which to articulate claims responsive to both racial oppression and economic subordination. Whatever the cause, this evasion has yielded a modern egalitarian constitutional view that has successfully established principles without securing the concomitant material changes.

Taking Dignity Seriously

Despite the doctrinal abandonment of a materialist civil rights agenda, the basic insight into the materialist underpinnings of freedom and equality remains theoretically robust and promising, at least among a handful of welfare and "good society" theorists (such as Frank Michaelman, Michael Sandel, Amartya Sen, Martha Nussbaum, Robin West, and William Forbath). Indeed, Amartya Sen and Martha Nussbaum's work on "capabilities" proves particularly illuminating on the possibilities of securing dignity, freedom, and equality in a liberal democratic state.[15]

By capabilities, Sen and Nussbaum refer to valuable human freedoms that can be meaningfully exercised by individuals. The focus is not on freedom in some abstract sense, but on the individual capacity for freedom that is contingent on material disparities and the exercise of limited human agency. Under this view, the benchmark of equality is, not formal opportunity, but real opportunity for individuals to determine their own conceptions of the good with dignity and respect.

Importantly, the capabilities approach does not impose a requirement on government to secure minimum welfare for all citizens. Instead, it demands that the state ensure that all citizens possess certain capabilities, such as the capability to live a safe, well-nourished, productive, educated, social, and politically and culturally participatory life of normal length. Thus, the state need not provide the full range of welfare goods to every citizen (food, shelter, clothing, physical safety, nondiscriminatory and nonhumiliating work, and the like), but it must ensure that each individual has the capacity to attain them. Access to the material precondition of these capabilities is the truest measure of freedom and equality in a liberal state.

These historical and philosophical insights into the relationship between dignity, freedom, and materialism inform what I call the dignity-centered approach to race jurisprudence. A jurisprudence of race that takes dignity seriously has profound materialist implications because the idea of dignity is powerfully linked not only with formal notions of freedom and equality but also with the material wherewithal to exercise that freedom on an equal basis. Put differently, freedom and equality, viewed through the prism of dignity, demand not only formal equal opportunity for all, but that each of us possess the equal capacity to exercise basic freedoms. It embraces a more compelling and robust conception of freedom and equality responsive to all aspects of racial inequality, including the material aspects of economic oppression.

Dignity therefore demands more than a chimera of equal opportunity premised on abstracted negative rights and prohibitions on racial discrimination. Instead, it focuses upon real freedom and real opportunities and, in this way, places fairly concrete material demands upon the state—demands that present real promise in terms of generating a culture of racial equality that can produce and sustain meaningful changes in the material lives of racially subordinated individuals.

So how does it work? That is, how does a dignity-centered race jurisprudence produce the effects I have described? How does this approach address the culture of complacency and indifference to racial inequality that is reinforced under conventional race jurisprudence?

Let me offer two illustrations. First, consider generally the material disparities in wealth, health, and society between whites and nonwhites. Along virtually every metric of social well-being, racial minorities lag behind whites. Minorities with the same level of education as whites continue to earn substantially less. People of color continue to occupy proportionally fewer managerial positions and proportionally greater service and unskilled-labor positions. Median family income for racial minorities is roughly two-thirds that of whites. Minority youth continue to lag behind whites in performance on standardized tests for mathematics and reading comprehension. The percentage of minority children under the age of eighteen who live in poverty is almost double that of whites. The same is true for the number of births to unwed mothers. Homicide victimization rates for blacks are nearly double the rates for whites. Incarceration rates for black men are seven times those of white men. Minority adult men and women have a shorter life expectancy than their white counterparts, with infant mortality rates approximately double those for whites.[16]

What does conventional race jurisprudence have to say in response to this evidence? As an initial matter, conventional race jurisprudence either assumes baseline equality of natural and material endowments, or deems this matter entirely irrelevant. It asks whether nonwhites enjoy formal equality with whites. Have nonwhites been denied the negative right to be free from invidious racial and ethnic classification? Has there been a formally recognized abridgment of these negative rights that bears directly on the criteria of comparison? If both questions can be answered in the negative, then there is no reason under this conventional view to be suspicious of racially correlated disparities. Such disparities may be unfortunate, but there is nothing that conventional race jurisprudence can do about them.

A dignity-centered approach departs from the conventional view in a number of key ways. First, unlike the conventional view, a dignity-centered approach neither assumes baseline equality of material endowments (although it does presume equal humanity and social worth) nor deems this matter irrelevant. Instead, it meaningfully interrogates the baseline and asks whether racial minorities and whites possess equal capabilities to flourish under a regime of formal equality. Does society presume the equal humanity of nonwhites and whites and provide each with the material wherewithal to exercise basic freedoms on an equal basis? Only if one can answer this question in the affirmative does it then pursue the conventional inquiry as to whether racial minorities and whites possess the negative right to be free from invidious racial and ethnic classification, and whether there has been a formal abridgment of that right. If the initial inquiry must be answered in the negative, however, then there is good reason to be suspicious of the racially correlated disparities, even if the regime of formal equality is in tact and there has been no formal abridgment.

So we can begin to see how a dignity-centered approach opens up the possibilities of substantive racial justice. Unlike the conventional view, which focuses exclusively on the project of negating dignity-expropriative behaviors after the fact, the dignity-centered approach places an affirmative obligation on the state to secure *ex ante* baseline equality by providing the material preconditions for racial minorities to exercise freedom on par with whites.

A second and more concrete example—work—further clarifies the redeeming qualities of the dignity-centered approach. Work is a powerful constituent element of personal identity. It goes beyond mere cash accumulation. Work can be understood as a person's contribution to society, which triggers a host of other values including respect, dignity, and recognition. Among the range of status hierarchies, perhaps the most obvious and accessible is the distinction between those individuals who are gainfully employed and those who are not.

It is perhaps unsurprising to learn that, on average, people of color have fewer and less lucrative employment opportunities than whites. As an initial matter, workers of color tend to be disproportionately unemployed.[17] In the economic downturn from 2000 to 2002, people of color lost annual real income more than three times as fast as whites. Illinois was typical in this regard, where after a substantial number of blue-collar jobs were lost, 75.2 percent of all white men over sixteen years old were employed while the black-male employment rate was but 56.6 percent.[18]

It is perhaps equally unsurprising to learn that disparities persist even among those gainfully employed. Census data show, for instance, black women's wages are 62 percent of similarly situated white men and 85 percent of similarly situated white women.[19] Among the college-educated males, white men earn $66,000 a year while Hispanics earn $49,000 and blacks earn $45,000. In blue-collar workplaces, immigrants, women, and people of color remain largely segregated in jobs with the worst conditions. Women and African Americans are overrepresented in temporary and part-time employment, where jobs are low paying and workers have little or no control over their hours. Immigrants and women of color also number disproportionately among those who toil in sweatshops, contending with subminimum wages, nonpayment of wages, compulsory overtime, and long hours leading to damaged health.[20]

The conventional response, as I described earlier, is one that looks to formal equal opportunity. Under this view, one might reasonably conclude employment opportunities have been equalized and that the "achievement gap" accounts for the continuing gaps in wages and employment between whites and minorities.[21]

What might a dignity-centered race jurisprudence demand in this particular context? If we view the ability to work and reap the fruits of one's labor as an important basic freedom, then a dignity-centered approach might ask what preconditions need to be in place in order for all citizens, regardless of race, to exercise this basic freedom on an equal basis. This may entail obligations on the state to provide free and equal access to decent health care, education, and protection from physical violence. Moreover, once employed, the state may have the further obligation to ensure that individuals possess free and equal opportunities to earn comparable wages in dignified working conditions and to seek promotion.

The dignity-centered approach therefore contemplates serious structural changes in the institutional obligation of the state to citizens of color. In demanding rigorous, contextual scrutiny of material preconditions of freedom, the dignity-centered approach to race jurisprudence promotes a culture of racial equality that enables the human flourishing of racial minorities—a culture that conventional race jurisprudence is fundamentally unable to realize.

Anticipated Difficulties with the Dignity-Centered Approach

This approach is not without its problems, however. Perhaps the strongest objection to a dignity-centered race jurisprudence is that the imposition of some affirmative obligation on the state to ensure material preconditions to exercise freedom on an equal basis is fundamentally inconsistent with the prevailing conception of liberal constitutional rights.

The argument is essentially as follows: the conventional view of liberal constitutional rights are that they are negative rights—rights that place explicit limits on the ability of the state to interfere in the private lives of citizens. Individual rights to liberty, property, contract, and privacy protect us against paternalistic meddling by the state, including intervention that some view as promoting a "good and just society." Because individual rights are both conceived and deployed to protect against an overreaching state, the logic of these negative rights would appear diametrically opposed to any affirmative obligation on the state to ensure that citizens possess the material wherewithal to exercise basic freedoms. Put differently, our negative-rights regime has the effect of disempowering the state from interfering in the private lives of citizens, even for progressive democratic purposes. If the state is to have an obligation to secure the material aspects of equal dignity, it must do so through some mechanism other than individual rights.

There are at least two responses one might offer in defense of the dignity-centered approach. First, although the prevailing view is one that fetishizes negative liberties, this need not be the case. Indeed, the Constitution certainly implies positive rights that arguably interfere with traditional individual rights to be free from state meddling in private affairs. Consider the Thirteenth Amendment's prohibition of slavery. Although the Supreme Court has invoked it only to strike down state legislation, it is a fair assumption that the Thirteenth Amendment also imposes an obligation on the federal government to protect people against private violations of this right as well. Similarly, the Seventh Amendment requires the federal government to provide jury trials in civil and federal cases even though, unlike criminal cases, the state is not directly involved. And in the criminal context, the Supreme Court has required the state to provide counsel, trial transcripts, and other aids to defendants.[22]

Similarly, one might plausibly read the Fourteenth Amendment's prohibition on the abridgment of the privileges and immunities of citizens and the denial of equal protection of the laws as an affirmative obligation on the state to ensure equal citizenship of the sort discussed above. The first sentence of Section 1 declares that "No State shall deny" various entitlements, including equal citizenship and protection of the laws. As Robin West notes, "It may be unfortunate that the drafters chose to use a double negative, but the meaning is not obscure. If no state is allowed to deny, then all states must provide."[23] To be sure, this is not the conventional reading of the Amendment's guarantee. It is certainly a plausible interpretation, however, one that seems more consistent with both the promise of Reconstruction and the overall struggle for racial equality.

Moreover, almost all state constitutions provide for a right to an education, and a substantial number recognize constitutional rights to welfare, housing, health, and abortions. One can debate whether positive rights are best located at the state or federal level. It is clear, however, that positive rights are not wholly outside the American constitutional tradition.

Second, it is important to realize that the distinction between negative and positive rights is more theoretical than real. Consider the right to possess private property. There seems to be little controversy about the appropriateness of protecting property and other forms of private economic activity against governmental action. This is justified on the ground that this involves only a negative right, that is, preventing the state from interfering with property. However, this conveniently overlooks the vast array of resources and protections that property owners expect the state to provide in order to give substance to property rights. Negative property rights necessarily impose affirmative obligations on the state to provide adequate record keeping, law enforcement, and the provision of a legal structure to resolve property rights disputes.

At bottom, whether we are talking about positive-right features of negative rights, or positive rights explicitly, the animating principle is simply that, in civil society, one can always make a claim on government to create institutions and programs that provide for the common defense of individual rights and promote the general welfare. We demand that the government provide certain things and, to that end, obligate it to create certain programs, because we believe that as citizens we are entitled to them.

One might also object that the dignity-centered approach runs afoul of America's deep commitment to merit. The belief in individual merit and the corresponding denunciation of unearned privilege permeates nearly every aspect of American life, from club memberships to education to employment. The problem, of course, is that merit is perhaps more mythology than truth. In reality, the idea of merit has always been situated as an ideal against the prevailing backdrop of privilege and inheritance. Not surprisingly, the idea of merit is increasingly exposed as largely illusory. As Fred Schauer explains, "We are rapidly in the process of burying the myth of Horatio Alger [because it is becoming increasingly apparent that] [y]ou cannot get rich (or even not poor) in contemporary America just by working hard."[24]

In any event, a dignity-centered approach can be understood to correct a fundamental anomaly of the merit argument. The idea of merit presupposes baseline equality and then seeks to explain or ameliorate suspicion of injustice triggered by demonstrable disparities in socioeconomic well-being by attributing them to varying degrees of individual effort. The merit argument masks these disparities within an aura of "naturalness" and evades serious contemplation of exogenous explanations for the purported "natural" hierarchy.

Whatever one might think about merit, it is clear that, if we are to subscribe fully to the merit principle and the outcomes it produces, we must be confident in the assumption of baseline equality. The progressive appeal of the dignity approach to race jurisprudence is that it poses a direct challenge to the legitimacy of racial hierarchy by calling attention to baseline inequalities among groups and highlights the social and cultural insecurities of those with whom they interact. In this sense, the approach enhances the reliability of merit-based assessments by ensuring baseline equality through equal investment in all citizens.

A third potential objection is that an explicitly materialist response to perceived racial injustice may prove stigmatizing to recipients of material transfers. The logic of this argument pervades debate over the potentially stigmatizing effects of affirmative action policy. Justice John Paul Stevens, in his concurring opinion in *Richmond v. Croson* observed that "although [a race preference policy] stigmatizes the disadvantaged class with the unproven charge of past racial discrimination, it actually imposes a greater stigma on its supposed beneficiaries."[25] Similarly, Justice Lewis Powell, in the landmark *Bakke* decision, observed that "preferential programs may only reinforce common stereotypes holding that certain groups are unable to achieve success without special protection based on a factor having no relationship to individual worth."[26] Justice Anthony Kennedy, in *Metro Broadcasting v. Federal Communications Commission,* offered a similar warning: "The history of governmental reliance on race demonstrates that racial policies defended as benign often are not seen that way by the individuals affected by them. . . . Special preferences . . . can foster the view that members of the favored groups are inherently less able to compete on their own."[27]

Again, one might offer a twofold response. First, although some whites may view material transfer to nonwhites as stigmatizing, it is not entirely clear whether that view is shared by racial minorities. A number of commentators have pointed out that proponents of this view rarely seek confirmation that such stigmatization actually occurs. As Alexander Aleinikoff comments, "Despite assertions by whites that race-conscious programs 'stigmatize' beneficiaries, blacks remain overwhelmingly in favor of affirmative action. Would we not expect blacks to be the first to recognize such harms and therefore to oppose affirmative action if it produced serious stigmatic injury?"[28] Indeed, Derek Bok and William Bowen's landmark study on the beneficiaries of affirmative action suggests race-conscious material transfers have the effect of boosting self-esteem and self-confidence because the beneficiaries have been given the opportunity to learn and compete with the best and brightest students.

Second, even if one believes that special preferences are stigmatizing to beneficiaries, there is no reason to conclude that a policy that secures baseline equality would produce the same effect. The dignity-centered approach is grounded in the idea of equal humanity and social worth. By focusing on baseline equality of opportunity, it seeks to eliminate the "special preference" afforded to whites in a culture of racial inequality that nurtures and sustains racial oppression. It is hard to imagine how providing the material preconditions to exercise freedom on an equal basis would prove stigmatizing. Indeed, in a culture committed to racial equality, stigma would presumably attach to those who seek to retain special privilege derived from structural barriers that prevent others from exercising social and economic mobility on a free and equal basis.

The achievement of racial equality in American society remains one of the most perplexing and profound challenges of our time. The principal obstacle is how best to promote a freedom-loving culture that empowers racial minorities to exercise that freedom on equal terms. I have argued that the critical lesson of the *Dred Scott* case, and the corresponding denial of dignity the Scotts experienced, is clear: law can be better utilized to promote a culture of racial equality when we come to understand the role of race jurisprudence as one that seeks to secure and promote the dignitary interests of racial minorities.

In many ways, the argument advanced in this chapter is deeply utopian insofar as it provides a vision of social citizenship and good society that is profoundly in tension with the prevailing conception of the nature of the welfare state and conventional beliefs in status and hierarchy in a liberal capitalist society. But, like any good society theorist, I believe that progress occurs when one not only articulates but presses for realization of the ideal. My hope is that some aspect of this enterprise might yield changes in institutional arrangements that meaningfully improve the lives of everyday people—an enterprise that moves us away from the kinds of law and legal reasoning that gave us the *Dred Scott* decision and toward a culture of equality that takes human dignity seriously.

Notes

1. Dred Scott v. John F. A. Sandford, 60 U.S. (19 How.) 393 (1857).
2. Ibid., 407.

3. Ibid., 403 (emphasis added).

4. Ibid., 410 (emphasis added).

5. Ibid., 407.

6. Akhil Reed Amar, "Foreword: The Document and the Doctrine," *Harvard Law Review* 114, no. 1 (2000): 105.

7. The Slaughterhouse Cases, 83 U.S. 36 (1873).

8. Ibid., 71.

9. Strauder v. West Virginia, 100 U.S. 303, 309 (1880).

10. Martin Luther King Jr., *Why We Can't Wait* (1964), reprinted in *A Testament of Hope: The Essential Writings and Speeches of Martin Luther King, Jr.,* ed. James Melvin Washington (San Francisco: Harper and Row, 1986), 538 ("The Negro in Birmingham, like the Negro elsewhere in this nation, had been skillfully brainwashed to the point where he accepted the white man's theory that he, as a Negro, was inferior. He wanted to believe that he was the equal of any man; but he didn't know where to begin or how to resist the influences that had conditioned him to take the least line of resistance and go along with the white man's views"); Kwame Ture (Stokely Carmichael) and Charles V. Hamilton, *Black Power: The Politics of Liberation in America,* Vintage ed. (New York: Vintage Books, 1992), 29 ("From the time black people were introduced into this country, their condition has fostered human indignity and the denial of respect. Born into this society today, black people begin to doubt themselves, their worth as human beings. Self-respect becomes almost impossible").

11. In a previous article, I explored in detail the various ways in which philosophers and legal scholars have conceptualized and deployed the idea of dignity in a variety of settings dating back to the eighteenth century. See Christopher Alan Bracey, "Dignity in Race Jurisprudence," *University of Pennsylvania Journal of Constitutional Law* 7, no. 3 (2005): 677–705.

12. Here, I am thinking of Glenn Loury's theory of social capital, as developed in the work of economists and political scientists such as Robert Putnam, George Borjas, and others. See Glenn Loury, "A Dynamic Theory of Racial Income Differences," in *Women, Minorities, and Employment Discrimination,* ed. Phyllis Ann Wallace and Annette M. Lamond (Lexington, Mass.: Lexington Books, 1977); Robert Putnam, *Making Democracy Work: Civic Traditions in Modern Italy* (Princeton, N.J.: Princeton University Press, 1993); James Coleman, *Foundations of Social Theory* (Cambridge, Mass.: Belknap Press of Harvard University Press, 1990); Kenneth Arrow, "What Has Economics to Say about Racial Discrimination?" *Journal of Economic Perspectives* 12, no. 2 (1998): 97–98; George Borjas, "Ethnic Capital and Intergenerational Mobility," *Quarterly Journal of Economics* 107, no. 1 (1992): 123–50.

13. Risa Goluboff, "'Let Economic Equality Take Care of Itself': The NAACP, Labor Litigation, and the Making of Civil Rights in the 1940s," *UCLA Law Review* 52, no. 5 (2005): 1464.

14. Tomiko Brown-Nagin, "Race as Identity Caricature: A Local Legal History Lesson in the Salience of Intraracial Conflict," *University of Pennsylvania Law Review* 151, no. 6 (2003): 1913–76.

15. See Amartya Sen, *Development as Freedom* (New York: Knopf, 1999); Amartya Sen, "Capability and Well-Being," in *The Quality of Life,* ed. Martha C. Nussbaum and Amartya Sen (New York: Oxford University Press, 1993).

16. See Glenn C. Loury, *The Anatomy of Racial Inequality* (Cambridge, Mass.: Harvard University Press, 2002), 175–76, 180–82, 184, 190, 196, 200–204.

17. In 2003, for instance, 10.8 percent of blacks, 7.7 percent of Hispanics, and 6.0 percent of Asians were unemployed, compared to 5.2 percent of whites. See Lawrence R. Mishel, Jared Bernstein, and Sylvia A. Allegretto, *The State of Working America, 2004/2005* (Ithaca, N.Y.: ILR Press, 2005).

18. See Robert Cherry, *Who Gets the Good Jobs? Combating Race and Gender Disparities* (New Brunswick, N.J.: Rutgers University Press, 2001), 9.

19. Women's Bureau, U.S. Department of Labor, *Facts on Working Women: Black Women in the Labor Force,* available at http://www.dol.gov/dol/wb/public/wb_ publs/bwlf97.htm.

20. See Donna E. Young, "Racial Releases, Involuntary Separations, and Employment At-Will," *Loyola of Los Angeles Law Review* 34, no. 2 (2001): 363–73; Clyde W. Summers, "Contingent Employment in the United States," *Comparative Labor Law and Policy Journal* 18, no. 4 (1997): 506–14; Shirley Lung, "Exploiting the Joint Employer Doctrine: Providing a Break for Sweatshop Garment Workers," *Loyola University Chicago Law Journal* 34, no. 2 (2003): 297. See generally Miriam Ching Yoon Louie, *Sweatshop Warriors: Immigrant Women Workers Take On the Global Factory* (Cambridge, Mass.: South End Press, 2001), 41.

21. See, for example, Abigail Thernstrom and Stephan Thernstrom, *No Excuses: Closing the Racial Gap in Learning* (New York: Simon and Schuster, 2003); Richard A. Epstein, *Forbidden Grounds: The Case against Employment Discrimination Laws* (Cambridge, Mass.: Harvard University Press, 1992), 263 (suggesting that less-educated blacks should take jobs on an at-will basis and at lower wages to develop the skills they need to move ahead). Indeed, the Thernstroms adhere to this position, despite the significant gaps in employment and wages that remain even after controlling for educational attainment and test scores. William R. Johnson and Derek Neal, "Basic Skills and the Black-White Earnings Gap," in *The Black-White Test Score Gap,* ed. Christopher Jencks and Meredith Phillips (Washington, D.C.: Brookings Institution Press, 1998).

22. See Gideon v. Wainwright, 372 U.S. 335 (1963) (holding that an indigent defendant in state criminal prosecution has the right to have counsel appointed to him); Griffin v. Illinois, 351 U.S. 12 (1956) (holding that indigent defendants have the right to be furnished with trial records and transcripts, without cost, for appellate purposes).

23. Robin West, "Rights, Capabilities, and the Good Society," *Fordham Law Review* 69, no. 5 (2001): 1912.

24. Frederick Schauer, "Community, Citizenship, and the Search for National Identity," *Michigan Law Review* 84, no. 7 (1986): 1516.

25. Richmond v. Croson, 488 U.S. 469, 517 (1989) (Stevens, J., concurring).

26. Regents of the University of California v. Bakke, 438 U.S. 265, 298 (1978).

27. Metro Broadcasting v. Federal Communications Comm'n, 497 U.S. 547, 635–36 (1990) (Kennedy, J., dissenting).

28. See Alexander Aleinikoff, "A Case for Race Consciousness," *Columbia Law Review* 91, no. 5 (1991): 1091.

EIGHT

Dred Scott, Racial Stereotypes, and the "enduring marks of inferiority"

Leland Ware

A COUPLE of years ago, I was in the lobby of the Hotel du Pont in Wilmington, Delaware, one of the most lavish hotels from America's Gilded Age. It has rich woodwork, mosaic and terrazzo floors, handcrafted chandeliers, and gilded hallways. It is the annual meeting place for many of the Fortune 500 companies that are incorporated in Delaware. I was on my way to a reception dressed in a banker's gray Brooks Brothers suit, a crisp white shirt, and an understated tie. I paused in the sumptuous lobby to find out in which of the ballrooms the reception was being held. As I stood there, a middle-aged white man walked up to me, handed me his keys, and asked me to retrieve his car.

The lived experiences of African Americans remain burdened by what Chief Justice Roger Taney called the "enduring marks of inferiority."[1] Despite tremendous racial progress and a broad societal commitment to the principle of racial equality, interactions such as the one described above reveal that old habits, attitudes, assumptions, and beliefs—particularly those involving race—die hard, slow deaths. The *Dred Scott* case played a vital role in legitimizing perceptions of black inferiority in the eyes of the law and the American public. In this chapter, I will trace the progression and evolution of this basic idea of black inferiority that animated Taney's majority opinion for the Court. I intend to highlight the ways in which the legacy of black inferiority influenced the trajectory of American legal and cultural history on race. Importantly, I suggest that, despite two civil rights revolutions and the proliferation of civil rights laws designed to normalize the principle of racial equality, the legacy of black inferiority lingers to this day, occasionally animating the unconscious or unthinking behaviors of otherwise well meaning whites.

Inferiority and the Inculcation of Stereotypes

One of the great tragedies of the *Dred Scott* decision was that it constitutionalized the ideology of racial inferiority. To buttress his interpretation of the legal status of enslaved persons, Taney claimed that African-descended people were an "inferior class of beings" lacking any rights that "the white man was bound to respect."[2] Taney purported to represent the views of the Constitution's framers concerning an "unfortunate race" and contended that he was revealing the true intent and meaning of constitutional text and, specifically, citizenship as it governed Article 3 questions. The central thesis of Taney's opinion was his assertion that the Constitution's framers did not consider African slaves and their descendants to be citizens.

Dred Scott v. Sandford presented complex and intriguing questions of jurisdiction, territoriality, estoppel, comity, federalism, appellate procedure, property rights, and the legal status of slavery and enslaved persons during the antebellum era. As the dissenting opinions in *Dred Scott* indicated, the majority's resolution of those issues rested on questionable reasoning, and some were not addressed at all.[3] *Dred Scott* was decided in a context of long-simmering tensions among states where slavery was sanctioned and those in which the practice had been outlawed. Proslavery and antislavery forces were locked in a fierce debate. The legal issues in *Dred Scott* reflected a bitter political battle over slavery and the balance of power in Congress. The decision was intended to end the legal controversy. But instead of resolving the many issues surrounding slave ownership, the *Dred Scott* decision represented another step on a long path that led to the Civil War.

Dred Scott was overruled by the post–Civil War amendments to the Constitution. For a brief period, African Americans made remarkable strides toward equality. By the final decades of the nineteenth century, the ideology of black inferiority that animated the *Dred Scott* decision was redeployed in a post–Civil War regime of racial subordination. The collective antiblack sentiment was such that very few white Americans gave any serious consideration to the equality of African Americans. Although the Thirteenth and Fourteenth amendments of the U.S. Constitution abolished slavery and prohibited states from denying persons equal protection of the laws, the assumptions about black inferiority lived on. Not surprisingly, by the close of the nineteenth century, racial segregation and concomitant subordination was officially sanctioned by the Supreme Court in the landmark decision *Plessy v. Ferguson*.[4]

Theories of "scientific" racism that purported to prove black inferiority were widespread in the 1850s, when *Dred Scott* was decided. Samuel Morton, a professor of medicine at the University of Pennsylvania, claimed that differences in head shapes could predict a racial group's intelligence and other personality traits.[5] Morton's theory of polygenesis also hypothesized that racial groups did not share a common origin. This provided a "scientific" basis for viewing African-descended people as different and inferior species. Eugenics was introduced in the late nineteenth century by Francis Galton, a British scientist who theorized that the traits and behaviors of humans could be predicted and controlled by breeding people with the "best" genes. Adherents of phrenology, another popular theory, believed that personality traits and characteristics could be ascertained by measuring the shape of an individual's head.

The ideology of black inferiority was reinforced in literature and popular culture. Some of the best-selling popular literature of the late nineteenth and early twentieth centuries reflected and perpetuated stereotypes. Thomas Dixon Jr., a popular author of the period, published *The Clansman: An Historical Romance of the Ku Klux Klan*, which glorified the Klan and portrayed it as a protector of the Southern way of life. Charles Carroll's *The Negro a Beast; or, In the Image of God* was patterned along the same lines. African American stereotypes became a popular vehicle for entertainment in minstrel shows and other productions. White performers darkened their faces with burnt cork, exaggerated their lips with paint, donned wigs, and took to the stage. The common theme in all these performances, a popular mainstay of traveling shows and vaudeville productions, were jokes highlighting laziness, ignorance, and other negative traits using crude versions of the black dialect.[6]

With the advent of motion pictures in the early twentieth century, stereotypical depictions of African Americans moved from the stage to the screen and into the collective psyches of whites. Stereotypes were prominently featured in films for most of the twentieth century. In *Toms, Coons, Mulattoes, Mammies, and Bucks,*[7] film historian Donald Bogle identified the principal stereotypes depicted in motion pictures. The name "Tom" was derived from the character in Harriett Beecher Stowe's nineteenth-century best seller, *Uncle Tom's Cabin.* In films, Toms were always loyal to their owners and employers.[8] They were depicted as obsequious, selfless, and kindly, traits that endeared them to white audiences. "Coons" were irresponsible, lazy, and dishonest. They were frequently shown eating watermelons, stealing chickens, and shooting dice while speaking ungrammatical English.[9] The "Mammy" character was depicted as a cantankerous, overweight female.[10] The "Tragic Mulatto" was a light-skinned black (usually female) attempting to pass for white.[11] The mulatto was a tragic but sympathetic character who was emotionally scarred by a mixed racial heritage. Another stereotype, the "Jezebel," was a promiscuous black woman who used her sexuality for personal gain. The "Black Buck" character was a large, fearsome, and hypersexualized male.[12]

D. W. Griffith's 1915 production, *Birth of a Nation,* depicted the Jim Crow South in a way that glorified the Ku Klux Klan and featured stereotypes that included the Black Buck, who had an uncontrollable lust for white women, and a mulatto Jezebel. In the popular, Academy Award–winning 1939 classic, *Gone with the Wind,* the Mammy character was a humorous and loyal servant to Scarlett O'Hara as they endured the hardships of a Southern city destroyed by the Civil War. *Song of the South* was a popular Walt Disney adaptation of African American folk tales transcribed in the late nineteenth century by Joel Chandler Harris in *Uncle Remus: His Songs and His Sayings.* Disney's 1946 movie presented a romanticized version of the South and was replete with stereotypes. The African American characters were portrayed as happy and content in their subservient occupations in the Jim Crow South.[13]

Amos 'n' Andy was one of the most popular radio programs in the 1930s and 1940s, and it moved to television in the 1950s. One of the principal characters, Kingfish, was a dishonest schemer who fit Bogle's "Coon" paradigm, entertaining audiences with his failed schemes and mangled grammar. Andy was slightly dim-witted and gullible to Kingfish's schemes. Sapphire, Kingfish's loud and abrasive wife, was another stereotyped portrayal of African American women.[14]

African American stereotypes were featured prominently in product advertisements. Aunt Jemima promoted pancake mixes, Uncle Ben sold rice, and Uncle Rastus was the Cream of Wheat chef. Aunt Jemima's character, an example of the "Mammy" image, was based on a real woman, Nancy Green; her image is still the icon for pancake mixes. Rastus, the Cream of Wheat chef, was derived from a photograph of a black Chicago waiter. The product is still marketed with that image.[15] Throughout the first half of the twentieth century, stereotypes were ubiquitous and taken for granted as accurate portrayals of African Americans, reinforced on a daily basis in newspapers, books, radio programs, and films.

The Perpetuation of Racial Stereotypes Today

"Scientific" racism against blacks was on the wane by the late 1940s, and the explicit racial caricatures that were ubiquitous as late as the 1960s have largely disappeared. But harmful stereotypes endure. In *The Black Image in the White Mind,* Robert Entman and Andrew Rojecki examined the ways in which African Americans are depicted by the media and found that the media contributes to the perpetuation of stereotypes in whites' perceptions of blacks.[16] One example of this can be seen in analyses of televised news programming and the depiction of blacks as criminals.[17] Entman and Rojecki found that crime reporting conveyed a strong impression that violent crime is a threat to public safety and that the perpetrators are usually racial minorities. The majority of Americans obtain information about current events through local news reports. Entman and Rojecki presented data that showed 72 percent of Americans regularly watched local news programming, compared to 56 percent who read daily newspapers and 41 percent who regularly watched network news programs. Most Americans "get most of their information about their communities from local television news and in general terms, they believe what they are being shown and told."[18]

Local news programming relies heavily on crime reporting, because crime is easy to find, inexpensive to report, and provides provocative visuals: "If it bleeds it leads."[19] Television broadcasters operate in a highly competitive marketplace, driven by ratings that determine, among other things, what stations can charge advertisers for commercial time, and attention-grabbing visuals attract viewers. African Americans were depicted in crime stories at a disproportionately high rate. Although African Americans do commit crimes at a disproportionate rate compared to their representation in the population, researchers found that whites believed that 60 percent of all people arrested for violent crimes in the United States were black, which was far higher than the actual rate.[20]

In a study of local television news in Philadelphia, whites were typically depicted as victims of violent crime and blacks shown as the perpetrators. In a study examining local news broadcasts in Chicago, white crime victims outnumbered blacks in local news reports, even though blacks were more likely to be crime victims. Black perpetrators of crimes were overrepresented; black victims, underrepresented.[21] In the same study, African Americans were shown in the custody of police officers in handcuffs or otherwise restrained twice as often as whites in the same circumstances. Black defendants were more likely to be shown in street clothes or prison clothing than white defendants, who were more often shown wearing suits. Blacks were depersonalized, as the names of individuals accused of committing crimes were more often given for whites than for blacks. Local news broadcasters' heavy reliance on crime reporting fuels the widespread impression that violent crime is more prevalent than it actually is and that African Americans are the primary perpetrators. Entman and Rojecki concluded that "the mass media convey impressions that blacks and whites occupied different moral universes, that blacks are somehow fundamentally different from whites."[22]

Media outlets contribute to the perpetuation of other stereotypes. In *Why Americans Hate Welfare,* Martin Gilens described the racialization of poverty and analyzed the role that the media plays in fostering this stereotype. In one example, Gilens examined photographs that accompanied poverty stories in *Time, Newsweek,* and *U.S. News and World Report.* He found that 53.2 percent were pictures of black people, at a time that blacks represented only 29 percent of America's poor.[23] White Americans believe that the majority of welfare recipients are black, even though most of the recipients are white, because the news media consistently use images of African Americans when reporting on poverty and welfare. Gilens's data showed that many Americans dislike public assistance programs mainly because they associate welfare with blacks, consistently overestimating the black proportion of the poor and of welfare recipients. The media's depictions of poverty contribute to the stereotypes of blacks as lazy, unintelligent, and undeserving recipients of public assistance.

The entertainment industry is making large profits from the exploitation of racial stereotypes. Rap music is a multibillion-dollar industry that sold more than 80 million records in the United States in 2002, which represented nearly 13 percent of all recordings sold. Many of the most popular rap songs contain lyrics explicitly portraying the violence and drug use associated with urban gang life. The music of rappers such as 50 Cent, Lil Wayne, The Game, and Soulja Boy contains expressions of hostility toward whites, women, and law-enforcement authorities. Their songs depict a ghetto culture where the "Code of the Streets" prevails, which is represented by oppositional behavior and attitudes that reject the mainstream and glamorize individuals who engage in self-destructive, dangerous behavior. Conspicuous consumption, ostentatious displays of jewelry, fast cars, and scantily clad women are the images that predominate in music videos.[24]

There is diversity among viewpoints within the rap industry, but many of the songs and videos are replete with stereotypical and misogynist depictions of black women. In this contemporary iteration, the "Jezebel" character is the "ho" (whore), a prominent character in rap songs, who represents a promiscuous woman who uses sex as a means to obtain her physical and material desires. Another stereotype is the "Sapphire" character, referred to as the "bitch" in rap songs, who is depicted as a domineering and devious African American woman who manipulates the men in her life. She has a combative disposition and undermines the aspirations of her man.[25]

Many of the images in rap videos commodify and exploit blackness much in the same way that pornography objectifies and commodifies women. Blacks are presented as objects for entertainment and consumption. Rap's product is an extravagant, "ghetto fabulous" portrayal of life in inner-city neighborhoods. Young blacks and whites are attracted to the "gangsta" images of tough ghetto youths driving luxury cars, "iced down" in flashy jewelry, wearing oversized shirts and baggy pants, and surrounded by voluptuous "video hos."[26] These images are little more than adolescent male fantasies, but the entertainment industry is profiting handsomely from a product manufactured in recording studios.

Wynton Marsalis, a prominent musician and musical director of jazz at Lincoln Center, denounced rap as "ghetto minstrelsy."[27] And it is no small irony that African American performers and record producers are complicit in this project. The "thug" image that many rappers work hard to project is an updated version of the "Buck" character depicted in *Birth of a Nation:* a large, fearsome, and hypersexualized black male. Rap performers are profiting from their products, but as one commentator observed, when young Black males "labor in the plantations of misogyny and sexism to produce gangsta rap," it is a reflection of their own humiliation and subjugation by powerful economic forces.[28] Rap music is consumed by a large, international audience, and it contributes to the ways in which young African Americans are perceived.[29]

Racial Resentment and Unconscious Discrimination

Discrimination is often seen as a behavioral component of racial prejudice. It is better understood, however, as an interaction of social cognitions about race and behavioral outlets that bring congruence to a person's racial preferences and social settings.[30] Many of the ideas and beliefs held by adults were formed during their early childhood years, and those beliefs serve as a basis for judgments during the adult years.[31] Socialized beliefs can create stereotypes about the social environment. Stereotypes, which involve the creation of a mental image of a typical member of a particular category, are cognitive shortcuts that provide meaning to concepts and phenomena in society.[32] Individuals are perceived as undifferentiated members of a group, lacking any significant differences from the others. Common traits are assigned to the entire group. When a particular behavior by a group member is observed, the viewer evaluates the behavior through the lens of the stereotype.[33]

After the success of the civil rights movement in the 1960s, overt racism slowly diminished. Civil rights laws made racial discrimination socially unacceptable and legally impermissible, and a societal commitment to the principle of racial equality emerged. Today, most whites subscribe to the norm of racial equality, but stereotypes and negative attitudes about African Americans persist.[34] An example of this can be found in the opposition of some to public policies designed to advance racial equality. Racial resentment is the adherence of many whites to a belief that African Americans are too demanding and are undeserving of any special government assistance.[35] Racial resentment differs from traditional prejudice because the adherents do not subscribe to the notion of biological inferiority.[36] Instead, the attitude is derived from social constructs and beliefs that are developed by individuals at an early age. These sentiments often operate at an unconscious level, originating from social-dominance orientations and other personality traits, and they are expressed through stereotypes and other biases.[37]

Polling data shows that many whites hold attitudes that are attributable to racial resentment, believing that blacks are deficient in values such as patriotism, hard work, discipline, and self-sacrifice.[38] They believe that, as the legal barriers were removed decades ago by civil rights laws, the continuing levels of violence and poverty in inner-city communities reflect the failure of blacks to take advantage of the opportunities available to them. Fraud and abuse in the welfare system, escalating crime rates, and the dissolution of the traditional family are seen as reflections of those shortcomings.[39]

Unconscious discrimination is closely related to racial resentment. It stems from beliefs so deeply embedded in American culture that they are not explicitly learned.[40] In "The Id, the Ego, and Equal Protection: Reckoning with Unconscious Racism," Charles Lawrence explains that racism is deeply ingrained in our culture and is transmitted from one generation to another through a set of tacit understandings. These beliefs, Lawrence explained, are part of an individual's understanding of the society in which we reside. A white child is not taught that blacks are inferior, but he or she learns this is so by observing the behavior of others. These unarticulated understandings are not present in an individual's conscious memory; they are stored deep in the psyche where they reside at an unconscious level.[41]

Scholars representing a range of academic disciplines have produced an extensive body of research that demonstrates the existence of unconscious discrimination. In *The Content of Our Categories,*[42] Linda Krieger explains that much of the discriminatory conduct that occurs now is not the product of conscious animus. Krieger explains that decision making relies on "categorization," a process in which similar objects are grouped together in a person's thought processes. An individual determines what something is by ascertaining to what it is similar and from what it differs. Categorization simplifies and expedites this task, allowing individuals to identify objects, make predictions about the future, draw inferences, and attribute outcomes to specific events. At an unconscious level, individuals perceive, categorize, and evaluate information depending on the ways in which information is presented and the context in which it is received. The danger is that categorization can make it difficult for an observer to recognize a person's individual characteristics.

Stereotyping is a form of categorization. Stereotypes are embedded in children's memories long before they have ability to evaluate differences in groups.[43] Stereotypes are the natural by-products of ordinary perception, categorization, learning, memory, and judgment. Categorization, including racial stereotyping, is virtually automatic, operating at a level independent of conscious attitudes, beliefs, and perceptions. Stereotypes can be so deeply embedded that they persist after an individual is presented with clear and convincing evidence that refutes the stereotype.[44] Unconscious discrimination can influence decision making long before any final decision is made. The biases function outside of the decision maker's conscious awareness; they can influence the ways information is processed and used. Stereotypes can shape the interpretation of information and influence the ways in which that information is stored and retrieved from memory. A decision maker can treat a person differently on the basis of race or sex, believing that he or she is acting on the basis of some legitimate, nondiscriminatory reason.[45]

An extensive body of research explains how unconscious stereotypes function in the human mind.[46] John Dovidio and Samuel Gaertner use the term "aversive racism" to describe the actions of individuals who support policies that promote racial equality and consider themselves as not prejudiced but act in ways that disadvantage minorities. Aversive racists often experience feelings of *uneasiness or fear* in the presence of racial minorities. Their negative attitudes are usually unacknowledged because they conflict with their egalitarian value systems. Aversive racists typically do not discriminate against African Americans when it would be obvious to others and themselves, but they are likely to do so when there are race-neutral justifications for their behavior.[47] Individuals who harbor bias would find it aversive to recognize their own racism.[48]

In one frequently cited experiment concerning the provision of emergency assistance, white bystanders were as likely to help a black victim as a white victim when they were the only witness to an emergency and their personal responsibility was clear. In circumstances in which there were other witnesses to the emergency, they would justify not helping on the belief that someone else would intervene. In this situation, whites helped the black victim half as often as they helped the white victim. Racial bias was expressed in a way that could be justified on the basis of a race-neutral reason.[49]

The Implicit Association Test (IAT) is another experimental model that detects unconscious discrimination. The IAT measures association response times between representations for race, gender, age, and other classifications and positive and negative characteristics.[50] To measure racial associations, test takers' preferences are measured by their response times in pairing positive words or negative words with depictions of alternating white and black faces. Quicker response times to pairing black faces with negative words and white faces with positive words indicate a subtle preference for associating a black or white face with a negative or positive word. The test is premised on the observation that it takes participants longer to associate words and faces that the test takers consider incompatible.

The test developers determined that the time differential could be quantified to provide an objective assessment of a test taker's unconscious attitudes. Because reaction times are mapped in milliseconds, the associative process is automatic and not subject to the sort of conscious control that could make it difficult to determine whether the participants were producing consciously desired outcomes. Using the IAT, researchers have documented a preference for whites among test takers of different races who believed that they did not harbor any racial prejudices. The test results indicate that the test taker's attitudes about race were influenced by unconscious bias. The extensive body of quantitative research and commentary produced over the last two decades shows that the existence of unconscious discrimination cannot seriously be disputed—racial bias is still prevalent, and it burdens the lived experiences of African Americans and other minorities.

Notions of black inferiority have a long history in America. During the Constitutional Convention in Philadelphia, the legal status of slavery was debated and finally resolved with the "three-fifths clause," which implicitly acknowledged slavery. The Constitution also recognized slavery in a provision that allowed for the return of runaway slaves to their owners. After the Constitution was ratified, the debate over slavery continued as the Northern states began to prohibit slave ownership while the laws of other states sanctioned the institution. When the United States acquired new territories, the conflicts over slavery intensified. The questions then were whether the territories should be admitted as free or slave states and the effect this would have on the balance of power in Congress. The majority in *Dred Scott* hoped the decision would end the legal debate. Taney's opinion relied on "scientific" racism to justify involuntary servitude. He claimed that African-descended people were beings of an inferior order that had no rights that whites were bound to respect. Taney's opinion added fuel to a firestorm of conflicts that led to the Civil War.

The legacy of black inferiority exemplified by *Dred Scott* profoundly shaped the trajectory of racial progress in the decades following the decision. An assumption of black inferiority was the subtext of nineteenth-century Supreme Court decisions that undermined the Fourteenth and Fifteenth amendments. States were prohibited from treating African Americans differently and less favorably, but individuals were free to discriminate as much as they pleased.[51] State officials were allowed to use subterfuges to prevent African Americans from voting in the South as long as the laws on which they relied were couched in race-neutral terms.[52] Racial inferiority was the underlying assumption of the 1896 decision in *Plessy v. Ferguson.* Legal equality and "social" equality were viewed as separate and distinct. During this period, the ideology of inferiority was institutionalized and woven deeply into the fabric of American culture. The legal status of African Americans as second-class citizens continued until the 1960s, when the enactment of federal laws prohibited official discrimination and segregation.

Of course, conditions for African Americans have improved immensely in the generation since the 1960s. President Barack Obama's election is a testament to the strides that have been made. His leadership of the world's most powerful nation will diminish considerably the stereotypes that linger. The next generation will have an entirely different frame of reference and a different set of experiences from those we had growing up. Despite the almost immeasurable progress, however, racial discrimination persists, and its nature is not altogether different from what it was when *Dred Scott* was decided. Today's racial discrimination is a complex amalgam of overt discrimination, internalized stereotypes, and implicit biases that operate in ways that disadvantage African Americans. More than 150 years later, the "marks of inferiority" endure.

Notes

1. Dred Scott v. John F. A. Sandford, 60 U.S. (19 How.) 393, 416 (1857).
2. Scott, 60 U.S. at 407.
3. Ibid., 529–64 (McLean J., dissenting), 564–633 (Curtis, J., dissenting).
4. Plessy v. Ferguson, 163 U.S. 537 (1896).
5. Bruce Dain, *A Hideous Monster of the Mind: American Race Theory in the Early Republic* (Cambridge, Mass.: Harvard University Press, 2003).
6. Elizabeth Ewen and Stuart Ewen, *Typecasting: On the Arts and Sciences of Human Inequality* (New York: Seven Stories Press, 2006), 407–13; J. Stanley Lemons, "Black Stereotypes as Reflected in Popular Culture, 1880–1920," *American Quarterly* 29, no. 1 (1977): 102–16.
7. Donald Bogle, *Toms, Coons, Mulattoes, Mammies, and Bucks: An Interpretive History of Blacks in American Films,* rev. ed. (New York: Continuum, 1989).
8. These depictions were a staple of popular films featuring African American dancer and actor Bill Robinson and child star Shirley Temple. Robinson performed the role of Uncle Billy, a kind and good-natured Tom. See *The Little Colonel* (1935); *The Littlest Rebel* (1935); *Rebecca of Sunnybrook Farm* (1938).
9. Lincoln Theodore Perry's character, Stepin Fetchit, is a classic portrayal of the Coon. See *In Old Kentucky* (1929); *Stand Up and Cheer* (1934); *David Harum* (1934).
10. *Gone with the Wind* (1939).
11. *Imitation of Life* (1934 and 1959); *Pinky* (1949).
12. *Birth of a Nation* (1915).
13. Steven Watts, *The Magic Kingdom: Walt Disney and the American Way of Life* (Columbia: University of Missouri Press, 2001).
14. Donald Bogle, *Primetime Blues: African Americans on Network Television* (New York: Farrar, Straus and Giroux, 2001), 26–42.

15. Marilyn Kern-Foxworth, *Aunt Jemima, Uncle Ben, and Rastus: Blacks in Advertising, Yesterday, Today, and Tomorrow* (Westport, Conn.: Greenwood Press, 1994).

16. Robert M. Entman and Andrew Rojecki, *The Black Image in the White Mind: Media and Race in America* (Chicago: University of Chicago Press, 2000).

17. Jerry Kang, "Trojan Horses of Race," *Harvard Law Review* 118, no. 5 (2005): 1489–1593.

18. Danilo Yanich, "Crime Creep: Urban and Suburban Crime on Local TV News," *Journal of Urban Affairs* 26, no. 5 (2004): 535–63.

19. Ibid., 537.

20. Ibid. See also Dennis Rome, *Black Demons: The Media's Depiction of the African American Male Criminal Stereotype* (Westport, Conn.: Praeger, 2004). The Federal Bureau of Investigation estimated in 1997 that 41 percent of those arrested for violent crime were black and 57 percent were white; blacks make up approximately 12 percent of the U.S. population. See Entman and Rojecki, *Black Image in the White Mind,* 79; see also Patricia G. Devine and Andrew J. Elliot, "Are Racial Stereotypes Really Fading? The Princeton Trilogy Revisited," *Personality and Social Psychology Bulletin* 21, no. 11 (1995): 1139–50 (consistent and negative contemporary stereotypes of blacks).

21. Entman and Rojecki, *Black Image in the White Mind;* see also Franklin D. Gilliam Jr. and Shanto Iyengar, "Prime Suspects: The Influence of Local Television News on the Viewing Public," *American Journal of Political Science* 44, no. 3 (2000): 560–73. A study using data from Los Angeles, California, showed that African Americans were overrepresented in crime reports on local news broadcasts. Travis L. Dixon and Daniel Linz, "Overrepresentation and Underrepresentation of African Americans and Latinos as Lawbreakers on Television News," *Journal of Communication* 50, no. 2 (2000): 131–54.

22. Entman and Rojecki, *Black Image in the White Mind,* 6.

23. Martin Gilens, *Why Americans Hate Welfare: Race, Media, and the Politics of Antipoverty Policy* (Chicago: University of Chicago Press, 1999), 113.

24. Ronald L. Jackson II, *Scripting the Black Masculine Body: Identity, Discourse, and Racial Politics in Popular Media* (Albany, N.Y.: State University of New York Press, 2006), 110–13.

25. Terri M. Adams and Douglas B. Fuller, "The Words Have Changed but the Ideology Remains the Same: Misogynistic Lyrics in Rap Music," *Journal of Black Studies* 36, no. 6 (2006): 938–57.

26. Michael Eric Dyson, *The Michael Eric Dyson Reader* (New York: Basic Civitas Books, 2004), 411–17.

27. "Shock of the New," *Guardian,* March 7, 2007, http://www.guardian.co.uk/music/2007/mar/02/jazz.

28. bell hooks, "Sexism and Misogyny: Who Takes the Rap?" *Z Magazine* (February 1994).

29. Jeffrey O. G. Ogbar, *Hip Hop Revolution: The Culture and Politics of Rap* (Lawrence: University Press of Kansas, 2007).

30. James M. Jones, *Prejudice and Racism* (New York: McGraw-Hill, 1997), 425–27.

31. Jody Armour, "Stereotypes and Prejudice: Helping Legal Decisionmakers Break the Prejudice Habit," *California Law Review* 83, no. 3 (1995): 733–72.

32. Jones, *Prejudice and Racism,* 164–201.

33. Ibid.

34. Donald R. Kinder and Lynn M. Sanders, *Divided by Color: Racial Politics and Democratic Ideals* (Chicago: University of Chicago Press, 1996), 92–127. This disposition has been variously labeled "symbolic racism," "modern racism," and "racial resentment." These attitudes include a belief that discrimination does not impose a significant impediment to black advancement. African Americans should simply work harder to improve their economic and social status. The more overt forms of prejudice and racism have declined, but stereotypes about blacks persist. Patrick J. Henry and David O. Sears, "The Symbolic Racism Scale," *Political Psychology* 23, no. 2 (2002): 254–58.

35. Kinder and Sanders, *Divided by Color,* 37.

36. Ibid., 113.

37. Ibid., 113–15.

38. Lawrence Bobo and James R. Kluegel, "Status, Ideology, and Dimensions of Whites' Racial Beliefs and Attitudes: Progress and Stagnation," in *Racial Attitudes in the 1990s: Continuity and Change,* ed. Steven A. Tuch and Jack K. Martin (Westport, Conn.: Praeger, 1997), 99–105.

39. Donald R. Kinder and David O. Sears, "Prejudice and Politics: Symbolic Racism versus Racial Threats to the Good Life," *Journal of Personality and Social Psychology* 40, no. 3 (1981): 414–31.

40. Charles R. Lawrence III, "The Id, the Ego, and Equal Protection: Reckoning with Unconscious Racism," *Stanford Law Review* 39, no. 2 (1987): 317–88.

41. Ibid.

42. Linda Hamilton Krieger, "The Content of Our Categories: A Cognitive Bias Approach to Discrimination and Equal Employment Opportunity," *Stanford Law Review* 47, no. 6 (1995): 1161–1248.

43. Armour, "Stereotypes and Prejudice."

44. See Peggy C. Davis, "Law as Microaggression," *Yale Law Journal* 98, no. 8 (1989): 1561–62 (explaining how racial stereotypes affect the cognitive processes of categorization in individuals).

45. Linda Hamilton Krieger and Susan T. Fiske, "Behavioral Realism in Employment Discrimination Law: Implicit Bias and Disparate Treatment," *California Law Review* 94, no. 4 (2006): 1034. See also James M. Jones, "Psychological Knowledge and the New American Dilemma," *Journal of Sociological Issues* 54, no. 4 (1998): 641–62 (discussing, among other things, categorization and stereotyping);

Kang, "Trojan Horses"; Anthony G. Greenwald and Linda Hamilton Krieger, "Implicit Bias: Scientific Foundations," *California Law Review* 94, no. 4 (2006): 954–58.

46. Leland Ware, "A Comparative Analysis of Unconscious and Institutional Discrimination in the United States and Britain," *Georgia Journal of International and Comparative Law* 36, no. 1 (2007): 89–157; see also John F. Dovidio, Samuel L. Gaertner, and Kerry Kamakami, "Implicit and Explicit Prejudice and Interracial Interaction," *Journal of Personality and Social Psychology* 82, no. 1 (2002): 62–68.

47. Samuel L. Gaertner and John F. Dovidio, "The Aversive Form of Racism," in *Prejudice, Discrimination, and Racism,* ed. John F. Dovidio and Samuel L. Gaertner (Orlando, Fla.: Academic Press, 1986), 61–89.

48. "Racial bias is expressed in indirect ways that do not threaten the aversive racist's non-prejudiced self-image. . . . [D]iscrimination occurs when [that] bias is not obvious or can be rationalized on the basis of some factor other than race." John F. Dovidio and Samuel L. Gaertner, "Aversive Racism and Selection Decisions: 1989 and 1999," *Psychological Science* 11, no. 4 (2000): 315–19.

49. Samuel L. Gaertner and John F. Dovidio, *Reducing Intergroup Bias: The Common Ingroup Identity Model* (Philadelphia: Psychology Press, 2000), 24–26.

50. The tests were developed by Professors Anthony Greenwald and Mahzarin Banaji. See Project Implicit, IAT Home, at https://implicit.harvard.edu/implicit/demo/; see also Anthony G. Greenwald, Debbie E. McGhee, and Jordan L. K. Schwartz, "Measuring Individual Differences in Implicit Cognition: The Implicit Association Test," *Journal of Personality and Social Psychology* 74, no. 6 (1998): 1464–80.

51. The Civil Rights Cases, 109 U.S. 3 (1883). Key provisions of the 1875 Reconstruction Civil Rights Act were declared unconstitutional. The decision established the "state action" doctrine, holding that Congress did not have the authority to regulate private acts of discrimination.

52. Williams v. Mississippi, 170 U.S. 213 (1898). The Supreme Court approved Mississippi's constitutional amendment requiring voters to pass literacy tests and to pay poll taxes. The laws applied to all of the state's residents but were used to disfranchise black voters.

NINE

Unmasking the Lie

Dred Scott *and the Antebellum Southern Honor Culture*

Cecil J. Hunt II

ALTHOUGH IT is possible for a nation to deny its history, it is not possible for it to escape responsibility for the consequences of that history. A significant part of America's history consists of the sordid practice of black chattel slavery. Integral to that peculiar institution was the Supreme Court's 1857 decision in *Dred Scott v. Sandford*,[1] which notoriously validated the constitutionality of America's unique form of slavery.[2] This case, decided more than a century and a half ago, represents far more than a shameful part of America's long forgotten past. As historian Don Fehrenbacher observed, "[T]he spirit of the opinion survived for a century in the racial sequel to emancipation," and the decision "had a distinctly modern ring." Thus, careful reflection on the bitter legacy of *Dred Scott* continues to have significant contemporary "revelatory value."[3]

In this essay, I discuss matters of humanity, honor, and respect. I suggest that when Chief Justice Roger Taney, author of the majority opinion in *Dred Scott*, characterized black people as "a subordinate and inferior class of beings who . . . whether emancipated or not . . . had no rights which the white man was bound to respect,"[4] he was also saying that blacks had *no right to be respected* by whites.[5] In this way, beyond characterizing blacks as members of "that unfortunate race,"[6] Taney was also saying that blacks were not at all human but rather just *things—things* that were "so far below [whites] in the scale of created beings" that they should be regarded as "ordinary article[s] of merchandise."[7] By characterizing blacks as degraded *things,* rather than people, Taney was arguing not only that blacks had no legal rights to be respected, but also that they had no human rights to be respected as members of the human family.

Whether Taney subscribed to these views in his personal affairs is a matter of much debate. Consider, for instance, the fact that Taney freed his own slaves more than thirty years before *Dred Scott* was decided.[8] He also once wrote to a friend that "I do not consider it any degradation to kneel side by side with a Negro" in church.[9] Furthermore, on at least one recorded occasion, Taney represented a client that "had been described as a negro" before the Supreme Court.[10] Nevertheless, the racial ideology of white disrespect of blacks infamously articulated in his written opinion in *Dred Scott* has exerted a powerful influence on virtually every aspect of America's racial discourse for the past 150 years.

One of the unfortunate legacies of *Dred Scott* is the manner in which this ideology of racial disrespect has, over time, worked to sabotage and undermine national efforts to achieve meaningful racial equality in America. This historical legacy of racial disrespect can be seen in the violence and fraud of the white redemption of the South following Reconstruction and in the orgy of lynch law and violence, which reached its peak in the 1890s but continued sporadically throughout the South through the 1930s; in Jim Crow segregation, first authorized by the Supreme Court in *Plessy v. Ferguson* in 1896, and typified by virtually every aspect of American public life from then until the Supreme Court decided *Brown v. Board of Education* in 1954; in the violence and resistance to educational integration in grade school and colleges and universities in the late 1950s and early 1960s; in the civil rights movement of the 1950s and 1960s; in discrimination in housing and lending redlining from the 1940s through the 1970s; in white resistance to affirmative action in the 1980s and 1990s; and in racially targeted financial fraud often found in present-day predatory lending.

Despite this extended legacy of racial disrespect, there are a number of hopeful signs that bode well for the future of race relations in America. These signs include, but are not limited to, high level governmental appointments of blacks such as Clarence Thomas to the Supreme Court Condoleezza Rice and Colin Powell as secretaries of state, and the election of Barack Obama as the first African American president of the United States in 2008. At the same time, these racially significant events have done little to change the lives of millions of ordinary black people for the better, many of whom continue to suffer disproportionately from inferior public schools and high dropout rates, crime-plagued inner cities, high rates of infant mortality, high rates of HIV/AIDS infection, high levels of poverty and joblessness, and the indignity of both criminal and commercial racial profiling. The persistence of these social problems and the relatively modest degree of outrage they provoke among the majority of Americans reflect, in my view, this legacy of racial disrespect.

Honor, Respect, and the Southern Way of Life

In the Southern honor culture, where Taney and many of his fellow Southern justices were raised, the terms "respect" and "honor" had particular meanings that reflected traditional regional beliefs and deep-rooted values, and they were all men who had a high sense of honor.[11] Their upbringing in the Southern honor culture meant that the meanings and implications that the justices associated with those terms were not the same as could be found in the North. By viewing Taney's opinion in *Dred Scott* through the analytical lens of honor and respect as expressed in the historical context and language of the Southern honor culture, it is possible to gain a deeper understanding of the case, its implications on contemporary racial reality, and the possibility of significant progress in achieving racial equality in America.

From a contemporary perspective, the values of honor and respect may seem old-fashioned and perhaps of little value in scholarly analysis.[12] In the Old South, however, these values were and continue to be a part of a "culture of honor ideology" that embodied important standards of public and private behavior.[13] As Chandra Manning points out, "Though difficult to define precisely (and significantly different from what we mean by 'honor' today) a specific notion of honor was central to white Southerners' values and culture. It encapsulated white southern men's concern with personal reputation, and rested on acknowledgment by one's peers of attributes like courage, right morals, and masculinity."[14] Such values can have a significant effect on the "laws and institutional behaviors . . . and public representations" of those who share these ideologies.[15] Importantly, these values were powerful social and political determinants of the southern mentality in 1857, when the *Dred Scott* case was decided.[16]

Taney understood that, in the Southern mind, there was more at stake in *Dred Scott* than simply economic property rights in slaves. Thus, Taney's characterization of blacks, both free and slave, as being unworthy of white respect, both personally and in their legal rights, was no casual choice of words. By using the language of honor and respect, he was signaling to the South that white honor, which was delicately balanced by black dishonor, was being not only protected and vindicated but also enshrined into national constitutional law that the entire country would be bound to recognize and respect. Thus, Taney's decision was not simply a justification for the economic system of Southern slavery. It was a validation for the entire Southern way of life.

Honor and respect are in many ways functional equivalents.[17] However, a subtle and important distinction can be made between the two terms in that honor might be understood as a predicate to respect. In the antebellum South, a man deserved to be respected by society and other men because he was honorable. As one scholar has explained, "Any accurate description of Southern honor must be couched in qualified language and described with care, for it was simultaneously potent and elusive."[18] Southern honor was an outward-looking value that involved an extreme concern with public appearances and the opinions of others and "led people to pay particular attention to manners, to ritualized evidence of respect."[19]

In the context of Southern honor and respect, the "being and truth about a person are identical with the being and truth that others acknowledge in him."[20] Thus the "heart of honor was the respect of others . . . and the willingness to defend [one's] honor . . . and to possess honor worthy of defense."[21] The defense of this sense of honor often took the form of violence and the expression of a willingness to use violence.[22] Thus the "difference between having and not having honor was the difference between having and not having power."[23]

At the same time, it is worth emphasizing that honor was not simply an artifact of social elites. As Bertram Wyatt-Brown has pointed out, "[H]onor is not confined to any rank of society; it is the moral property of all who belong within the community."[24] In fact honor is such a galvanizing and insular concept that it "determines the community's own membership."[25] As Edward L. Ayers perceptively observed, within the "broad spectrum of Southerners" men who "were neither rich nor poor . . . considered themselves men of honor."[26] Ariela J. Gross captured this democratic sense of honor:

> [T]he Southern code of honor was not the exclusive possession of gentlemen. Men of the lower classes took part in their own rituals of honor. . . . Most basically, Southern common folk though not given to gentlemanly manner, duels and other signs of superior elan, also believed in honor because they had access to the means for its assertion themselves—the possession of slaves—and because all whites, nonslaveholders as well, held sway over all blacks. Historians have referred to this unifying principle as "herrenvolk democracy" or "white men's timocracy."[27]

Thus, poor white men who did not own slaves had to assert and affirm their whiteness and manhood through the very existence of slavery, however removed the actual institution was from their everyday lives. To be sure, poor whites had and exercised dominion and violence upon the bodies of both free and enslaved blacks whenever they happened to encounter them in public. But a poor white man who never even saw a slave was confirmed in his whiteness, manhood, social station in Southern society, and personal value by the very existence of black slavery. By this metric, no matter how poor, propertyless, and degraded any white man was, slavery established a social floor below which no white person could fall. Only blacks, whether slave or free, "constituted the mudsill class."[28] The very nature of "Southern politics depended on a belief that all white men were equals" in their distance from blacks, which "resulted in a democratization of honor, a recognition that there were elements of honor in which all white men could partake, especially through acts of citizenship."[29]

Southern society was an honor-based culture.[30] In such an honor culture, "there is no higher goal than honor and glory and its corollary of shame avoidance."[31] Because of the cultural norms that such societies develop, as it has been accurately observed, the natural dynamic of an "honor culture erases any meaningful distinction between service to some noble principle and the avoidance of shame and the acquisition of honor. The entire moral order is subsumed under the larger goal of honor."[32]

As Orlando Patterson has correctly observed in his important study on slavery, the honor culture of the Old South "developed to its highest degree a slaveholder's ideology . . . and the most elaborate and deliberately articulated timocracy of modern times."[33] Therefore, honor, as well as the efforts made to achieve and maintain it, was the "pivotal . . . and central articulating principle of southern life and culture" for all white male segments of society, whether slaveholders or not.[34] John Hope Franklin captured the significance of honor in the timocratic Old South when he wrote, "[T]he honor of the Southerner caused him to defend with his life the slightest suggestion of irregularity in his honesty or integrity; . . . to him nothing was more important than honor. Indeed he placed it above wealth, art, learning, and the other 'delicacies' of an urban civilization and regarded its protection as a continuing preoccupation."[35]

"Lying" and "Unmasking" in Honor Cultures

In most honor cultures, being called a liar was an insult of the highest order. This was especially true in the honor culture of the Old South. Southern masculinity was inextricably tied to notions of honesty and integrity. As a consequence, to be called a liar was interpreted as an attack on both a man's masculinity and his honor. It was essentially an accusation that one's public image as a man was a sham, a fraud that had been perpetrated on the entire community. In the language of honor cultures, the assertion of a clear and apparent distance "between asserted appearance and reality" was tantamount to being exposed or "unmasked" in public and thereby "shamed."[36]

Since shame, or unmasking, is the direct opposite of honor, this connection between lying and shame helps explain why the South was so enraged by the harshness of Northern criticism of its slaveholding society. Deep criticism from antislavery segments in the North was, in essence, unmasking and thereby publicly shaming the entire South by pointing out the gap between their moral claims of legitimacy in their defenses of slavery and the stark moral reality of black humanity. Northern criticism of Southern slavery and Taney's conclusion about black disrespect "reinforced the loathing that Southerners (including Taney) felt for abolitionists."[37]

Although there was not universal disdain at the *Dred Scott* decision in the North, there was an insulting torrent of invective propelled against the *Dred Scott* decision in certain regions. Some Republican newspaper editorialists, such as the *New York Tribune's* Horace Greeley, "set the pace with editorials almost every day denouncing this 'atrocious,' this 'wicked, this 'abominable' judgment, which was no better than what might be obtained in any 'Washington bar-room'—denouncing also the 'cunning chief' whose 'collation of false statements and shallow sophistries' revealed a 'detestable hypocrisy' and a 'mean and skulking cowardice.'"[38] Similarly, the *Chicago Democratic Press* "expressed a 'feeling of shame and loathing' for 'this once illustrious tribunal.'"[39] Similar "flaming denunciations issued from the Republican press" and in religious meetings throughout the North.[40]

The viciousness of the attacks on Taney, in which he was accused of being both a liar and a coward, struck at the heart of the Southern honor culture. It would be an exaggeration to suggest that outraged and insulted Southerners were fatally provoked into war simply and solely on the basis of the ferocity of Northern insults concerning the *Dred Scott* decision. But given the core values of the South's culture of honor, it is reasonable to suggest that criticisms directed at the Southern way of life were an important contributing factor in "provok[ing] Southern extremists to disunion" and accelerating the nation's already headlong rush to the battlefield.[41] As historian Bertram Wyatt-Brown has accurately observed, "[I]n the South, vindicating an intense if not fanatical sense of honor was uppermost in the minds of disunionists. They argued that failure to answer the insult of Northern moral criticism . . . meant a loss of collective manhood and a feminization of the Southern spirit."[42]

Put differently, once a man of honor was insulted or shamed by being metaphorically "unmasked" in public, his only recourse was to resort to violence (or at least claim to be willing to use violence) to defend, vindicate, and reclaim his honor.[43] Originally this violence was played out in the Old South in the form of duels between members of the aristocracy, and by hand-to-hand fighting in the lower socioeconomic, nonslaveholding classes. The common glue in both groups was the willingness to use violence and the willingness in the use of violence to risk being killed.[44] The willingness to put one's life at risk for the cause of honor was the ultimate expression of manliness and honor because it articulated, in the eyes of one's honor group, that death was preferable to dishonor.[45]

Indeed, one of the clear distinctions between whites and slaves was that whites actually had the power and authority to use violence to protect their physical bodies and their public integrity. Slaves did not. Whether free or slave, almost universally, blacks had neither the power nor the authority to use violence to protect their physical bodies, their personal honor, or the honor of their families from insults by whites. In some instances, "southern states forbade [even] . . . free blacks . . . from owning firearms."[46] This prohibition struck at the very heart of black disrespect and dishonor because, by law, they were denied the power to protect both themselves and their families. The inability to defend oneself created an additional distance of honor between whites and blacks, at least with respect to black slaves, because a white man *could* risk his life for the sake of honor, because his life belonged to him, while a slave could not, because a slave's life did not belong to him but to his master.

Northern criticisms of the *Dred Scott* decision were tantamount to an insult to the South's collective sense of honor because, as the abolitionists had argued, the South had no moral right to rule, command, or protect their slave property or their way of life. In the Old South, an honorable man was expected to be willing and able to "protect one's person, family, and property," including most especially "the beliefs embodied in them." A sense of honor, then, is "the source of the protectiveness so characteristic of manliness."[47] In this way honor cultures like the Old South are by necessity patriarchal in structure. As one commentator has explained, "Honor is an asserted claim to protect someone, and the claim to protect is a claim to rule. How can I protect you properly if I can't tell you what to do?"[48] The Southern male was a man who claimed a right to command and protect his family, his way of life, and his slaves.[49] Any insult to his honor was therefore an assertion of his inability to protect himself, his family, and his property.

In the Southern honor culture, the very definition of slaves was based upon the idea of a person without honor. It is not an overstatement to say that in the South "all issues of honor related to slavery."[50] The homage to honor was not necessarily tied to slavery because it "existed before, during, and after slavery."[51] However, "the determination of men to have power, prestige, and self-esteem and to immortalize these acquisitions through their progeny was the key to the South's development."[52] Although the South did not invent slavery, it did raise the peculiar institution to a high art, in an effort to more finely define themselves. In this way, Southern honor depended on black dishonor, a connection evidenced by the founding principles of the Confederate States of America, which presaged the beginning of the Civil War. In his famous "cornerstone speech," the vice president of the Confederacy, Alexander H. Stephens, said that the new nation was dedicated to "the advancement of prosperity, happiness, safety, honor, and true glory of the confederacy." It would succeed because "our new government is founded upon . . . , its foundations are laid, its cornerstone rests upon the great truth, that the negro is not equal to the white man; that slavery—subordination to the superior race—is his natural and normal condition. This, our new government, is the first, in the history of the world, to be based upon this great physical, philosophical, and moral truth."[53] Stephens made it clear that the honor of the Confederate States was grounded in the presumption of inherent black inferiority and disrespect.

Honor, Respect, and the Contemporary Legacy of *Dred Scott*

The most divisive legacy of the *Dred Scott* decision has been the persistence of aspects of its underlying racial ideology of black disrespect.[54] At the heart of an honor culture lies a belief in a "natural order of rank [among men] . . . in which their manliness makes sense and deserves respect."[55] The most vivid contemporary expression of this ideology of black disrespect surfaces in the vast numbers of white supremacist websites on the internet and the proliferation of white supremacist groups such as the Aryan Nation. A vital part of the legacy of *Dred Scott* today is that, in the minds of many Southerners and those who follow their way of thinking, the ideological war to vindicate Taney's portrayal of blacks and thus Southern honor in the belief in a natural hierarchical ordering of man with whites at the top and blacks at the bottom remains unfinished. This longing for another time when white supremacy was unquestioned and enshrined in national law constitutes a type of continuing resistance to black racial equality and respect. This resistance to racial equality has manifested itself in a palpable sense of white disrespect and dishonor that attempts to deny the equality of blacks and whites—to deny, in short, their equal humanity.

This mentality on the part of many, but by no means the majority of whites, lay coiled as a motivating force at the very heart of Jim Crow segregation; massive white resistance to educational integration in public schools in *Brown v. Board of Education*;[56] antimiscegenation laws overturned by *Loving v. Virginia*;[57] the zeal seen in opposition, originally to *Regents of the University of California v. Bakke*[58] and more recently to *Grutter v. Bollinger*[59] upholding the limited constitutionality of affirmative action policies in higher education; and the Supreme Court's most recent action in striking down voluntary school integration policies in Seattle and Kentucky;[60] as well as racially targeted residential mortgage discrimination that denies so many blacks the equal opportunity to own homes; the racially targeted subprime and predatory lending practices that strip the relatively few black homeowners that exist of their home equity thorough fraud and misrepresentation.[61]

Viewed from this perspective, the disrespect and dishonor shown by some whites to blacks on a racial basis is not just a civil rights issue; it is a human rights issue.[62] In this way, the very essence of antiblack discrimination in all areas, from the most subtle to the most outrageous and egregious, constitutes a modern legacy of Taney's argument regarding the natural logic of white honor and supremacy and black dishonor and subordination. The sad legacy of the *Dred Scott* decision is that it suggested an expressly racialized line separating those worthy of respect from those who are not. This line continues to this very day to use a vague, inconsistent, and irrational racialized determination of who is white and who is black as a surrogate for one's worthiness of social, legal, and political respect . . . and disrespect.

As Derrick Bell has incisively observed, "To this day African Americans see their slave heritage . . . more as a symbol of dishonor than a source of pride. It burdened black people with an indelible mark of difference as we struggled to be like whites. In the end American slavery was peculiar because all slaves were defined by race."[63] As Bell's words suggest, the history of black people in North America, almost from their first arrival in 1619 to today, has been characterized and negatively impacted by an association with the elusive quality of a racial hierarchy of value and thus, by comparison, of honor and respect and their binary opposites, dishonor and disrespect.

It is beyond dispute that there have been dramatic improvements over the last 150 years in the recognition and enforcement of the rights of blacks in the political, economic, and social arenas that vividly culminated in the recent election of Barack Obama to be the first black president of the United States. Although black people have attained significant forms of legally recognized and government enforced formal rights of equal treatment and legal equality, in many areas race relations between blacks and whites in America continue to be strained and uncomfortable, and significant psychological and material racial disparities continue to exist and in some respects have intensified. Thus the goal of achieving any meaningful form of national racial equality on a large socioeconomic scale continues to appear frustratingly elusive. One of the principal underlying reasons for these continuing racial problems is that the struggle for the existing levels of formal racial equality that blacks have achieved has caused many whites to feel resentful for what they perceive as a loss of their deserved racial honor, respect, and supremacy—what scholars describe as "white privilege."[64]

One scholar has described the negative white reactions to black civil rights gains as consisting of some combination of "a nasty residue of racial contempt," "bitter resentment, cynicism," "deep dismissal," and "a denial of the prospect of reconciliation."[65] Thus, despite formal legal equality, blacks still remain the objects of some white disrespect, but more important, from the perspective of many whites, blacks continue, as Taney said, to have no right to *be* respected. The fact that many whites feel a fundamental disrespect for black people is deeply troubling and contributes either explicitly or implicitly to much of the continuing racial discord, strain, and psychological and material racial inequality in America.

Taney's explicit declaration that blacks have no right to be respected by whites gave a governmental imprimatur and a residual social tinge and license to all those who claim the mantle of being white to feel entitled to impose on all blacks a servile label and degrading treatment on their whim, to treat them as a means to whatever end whites desire, with no value as human beings as ends in themselves. This actual and residual governmental license could not help but lead to a sense of inferiority and loss of self-respect by blacks subjected to such treatment.

The disrespect against all blacks that Taney epitomized and thus encouraged in *Dred Scott* has not only practical, social, political, and psychological implications but also important moral considerations as well. Immanuel Kant argued that it was a "fundamental moral principle, a categorical imperative, that we should treat humanity, in every person, as an end in itself, never as a means only."[66] In terms of the effect this treatment has on the sense of self-respect felt by those subjected to disrespectful treatment, Kant also persuasively argued, according to philosopher Thomas Hill Jr., that self-respect "requires that we avoid servility and other forms of self-degradation," because "as a human being, everyone has an equal worth, independent of social standing and individual merits."[67] This characterization of the need that all humans have and are entitled to as a consequence of their humanity is directly tied to America's legacy of slavery generally and, particularly, to the type of racialized chattel slavery practiced in the honor culture of the Old South and endorsed by *Dred Scott*. From a moral standpoint, to subject or authorize by law the treatment of a human being that forces anyone to "grovel and humiliate oneself before others, in shame or even guilt, is to deny one's equal status as a human being."[68]

The historical disrespect toward blacks in America, so epitomized by the racist rhetoric of Taney's opinion in *Dred Scott*, has been passed down from the past to the present. In the minds of many whites on both sides of the political spectrum, both liberal and conservative, black people, as Taney suggested, still have no right to respect from whites . . . and frequently receive none. This basic and so far unaltered racial bias lies unspoken beneath all of the dramatic changes in race relations that have taken place in the last thirty to forty years in America. For whites, it is not consciously thought or actively expressed, but it is there, quietly manifesting itself in the nearly all-white social worlds that many whites construct for themselves outside of the workplace. Others wear this racial disrespect like a badge on their sleeves and express it in myriad ways, from revering and exhibiting the Confederate battle flag in its many forms, to continued open hostility to racial integration in education, housing, and employment, to joining extreme right-wing white supremacist groups.

Aristotle famously said that "we are what we repeatedly do." To the extent that America has repeatedly shown disrespect and dishonor to black people—in its courts, legislatures, workplaces, schools, and neighborhoods—racism has become one of the most traditional of American family values. The late Judge A. Leon Higginbotham has written that this kind of disrespect is the fuel that drives the American "precept of black inferiority [and it] is the hate that raged in the American soul through over 240 years of slavery and nearly 90 years of segregation. Once slavery was abolished, and once the more oppressive forms of segregation were eliminated, many whites' hate still had not lost its immediate object."[69] Whether this hate is expressed personally in snarling contempt or benignly in sterile institutional racism, the result is the same. Thus, Higginbotham concludes that "the ashes of that hate have, over the course of so many generations accumulated at the bottom of our memory. There they lie uneasily, like a heavy secret which whites can never quite confess, which blacks can never quite forgive."[70] The ultimate but deceptively simple answer to this distressing and persistent problem lies in the recognition of each person as possessing an equal humanity, deserving of equal respect and regard as human beings—nothing more, nothing less. This message was eloquently summed up on signs worn on the chests of black men marching silently during the civil rights movement—signs that read simply "I am a man."

Notes

1. Dred Scott v. John F. A. Sandford, 60 U.S. (19 How.) 393 (1857).

2. Paul Finkelman, ed., *Slavery and the Law* (Madison, Wis.: Madison House, 1997), 6, 7.

3. Don E. Fehrenbacher, *The Dred Scott Case: Its Significance in American Law and Politics* (New York: Oxford University Press, 1978), 5.

4. Scott, 60 U.S. at 406–7.

5. See Ronald Dworkin, *Taking Rights Seriously* (Cambridge, Mass.: Harvard University Press, 1978), 272.

6. Scott, 60 U.S. at 407.

7. Ibid., 409, 407.

8. Fehrenbacher, *Dred Scott Case,* 428.

9. Bernard C. Steiner, *Life of Roger Brooke Taney: Chief Justice of the United States Supreme Court* (Baltimore: Williams and Wilkins, 1922), 347.

10. Steiner, *Life of Roger Brooke Taney,* 352 (in LeGrand v. Darnel).

11. Ibid., 328.

12. See Sharon R. Krause, *Liberalism with Honor* (Cambridge, Mass.: Harvard University Press, 2002), 1.

13. Richard E. Nisbett and Dov Cohen, *Culture of Honor: The Psychology of Violence in the South* (Boulder, Colo.: Westview Press, 1996), 78.

14. Chandra Manning, *What This Cruel War Was Over: Soldiers, Slavery, and the Civil War* (New York: Vintage Books, 2007), 37.

15. Nisbett and Cohen, *Culture of Honor,* 78.

16. Ibid.

17. James Bowman, *Honor: A History* (New York: Encounter Books, 2006), 4.

18. Edward L. Ayers, *Vengeance and Justice: Crime and Punishment in the 19th Century American South* (New York: Oxford University Press, 1984), 19.

19. Ibid.

20. Ibid., 13.

21. Ibid., 16–17.

22. Nisbett and Cohen, *Culture of Honor,* 4.

23. Kenneth S. Greenberg, *Honor and Slavery* (Princeton, N.J.: Princeton University Press, 1996), 25.

24. Bertram Wyatt-Brown, *Southern Honor* (New York: Oxford University Press, 1982), xv.

25. Ibid.

26. Ayers, *Vengeance and Justice,* 15.

27. Ariela J. Gross, *Double Character: Slavery and Mastery in the Antebellum Southern Courtroom* (Athens: University of Georgia Press, 2000), 49.

28. Ibid.

29. Ibid. See also Manning, *What This Cruel War Was Over,* 15 (pointing out that white men's authority over blacks "identified them as men").

30. William Ian Miller, *The Mystery of Courage* (Cambridge, Mass.: Harvard University Press, 2000), 179.

31. Ibid. See also Wyatt-Brown, *Southern Honor,* xiv.

32. Ibid.

33. Orlando Patterson, *Slavery and Social Death* (Cambridge, Mass.: Harvard University Press, 1982), 94.

34. Ibid., 94–95.

35. John Hope Franklin, *The Militant South, 1800–1861* (Cambridge, Mass.: Belknap Press of Harvard University Press, 1956), 34–35.

36. Greenberg, *Honor and Slavery,* 9.

37. James F. Simon, *Lincoln and Chief Justice Taney: Slavery, Secession, and the President's War Powers* (New York: Simon and Schuster, 2006), 164.

38. Fehrenbacher, *Dred Scott Case,* 417.

39. Ibid.

40. Ibid.

41. William W. Freehling, *The Road to Disunion,* vol. 2, *Secessionists Triumphant, 1854–1861* (New York: Oxford University Press, 2007), 122.

42. Bertram Wyatt-Brown, *The Shaping of Southern Culture: Honor, Grace, and War, 1760s–1880s* (Chapel Hill: University of North Carolina Press, 2001), 305n5, xi, xiv, xvii.

43. Ibid., 178.

44. Ibid., 8.

45. Ibid, 178.

46. Finkelman, *Slavery and the Law*, 6.

47. Harvey C. Mansfield, *Manliness* (New Haven, Conn.: Yale University Press, 2006), 65.

48. Ibid., 66.

49. Interestingly, this is also the basis of the fact that a physical or other public insult to a man's slave by another white man was an insult to the master himself.

50. Nisbett and Cohen, *Culture of Honor*, xiii.

51. Wyatt-Brown, *Shaping of Southern Culture*, 16.

52. Ibid.

53. Alexander H. Stephens, "Cornerstone Address," March 21, 1861, in *Southern Pamphlets on Secession, November 1860–April 1861*, ed. Jon L. Wakelyn (Chapel Hill: University of North Carolina Press, 1996), appendix B.

54. See generally William C. Davis, *The Cause Lost: Myths and Realities of the Confederacy* (Lawrence: University Press of Kansas, 1996), 111 (describing the continuing myths indulged in by many in the geographical and ideological South to justify the Civil War and promote its "Lost Cause" as having nothing to do with slavery).

55. Mansfield, *Manliness*, 110.

56. Brown v. Bd. of Educ., 347 U.S. 483 (1954).

57. Loving v. Virginia, 388 U.S. 1 (1967).

58. Regents of the University of California v. Bakke, 438 U.S. 265 (1978).

59. Grutter v. Bollinger, 539 U.S. 306 (2003).

60. Parents Involved in Cmty. Schs. v. Seattle Sch. Dist. No. 1, 551 U.S. 701 (2007).

61. See generally Cecil J. Hunt II, "In the Racial Crosshairs: Reconsidering Racially Targeted Predatory Lending under a New Theory of Economic Hate Crime," *University of Toledo Law Review* 35, no. 2 (2003): 211 (describing the weighty evidence documenting that much of predatory lending is racially targeted toward blacks on both a racial and economic basis).

62. Ibid.

63. Finkelman, *Slavery and the Law*, 6, 7, quoting Derrick Bell.

64. Richard Delgado, ed., *Critical Race Theory: The Cutting Edge* (Philadelphia: Temple University Press, 1995), 75–95, 541–79.

65. Thomas E. Hill Jr., *Respect, Pluralism, and Justice: Kantian Perspectives* (New York: Oxford University Press, 2000), 60.

66. Ibid, 64 (citing Kant's *Metaphysics of Morals*).

67. Ibid.

68. Ibid.

69. A. Leon Higginbotham Jr., *Shades of Freedom: Racial Politics and Presumptions of the American Legal Process* (New York: Oxford University Press, 1996), 17.

70. Ibid.

TEN

Whose Ancestors Were Imported into This Country and Sold as Slaves?

John Baugh

MY OBSERVATIONS are inspired by the legal tenor of the vast majority of contributions to this volume. As an African American linguist I find Chief Justice Roger B. Taney's opinion in the *Dred Scott* case to be extraordinary and ironic. It is extraordinary because of his ability to restrict his ruling to a single race, namely, "Negroes." His opinion, ironically, could also provide a basis from which the United States can move beyond race. That is, Taney's effort to dehumanize slave descendants also contains the potential to deemphasize race and controversial policies based on a tenuous racial classification. His observations regarding the legal paradox that confronted "Negroes" did more than expose fundamental contradictions in a U.S. Constitution that tolerated slavery; they confirm that the legacy of enslavement, not race, could be the locus of American racial reconciliation.

As a linguist, I remain fascinated by Taney's carefully crafted wording and the distinction he makes when he writes, "It will be observed, that the plea applies to that class of persons only whose ancestors were negroes of the African race, and imported into this country, and sold and held as slaves."[1] It is because of Taney's distinction, which he repeats, that the title of this essay is drawn from his infamous landmark opinion: "Can a Negro, *whose ancestors were imported into this country, and sold as slaves,* become a member of the political community formed and brought into existence by the Constitution of the United States, and as such become entitled to all the rights, and privileges, and immunities, guaranteed by that instrument to the citizen?"[2]

His usage of the terms "Negro" and "citizen" are particularly worthy of close scrutiny because they are not compatible. Taney strives to make the distinction irreconcilable. By his logic, "Negroes," whose ancestors were imported and sold as slaves, were ineligible for any of the "rights, and privileges" afforded by the federal Constitution to "citizens." The *Dred Scott* decision attempted to make clear that descendants of slaves in the United States should never gain access to the courts or equal justice under the law.

However, slave descendants are currently a subset of the African American population, and debates pertaining to affirmative action based on race fail to appreciate the full range of cultural diversity represented by black citizens in the United States. John Ogbu's classification of "caste-like" minorities in the United States provides useful insight in this regard. He classifies U.S. citizens, not by race, but by family heritage regarding the immigrant status of their ancestors as "voluntary," "involuntary," or "anonymous."[3]

Elsewhere I have explored linguistic dimensions of Ogbu's categories as well as corresponding discrimination based on distinctive accents or dialects.[4] When viewed from a linguistic point of view, the African American population corresponds closely to Ogbu's caste-like categories, particularly with respect to the distinction between "voluntary" and "involuntary" immigrants. Stated in other terms, black Americans who have, or whose ancestors have, immigrated to the United States of their own volition tend to differ linguistically and culturally from black Americans whose ancestors were imported to this country and sold as slaves.

Taney was unquestionably referring to "involuntary" immigrants, according to Ogbu's classification. When important cultural, linguistic, educational, economic, and political differences are viewed in terms of broader (in)voluntary immigration to the United States, challenges to the empirical validity of racially based domestic policies emerge. In "The

Case for Reparations," Charles Ogletree devoted primary attention to disadvantaged U.S. slave descendants. "It's not designed to benefit the Tiger Woodses and Oprah Winfreys or so many others who have over-come the barriers of institutional discrimination," Ogletree noted, but he does not devote direct attention to distinctions between descendants of American slaves and, say, people of African origin whose ancestors were enslaved outside of the United States.[5] To his credit, Barack Obama ac-knowledged these important cultural distinctions in his first book, noting that his own African American experience was atypical. Although Barack Obama is an African American, as a biracial African American whose African father was a voluntary immigrant to the United States and whose mother is a European American, he has no direct historical familial ties to American slavery.[6]

Different linguistic labels pertaining to black people reveal significant diversity. Table 10.1 lists four prominent black politicians: President Nelson Mandela, President Barack Obama, former secretary of state Colin Powell, and former secretary of state Condoleezza Rice. For the purpose of this discussion we consider alternative labels and their relevance to all or some of these prominent political figures. Although all four can be classified as "black," only three are "African American." Of the African Americans only two are slave descendants; namely, Colin Powell and Condoleezza Rice. However, only Secretary Rice is descended from people enslaved in the United States. Secretary Powell's ancestors were enslaved elsewhere. All of those listed in table 10.1 are African descendants, but only Secretary Rice would fall under Taney's depiction of "*a Negro, whose ancestors were imported into this country, and sold as slaves.*"

TABLE 10.1
Diversity among Prominent Black Political Figures

	Black	Black/African American	Slave Descendant	U.S. Slave Descendant
Nelson Mandela	Yes	No	No	No
Barack Obama	Yes	Yes	No	No
Colin Powell	Yes	Yes	Yes	No
Condoleezza Rice	Yes	Yes	Yes	Yes

Based on this evidence, and more, I think it is important to reform many controversial race-based policies in favor of pinpointing assistance to U.S. slave descendants and Native Americans who are most in need of help. The slave descendant case is presented more fully by Ogletree. Blacks who have moved to the United States of their own volition as voluntary immigrants may differ considerably from those whose ancestors were brought to this country and sold as slaves. These distinctions are not trivial from a legal perspective, nor are they irrelevant to well-intended policies that frequently miss their intended target population. Again, Taney's insights prove helpful because of their unmitigated linkage to slavery in the United States.

Figure 10.1 illustrates this point with regard to the application of affirmative action policies, some of which draw upon the U.S. Census Bureau to define "blacks," which determined that "Black or African American" referred to people with "origins in any of the Black racial groups of Africa," including people who reported their race, for example, as "Black," "African Am.," "Nigerian," or "Haitian."[7] The Census Bureau uses the term "Black" or "African American" in correspondence to anyone of African descent. Taney's opinion, however, was concerned with those whose ancestors were once enslaved in America and thus did not conflate all people of African descent into a single category. *Brown v. Board of Education* perpetuated this trend, confirming that "minors of the Negro race" could not be "denied admission to schools attended by white children under laws requiring or

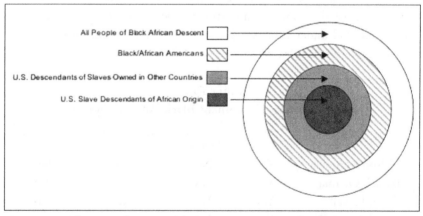

Figure 10.1. Alternative linguisitc labels pertaining to people of African descent in the United States.

permitting segregation according to race."[8] Again, using figure 10.1 as a point of reference, *Brown v. Board of Education* does not constrain itself to the plight of U.S. slave descendants, but instead to "Negro" children, who—by implication—are presumed to be descendants of enslaved Africans in America. Racial classification alone, however, is no longer sufficient to identify those blacks who still suffer the consequences of the legacy of American enslavement to which Taney makes most explicit reference. It is those who are among disadvantaged U.S. slave descendants for whom Ogletree's case for reparations can still be made.

In the meantime, the linguistic evidence is unmistakable. American vernaculars still include the linguistic legacy of the African slave trade, which left indelible traces of African and colonial dialects that are themselves the product of language contact on plantations throughout North and South America. Moreover, descendants of African slaves in Brazil, the Caribbean, and the United States all speak vernacular dialects of postcolonial European languages that have always been deemed as inferior to their dominant standard counterparts.

I turn now to Ogbu's "voluntary" immigrants, who, in striking linguistic and cultural contrast to people of African descent, have chosen to immigrate to the United States, usually long after slavery's demise. While these newer black Americans may suffer the consequences of racism long known to U.S. slave descendants, it is difficult to determine whether they are the intended recipients of the historical discrimination described by Taney, nor is it clear that they are the intended beneficiaries of affirmative action programs designed to overcome historical discrimination in the United States.

In the wake of the 2003 Supreme Court decisions regarding college admissions at the University of Michigan, I hope that linguists and other social scientists will lend further support to legal efforts to enhance the empirical precision with which we shall ultimately overcome the history of racial injustice born of slavery and the social disadvantages that still afflict so many U.S. slave descendants.[9] Although many hailed the divided Supreme Court decision regarding law school admission at the University of Michigan because it preserved the right to consider race along with other factors, that decision perpetuates the same flaw that has marked most legal rulings that pertain to race; namely, they have been reluctant to make explicit reference to slavery, thereby perpetuating a misleading connection between black Americans (i.e., as a race) and those "whose ancestors were brought to this country, and sold as slaves." I offer these observations in an effort to enhance precision across disciplines in the quest for fair and equal treatment of those who may be harmed because their ancestors, as slaves, were not free to participate fully in the Republic or the growing economy that their forced labor and ensuing military service helped create and sustain.

It strikes me as a fitting tribute to Taney's overtly racially divisive ambitions that we now acknowledge his exacting language with a resounding reply to the ponderous question he posed more than a century and a half ago. Toward that end, may it be said, and may it be so, that henceforth all those "whose ancestors were imported into this country, and sold as slaves," shall become full members of the political community formed and brought into existence by the Constitution of the United States, and as such become entitled to all the rights, privileges, and immunities guaranteed by that instrument to the citizen.

Notes

1. Dred Scott v. John F. A. Sandford, 60 U.S. (19 How.) 393, 399 (1857).

2. Ibid., 403 (emphasis added).

3. John U. Ogbu, *Minority Education and Caste: The American System in Cross-Cultural Perspective* (New York: Academic Press, 1978); Ogbu, "Understanding Cultural Diversity and Learning," *Educational Researcher* 21, no. 8 (1992): 5–14.

4. John Baugh, "It Ain't About Race: Some Lingering (Linguistic) Consequences of the African Slave Trade and Their Relevance to Your Personal Historical Hardship Index," *Du Bois Review: Social Science Research on Race* 3, no. 1 (2006): 145–59; Baugh, "Linguistic Contributions to the Advancement of Racial Justice within and beyond the African Diaspora," *Language and Linguistics Compass* 1, no. 4 (2007): 331–49.

5. Charles J. Ogletree Jr., "The Case for Reparations," *USA Weekend,* August 18, 2002.

6. Barack Obama, *Dreams from My Father: A Story of Race and Inheritance* (New York: Times, 1995).

7. U.S. Census Bureau, 2000 Census of Population, Public Law 94–171, at http://quickfacts.census.gov/qfd/meta/long_68178.htm.

8. Brown v. Bd. of Educ., 347 U.S. 483, 487–88 (1954).

9. Grutter v. Bollinger, 539 U.S. 306 (2003); Gratz v. Bollinger, 539 U.S. 244 (2003).

ELEVEN

Considering Reparations for *Dred Scott*

Alfred L. Brophy

AMONG THE many tragedies of our country's history of slavery is that it left a deep, virtually inexhaustible well of injury. There is no way to provide compensation for each injury of the past or for the unspeakable crimes of brutalization that took place under slavery.[1] And those crimes continue, in some ways, to multiply, for the injury and lack of hope continue from one generation to the next. As Randall Robinson has stated it, slavery "produces victims *ad infinitum,* long after the active state of the crime has ended."[2] It is humanly, as well as financially, well-nigh impossible to provide a complete remedy. Some argue that there have been offsets, from the Civil War to the war on poverty; but seemingly no matter how large the payments, a bill for tort damages—were it ever presented—would be astronomical.[3]

As a result, reparations advocates must find some principles for deciding which tragedies and which claimants will receive some form of compensation. But advocates of reparations have larger problems than trying to quantify the harms or select among recipients or apportion even limited payments. For those they would ask for compensation—the American voting public—do not want to hear those claims. When the *Mobile (Alabama) Register* polled on reparations for slavery in 2002, something like 67 percent of black Alabamians were in favor, while something like 5 percent of white Alabamians were in favor. It is "something like" because some white people became so enraged at the mere suggestion of reparations that they could not complete the poll. As a result, it was difficult to get an accurate sample.[4] We have a long way to go before people are even willing to contemplate, let alone vote for, reparations. The figures for apologies are somewhat more balanced. About 25 percent of white Alabamians believed in 2002 an apology for slavery was appropriate.

There are many places one might look for talk about reparations. There is talk of reparations (and occasionally action) for large-scale crimes, from the internment of more than 100,000 Japanese Americans during World War II to the deprivation of property from families of victims of the Holocaust. There is also talk of reparations for crimes that were large but more focused, such as the Tulsa riot of 1921. There has also been more general action: the Virginia, Maryland, North Carolina, Alabama, and Florida legislatures have offered apologies for their involvement in slavery, and even a few universities have investigated their roles in the institution of slavery and apologized. Brown University's Steering Committee on Slavery and Justice's comprehensive investigation of Brown's connections to slavery serves as a model for other schools.[5]

There remains resistance to talking about reparative action on a nationwide scale, which would address in significant ways such issues as the chasm between African American and non-Hispanic white income. The Great Society may provide a model for the scope and expense of such a program; as yet, we are too far away from such comprehensive plans to have a good idea of what they might look like or even what they would cost.[6] Those large-scale, often amorphous programs are part of an attempt to deal with general societal discrimination, which the Supreme Court (and the American public) have viewed with suspicion in recent years.[7] Something that is often missing from "reparations talk" is a specific plan for repairing past tragedies.

This volume on the *Dred Scott* case invites two sets of questions related to reparations. First, what was the culpability of the Supreme Court in *Dred*

Scott? How do we even measure that culpability? Should we ask questions like, Was the Supreme Court merely carrying out "the law" (however that is interpreted) or was it contributing its own proslavery interpretation? What effect did the decision have? Second, what are we to make of that legacy today? Is there something that should be done either by the Supreme Court or someone else to repair for this decision in particular? Should we separate *Dred Scott* from the rest of our nation's actions to protect slavery? This essay uses *Dred Scott* as a site for exploring the issues of reparations for specific past racial crimes in two ways: by understanding how we might measure the harm of a specific past event, and by trying to understand how we might pick among the matrix of possible responses to those events.

Culpability of the Supreme Court for *Dred Scott*

In assessing the Supreme Court's culpability in *Dred Scott,* we might start by remembering that the opinion is about a human being—in fact, about a number of human beings, as Lea VanderVelde's work reminds us, for the opinion implicated the freedom of Harriet Scott and their children as well as that of Dred Scott.[8] Even the name of the opinion ought to serve as a reminder of the human interests involved here, although perhaps there is something that also is disturbing about continuing to refer to a case by the name of the "property" involved, much as admiralty cases are named after the ship involved.

But beyond the opinion's role in keeping the shackles of slavery fastened upon the Scott family for at least a limited time, we ought to begin to assess the opinion's impact as well as its relationship to other proslavery actions by state and federal courts and legislatures. There are the other cases of people traveling in territories who could no longer claim freedom on that basis; one might call this the immediate doctrinal impact. Then there is the larger impact: the subordination of the rights of African Americans; the limiting of congressional power over the territories and, thus, the spread of slavery; and the legitimacy that it gave to a proslavery interpretation of the Constitution.

Throughout the antebellum period, the Supreme Court issued proslavery opinions. As a judge said in Harriet Beecher Stowe's 1856 novel *Dred: A Tale of the Great Dismal Swamp,* "from the communities—from the great institutions in society—no help whatever is to be expected."[9] The proslavery opinions were legion, especially in the years leading into *Dred Scott*. Those opinions, which rested on the understanding of the centrality of slavery to American life and the need to allow states extraordinary power over it include *Groves v. Slaughter* (essentially freeing Mississippi from the constraints of the federal regulation of interstate slavery) and *Prigg v. Pennsylvania* (setting the stage for federal intrusion into Northern states through the Fugitive Slave Act of 1850). At the state level, there are a number of opinions that upheld slavery at points where there might have been alternatives. The infamous 1829 North Carolina *State v. Mann* opinion delimited control over white people's physical punishment of slaves in their possession; other cases restricted, for example, emancipation by will.[10]

In its attempt to strip Congress of the power to decide for the territories, the Supreme Court adopted a decidedly Southern and proslavery interpretation of the Constitution. Much can be (and has been) said about whether that was appropriate; this is important in thinking about the Supreme Court's culpability. For if the Supreme Court was merely adopting what others had wrought, they would be a part of a larger system. If, however, the Court went beyond that, and became an advance advocate for proslavery thought, then it has additional culpability.

So what, then, do we make of the *Dred Scott* opinion's two prongs, which struck down the Congress's power over the territories (and, therefore, the Missouri Compromise) and excluded African Americans from the protection of citizenship. Until recently, the weight of historical opinion, illustrated by Don Fehrenbacher's 1978 *The Dred Scott Case* and William Wiecek's work,[11] was that the Taney Court was wrong, for several reasons. It decided issues that were not necessary to the decision of the case, such as the constitutionality of the Missouri Compromise. It supposed that there might be a "constitutional" settlement of largely political issues. And it substituted a Southern interpretation of the Constitution—developed largely in the 1840s—in place of what people had understood as constitutional up to that point.

By reference to the accepted notions of constitutionalism at the time, the Missouri Compromise would have appeared to be constitutional. In 1820 when the Missouri Compromise was adopted, no one thought it beyond the scope of Congress's authority to prohibit slavery in the territories.

In the subsequent years, under an increasingly proslavery interpretation of the Constitution, however, it became common doctrine among some that whatever was permitted by one state had to be allowed in the territories. John C. Calhoun advocated this strenuously. And in a series of other instances, from the crisis over abolitionist literature sent through the U.S. mail to the interstate sale of slaves to the rendition of fugitive slaves, proslavery constitutional doctrine took hold.[12]

Yet two recent books have called that account into question. Austin Allen's *Origins of the* Dred Scott *Case* maintains that Chief Justice Roger Taney's broad opinion was necessary, given the precedent and professional norms of the time.[13] Mark Graber's *Dred Scott and the Problem of Constitutional Evil* also interprets the case as in line with precedent.[14] However, it also suggests that certain problems, such as slavery, were inherent in the Constitution as drafted (hence the "problem of constitutional evil.") One aspect that separates Allen and Graber from the mainstream of writing on *Dred Scott* is the former's willingness to accept the opinion as reasonable constitutional doctrine at the time. If the opinion was, indeed, within the mainstream of constitutional thought, then that is testimony to just how far proslavery Southerners bent both constitutional thought and practice. If it was consistent with law, that testifies to the amount that the law was bent between the Missouri Compromise and 1857, by the steady proslavery drift of popular thought.

Certainly many people at the time believed it an extreme opinion and beyond what was necessary to keep the Scotts in slavery. For example, Benjamin Robbins Curtis, a dissenting justice, believed that the opinion was the result of a political, rather than a legal, interpretation: "When a strict interpretation of the Constitution, according to the fixed rules which govern the interpretation of laws, is abandoned, and the theoretical opinions of individuals are allowed to control its meaning, we have no longer a Constitution; we are under the government of individual men, who for the time being have power to declare what the Constitution is, according to their own views of what it ought to mean."[15] Antislavery forces, likewise, understood the nature of the proslavery constitution. In fact, there is a lot of wisdom about popular constitutionalism that appears in those works, as well as much learning on jurisprudence. For much of the abolitionist attack was a critique of the law of slavery, as well as the slave system. And while some, such as Lysander Spooner, argued fancifully (and unsuccessfully) that the Constitution was antislavery,[16] the collection of excerpts from James Madison's notes, *The Constitution a Pro-Slavery Compact,* was more accurate. William Goodell's *American Slave Code in Theory and Practice* and William Weld's *Slavery as It Is* both relied extensively on statutes and cases for evidence about the nature of slavery. Goodell's understanding of the legal system made his books important treatises on jurisprudence—about the gap between law and justice and the gap between law on the books and law in practice. In short, the Supreme Court's proslavery jurisprudence comes as no surprise.

That leads to the question: What was the effect of the opinion? Did it really lead, as some historians have suggested, to the Civil War? If it did, perhaps we ought to think about this as a critical piece of our liberation as a people, for it may have created an environment in which slavery was ended. At least after the war, it led in pretty direct ways to the adoption of the Fourteenth Amendment.

Perhaps, then, we ought to establish a monument to Taney for the contribution he made to the war and to Reconstruction afterward. There is a similar strain of reasoning about the Compromise of 1850—that the Compromise allowed the nation to stay together long enough that, when secession finally came, the United States was strong enough to fight and win the Civil War.[17] Whatever the merits of that argument regarding the Compromise of 1850, I suspect that argument is less meritorious when applied to *Dred Scott.* I suspect that the decision contributed relatively little to the coming of the Civil War; that in the multiple regression equation that explains our country's journey toward Civil War, the *Dred Scott* decision was relatively unimportant; and that its major contribution was, not in creating a backlash, but in undermining legitimate opposition to slavery.

Dred Scott's major "contribution" to antebellum politics and law was most likely to further legitimize the proslavery view of the Constitution and establish the framework for a new, proslavery federalism. In that way, it gave sustenance to the proslavery zealots in the years leading into Civil War. In the brief interval between its March 1857 announcement and the beginning of war in April 1861, it contributed to the intellectual machinery that supported slavery. It was part of a sophisticated defense of slavery by the leaders of American society. It also brought the Supreme Court and the rule of law into disrepute, though that was already under way because of the Fugitive Slave Act of 1850. The corrosive effects on respect for the rule of law is illustrated by a statement in the *New York Tribune* that the opinion is entitled to as much weight as "the judgment of a majority of those congregated in any Washington barroom."[18] Much as *Brown v. Board of Education* nearly one hundred years later seems to have legitimized the civil rights movement,[19] *Dred Scott* provided the Supreme Court's stamp of approval on the Southern interpretation of the Constitution.

What Is the Harm Now?

Leaving aside the history of *Dred Scott,* there is the separate and important question: What, if anything, ought to be done about it now? Part of this turns on an analysis of the opinion's continuing harm. It is a piece of the legacy of slavery, though it may be particularly hard to tease out what is unique about the harm it imposed. In fact, given *Dred Scott's* central role in the defense of slavery and its status as representative of the evil of slavery, perhaps it should occupy a central place in the discussion of reparations. Perhaps *Dred Scott* should be at the center of discussion of an attempt to correct for "general societal discrimination." It may stand for the damage that the institution of slavery has left upon our country.

If, however, we want to try to be more specific about the opinion's continuing effect, there may be two places to look. The most likely potential harm is the statement it makes about the nature of the Constitution and the role of African Americans in our country. One of the most frequently quoted phrases of the opinion is Taney's statement that blacks "had for more than a century before been regarded as beings of an inferior order, and altogether unfit to associate with the white race, either in social or political relations; and so far inferior, that they had no rights which the white man was bound to respect."[20] *Dred Scott* stands for twentieth-century jurists as evidence of the evil world of slavery.[21] The second harm is that there may be fragments of doctrine that have not yet been overturned. A number of Supreme Court cases recognized that the Fourteenth Amendment was designed to overturn *Dred Scott's* exclusion of African Americans from the privileges of U.S. citizenship.[22] Yet the Reconstruction-era Supreme Court narrowly interpreted the privileges and immunities clause and has not rebuilt a privileges and immunities clause jurisprudence since then.[23]

What to Do Now: Reparations Models

Given those assessments of the continuing harms, we can turn to the per-plexing question: What might be the appropriate remedy? Often repara-tions advocates address wholesale social issues. Charles Ogletree and Robert Westley, two leading advocates of reparations, are interested in widespread programs. Their models look like the Great Society.[24] *Dred Scott* will cer-tainly be at the center of discussion of slavery reparations, for it provides such critical evidence of the comprehensive government involvement in slavery.[25] One is left wondering, however, whether there is a way to bridge the gap between those grand designs and programs designed to repair for more specific past harms, like the *Dred Scott* opinion. What might the Missouri Supreme Court or the U.S. Supreme Court do to address their predecessors' decisions? Perhaps we can build upward from talk of *Dred Scott* to a better understanding of our history, to perhaps something more. If we are interested in understanding the connections of past and pres-ent and of the changes in public attitudes that may correlate with such altered understandings, then we should look for ways of achieving those goals. Which of the "multiple strategies" of reparations, to use Eric Miller's phrasing, are most likely to be successful?[26]

Considering Truth Commissions

In this task, there are some models of repair in specific locations. The most common and popular are truth commissions. In the recent past there have been the Tulsa Riot Commission,[27] the 1898 Wilmington Race Riot Commission,[28] the California Slavery Era Insurance Disclosure Act, which led to the "Slavery Era Insurance Registry," a registry of names of slaves who were insured by companies still doing business and the slave own-ers who insured them;[29] the Chicago Slavery Disclosure Era Ordinance, which has led to apologies by companies including JPMorgan Chase.[30] Na-tive Hawaiians received an apology from the federal government in 1993, which was subsequently used as a basis for granting relief in a case involv-ing a trust for the education of Hawaiian children.[31]

There may be a particular need for study of the *Dred Scott* decision and its impact, for public knowledge about the era of slavery seems inadequate. At a basic level, we need to address the public memory and understanding of our history, which respects the contributions of African Americans and respects and understands the suffering and disability that is the legacy of slavery and Jim Crow. We have an exceedingly long way to go in bringing understanding of basic facts of American history—like the horror that was slavery, as well as the role of slavery in impelling the South toward Civil War—to the public. James Horton reminded us in his presidential address to the Organization of American Historians that the president of Virginia's Heritage Preservation Association called "the slave plantation of the old South a place 'where master and slave loved and cared for each other and had genuine family concern.'" Horton concluded, "[T]his is the kind of reaction that most public historians who deal with these volatile history matters find all too familiar."[32]

This historical misinformation informs and structures how voters, legislators, and judges respond to issues of race. If one thinks that Reconstruction was an era of corrupt black politicians and Yankees, then you are unlikely to have a favorable view of the Reconstruction amendments or of the need for federal protection of voting rights or of the need for civil rights legislation, or of any kind of social programs, to say nothing of reparations.

In essence, what we need is an understanding of the past, what one might call "applied legal history," that is, a history of law—of court decisions, statutes, and the practices of law enforcement—that is both accurate and relevant to understanding questions we have today, giving rise to optimism that once people have facts they will think the same. We have seen some influential literature in this genre already, like C. Vann Woodward's *The Strange Career of Jim Crow,* which many credit for undermining support for Jim Crow shortly after *Brown* by disabusing us of the belief that Jim Crow was natural and had existed from the end of slavery.[33]

All of this invokes important questions about how ideology relates to action. Southern interpretations of war and Reconstruction helped win the hearts and minds of Americans in the era of Jim Crow, so that by 1896 it was almost unthinkable for the Supreme Court to uphold even a limited right of integration. Amid all of the talk of memory in the historical profession in recent years, there has been relatively little attention focused on the intellectual monuments left in the judicial opinions—the ways that courts attempted to channel and settle disputes and to portray the scientific and moral correctness of Jim Crow.

Individual justices have written about history.[34] In this process of recovering an understanding of the connections of the Supreme Court and the federal government to the institution of slavery, we are aided by some really fine histories of the case already.[35] Perhaps both the Missouri Supreme Court and the U.S. Supreme Court could use their institutional competence to disseminate a more accurate and complete history of *Dred Scott*. In fact, the Missouri State Archives has made significant and well-publicized strides in this direction.[36]

Considering an Apology

We are beginning to see truth commissions and apologies. Some may think them cheap. Given how difficult apologies are to obtain, they seem to have some significant meaning, and that may suggest their worth. That leads, naturally, to a discussion of the case for apologies. There has already been acknowledgment of error. Yet the opinion still sits on the shelf of every minimally equipped law library in the country. To some extent, we are fortunate for that, for it is not subject to erasure. As the successors to the courts that issued *Dred Scott,* both the Missouri and U.S. Supreme Courts might consider an apology. Those courts are the successors to the courts that issued the *Dred Scott* opinions, so there is a fairly direct connection between past and present. An apology could be part of recovering a more accurate and complete history and part of including people who have previously been excluded. In the case of *Dred Scott,* where the opinion so completely excluded African Americans from citizenship, perhaps the need for apology is greater than in other instances. And perhaps an apology holds out particular promise in this case because of the Supreme Court's role as one of our country's most revered institutions. In offering an apology, the courts would honor the memory of those who were enslaved. They would also acknowledge to Missouri and U.S. citizens that they understand that the sins of our country's past burden us still today. And they would help correct the ignorance of many Americans about our past.

Toward a New Reconstruction

While those symbolic and cultural actions may be attainable, there remains the question about something more tangible: a reconstruction of legal doctrine surrounding the privileges and immunities clause, for instance, as well as wholesale legislative action along the lines of the Great Society. Because *Dred Scott* stands as a monument to the institution of slavery, it may lie at the center of broader discussion of slavery, Jim Crow, and reparations.

In terms of judicial doctrine, a few glimpses of what that reconstructed doctrine might look like include an enlargement of Congress's power under Section 5 of the Fourteenth Amendment, premised on the idea that the amendment was designed to overturn the fragments of *Dred Scott* that empowered states. For we probably ought to take *Dred Scott* as a case about federalism (not just about slavery in the territories) and the Fourteenth Amendment as a wholesale repudiation of *Dred Scott*. We might also look to a revitalization of the privileges and immunities clause, which would do much of the work now performed by the equal protection clause. Even beyond legal doctrine, however, *Dred Scott* may then be a starting point for serious discussion of the place of slavery at the center of American life. As we discuss the legacy of slavery and the dark years of Jim Crow that followed, *Dred Scott* may illustrate the role that slavery and white supremacy played in leading to the wealth gap that yet exists between African Americans and non-Hispanic whites, and it might be the entering point for further, extended discussion of wide-ranging reparations. *Dred Scott* serves as a focal point for discussion of the federal government's support for slavery as well as the ubiquity of slavery in antebellum America.

Further Directions

There are yet other places to look for further investigation. There are certainly other Supreme Court decisions that deserve scrutiny; then there are other sites of intellectual support for slavery and Jim Crow. One example of the problems with the dissemination of erroneous histories is Thomas Dixon's 1905 book *The Clansman,* which appeared about the same time that Southern states were passing constitutional amendments to disfranchise black men. D. W. Griffith's movie *Birth of a Nation,* based on *The Clansman,* shows how all these diverse ideas fit together: the charges that a foolish, blundering generation brought us into Civil War; then the breakdown of the rule of law during Reconstruction; and the "redemption" of the South from corrupt Yankees and recently freed slaves.[37] This is what we ought to call the period of "de-construction" after the Civil War. We have seen progress already. President George W. Bush's speech at Goree Island in 2003 reminded us of the very way in which we have slowly improved. Abolitionists' moral vision, Bush said, "caused Americans to examine our hearts, to correct our Constitution, and to teach our children the dignity and equality of every person of every race." He also acknowledged the burden of the past and the road yet ahead: "The racial bigotry fed by slavery did not end with slavery or with segregation. And many of the issues that still trouble America have roots in the bitter experience of other times."[38] There have been apologies by national institutions, such as the U.S. Senate's apology for failure to pass an anti-lynching bill. So action by individual justices or by a court collectively may be appropriate. The road will be very, very long. Still, we can hope for that progress. And perhaps in that way, our better understanding of history will guide the way to remaking law and overcoming our past.

Notes

I thank Christopher Bracey and David Konig for inviting me to Washington University's symposium on *Dred Scott*. I was honored to be in such distinguished company and very much appreciate the help of the participants.

1. See Alfred L. Brophy, "Reconsidering Reparations," *Indiana Law Journal* 81, no. 3 (2006): 813 (discussing problems of trying to order claimants to reparations).

2. Randall Robinson, *The Debt: What America Owes to Blacks* (New York: Dutton, 2000), 216.

3. See Alfred L. Brophy, "Reparations Talk: The Tort Law Analogy in Reparations," *Boston College Third World Law Journal* 24, no. 1 (2004): 81, 115–30 (discussing analogies to tort law for measuring damage due to slavery).

4. See Alfred L. Brophy, *Reparations Pro and Con* (New York: Oxford University Press, 2006), 4–5.

5. Brown University, Steering Committee on Slavery and Justice, http://www.brown.edu/Research/Slavery_Justice/.

6. See, for example, Charles J. Ogletree, "Repairing the Past: New Efforts in the Reparations Debate in America," *Harvard Civil Rights–Civil Liberties Law Review* 38, no. 2 (2003): 279.

7. See Richmond v. Croson, 488 U.S. 469, 499 (1989) (requiring evidence of discrimination in the construction industry in Richmond, Virginia, in the past—rather than general evidence of societal discrimination). See also Wygant v. Jackson Bd. of Educ., 476 U.S. 267, 276–77 (1986).

8. See Lea VanderVelde and Sandhya Subramanian, "Mrs. Dred Scott," *Yale Law Journal* 106, no. 4 (1997): 1033; Lea VanderVelde, *Mrs. Dred Scott: A Life on Slavery's Frontier* (New York: Oxford University Press, 2009).

9. Harriet Beecher Stowe, *Dred: A Tale of the Great Dismal Swamp* (Boston: Phillips, Sampson, 1856), 2:76.

10. State v. Mann, 13 N.C. 263 (1830) (excusing a hirer of a slave from criminal liability for abusing her). See also, for example, Bailey v. Poindexter's Exec., 14 Gratt. 132 (Va. 1858) (denying enforcement to a will that permitted slaves to choose emancipation or continued slavery); Read v. Manning, 1 George 308 (Miss. Err. App 1855) (applying Mississippi statute that prohibited emancipation by will).

11. See Don E. Fehrenbacher, *The Dred Scott Case: Its Significance in American Law and Politics* (New York: Oxford University Press, 1978); William Wiecek, "Slavery and Abolition before the United States Supreme Court, 1820–1860," *Journal of American History* 65, no. 1 (1978): 34–59.

12. See Alfred L. Brophy, "Let Us Go Back and Stand upon the Constitution: Federal-State Relations in *Scott v. Sandford,*" *Columbia Law Review* 90, no. 1 (1990): 192, 204–6, 223–24.

13. Austin Allen, *Origins of the* Dred Scott *Case: Jacksonian Jurisprudence and the Supreme Court, 1837–1857* (Athens: University of Georgia Press, 2006).

14. Mark Graber, *Dred Scott and the Problem of Constitutional Evil* (New York: Cambridge University Press, 2006).

15. Dred Scott v. John F. A. Sandford, 60 U.S. (19 How.) 393, 621 (1857).

16. See, for example, Lysander Spooner, *The Unconstitutionality of Slavery* (Boston: B. Marsh, 1845).

17. See David M. Potter, *The Impending Crisis, 1848–1861,* ed. Don E. Fehrenbacher (New York: Harper and Row, 1976), 120.

18. Fehrenbacher, *Dred Scott Case,* 417.

19. See Paul Finkelman, "Civil Rights in Historical Context: In Defense of *Brown,*" *Harvard Law Review* 118, no. 3 (2005): 973–1029.

20. Scott, 60 U.S. at 407.

21. See, for example, Fullilove v. Klutznick, 448 U.S. 448, 516 (1980) ("In the history of this Court and this country, few questions have been more divisive than those arising from governmental action taken on the basis of race. Indeed, our own decisions played no small part in the tragic legacy of government-sanctioned discrimination.") (citing, among other cases, *Dred Scott*); McCleskey v. Kemp, 481 U.S. 279, 343 (1987) (citing *Dred Scott* for evidence of the history of white supremacy); Regents of University of California v. Bakke, 438 U.S. 265, 389–90 (1978) (same).

22. Sugarman v. Dougall, 413 U.S. 634, 652 (1973) (Rehnquist, J., dissenting) ("The paramount reason was to amend the Constitution so as to overrule explicitly the *Dred Scott* decision").

23. See, for example, Pamela Brandwein, *Reconstructing Reconstruction: The Supreme Court and the Production of Historical Truth* (Durham, N.C.: Duke University Press, 1999).

24. See, for example, Ogletree, "Repairing the Past"; Robert Westley, "Many Billions Gone: Is It Time to Reconsider the Case for Black Reparations?" *Boston College Law Review* 40, no. 1 (1998): 429–76.

25. See Don E. Fehrenbacher, *The Slaveholding Republic: An Account of the United States Government's Relations to Slavery,* ed. Ward M. McAfee (New York: Oxford University Press, 2001).

26. Eric L. Miller, "Reconceiving Reparations: Multiple Strategies in the Reparations Debate," *Boston College Third World Law Journal* 24, no. 1 (2004): 45.

27. Oklahoma Historical Society, Report by the Oklahoma Commission to Study the Tulsa Race Riot of 1921, http://www.okhistory.mus.ok.us/trrc/freport.htm.

28. North Carolina Office of Archives and History, http://www.ah.dcr.state.nc.us/1898-wrrc/.

29. California Department of Insurance, Slavery-Era Insurance Registry, http://www.insurance.ca.gov/0100-consumers/0300-public-programs/0200-slavery-era-insur/.

30. Brophy, *Reparations Pro and Con,* 144.

31. See Doe v. Kamehameha Schools, 295 F. Supp. 2d 1141, 1154 (D. Haw. 2003), affirmed en banc 470 F.3d 827, 831, 845 (9th Cir. 2006) (citing apology).

32. James O. Horton, "Patriot Acts: Public History in Public Service," *Journal of American History* 92, no. 3 (2005): 801.

33. See Howard N. Rabinowitz, "More Than the Woodward Thesis: Assessing the Strange Career of Jim Crow," *Journal of American History* 75, no. 3 (1988): 842–44.

34. See, for example, William H. Rehnquist, *Centennial Crisis: The Disputed Election of 1876* (New York: Knopf, 2004).

35. See, for example, Paul Finkelman, *Dred Scott: A Brief History with Documents* (Boston: Bedford Books, 1997); VanderVelde and Subramanian, "Mrs. Dred Scott."

36. Missouri State Archives, Dred Scott 150th Anniversary Commemoration, http://www.sos.mo.gov/archives/resources/dredscott.asp.

37. Thomas Dixon, *The Clansman* (New York: Doubleday, Page, 1905).

38. Remarks by the president on Goree Island, Senegal (July 8, 2003), http://www.whitehouse.gov/news/releases/2003/07/20030708-1.html.

PART FOUR

Judicial Perspectives

TWELVE

Lessons for Judges from *Scott v. Emerson*

Duane Benton

THE U.S. Supreme Court's *Dred Scott* decision[1] has been examined extensively, from 1857 until today.[2] The predecessor decision of the Missouri Supreme Court in *Scott v. Emerson*[3] has not been analyzed as comprehensively,
although Chief Justice Roger B. Taney concluded the Court's opinion by
invoking the state decision.[4] The Missouri opinion is crucial; a different
result by the state court would have foreclosed review by the highest court.
This essay analyzes *Scott v. Emerson,* emphasizing its lessons for judges.

The Missouri Opinion

Dred and Harriet Scott sued Irene Emerson for their freedom in state
court. Because the Scotts did not prove that Emerson owned them, the
jury ruled for her. As this could be rectified, the trial judge ordered a new
trial.[5] The new jury ruled for the Scotts.

The Missouri Supreme Court reversed, declaring the Scotts were still
slaves despite living in free territory. The court—Judge William Scott

writing, John F. Ryland concurring—reasoned that Missouri was not obligated to recognize other states' laws or federal territorial laws.

> The States of this Union, although associated for some purposes of government, yet, in relation to their municipal concerns have always been regarded as foreign to each other. . . . So of the laws of the United States, enacted for the mere purpose of governing a territory. These laws have no force in the States of the Union, they are local, and relate to the municipal affairs of the territory. Their effect is confined within its limits, and beyond those limits they have no more effect, in any State, than the municipal laws of one State would have in any other State.[6]

Scott posited, "No State is bound to carry into effect enactments conceived in a spirit hostile to that which pervades her own laws." After quoting Justice Joseph Story's treatise on conflicts of law, Scott continued, "It is a humiliating spectacle, to see the courts of a State confiscating the property of her own citizens by the command of a foreign law . . . the constitution of the State of Illinois, or the territorial laws of the United States . . . commonly called the Missouri Compromise."[7] And it was unjust to free a slave, Scott wrote, when the owner "very naturally supposed he had a right" to take the slave on free land without freeing him. "To construe this into an assent to his slave's freedom would be doing violence to his acts."[8] According to the court, in "states and kingdoms in which slavery is the least countenanced," a slave cannot sue for permanent freedom, as slavery reattaches upon return to slave territory.[9] The opinion closed with appeals to the changing times and God's will.[10]

Judge Hamilton R. Gamble dissented, relying on previous Missouri decisions and counseling calm detachment.[11] He concluded:

> Times may have changed, public feeling may have changed, but principles have not and do not change; and, in my judgment, there can be no safe basis for judicial decisions, but in those principles, which are immutable.
>
> It may be observed, that the principle is either expressly declared or tacitly admitted in all these cases, that where a right to freedom has been acquired, under the law of another State or community, it may be enforced by action, in the courts of

a slaveholding State; for, in every one of these cases, the party claiming freedom had not procured any adjudication upon his right in the country where it accrued.[12]

Lessons for Judges

While there are various styles of appellate judging, a consensus on fundamentals has existed since the nation's founding. The Missouri Supreme Court in *Scott v. Emerson* violated many basic principles of appellate review.

"The conventional theory is that an opinion should determine points raised by the parties and that it is wrong to inject new issues or apply legal principles neither urged nor mentioned by counsel."[13] This was the rule in the nineteenth century, as Taney stated: "This court must affirm or reverse upon the case as it appears in the record. We cannot look out of it, for testimony to influence the judgment of this court sitting as an appellate tribunal. And, according to the practice of the court of chancery from its earliest history to the present time, no paper not before the court below can be read on the hearing of an appeal."[14] Judge Scott, author of *Scott v. Emerson*, expressed a similar Missouri doctrine in an 1856 decision.[15]

The Missouri Supreme Court, in *Scott v. Emerson*, injected arguments not made by the parties. The state-court case did not raise far-reaching issues:

> The defense, then, was the technicality that Dred Scott had not legally proved that it was specifically Mrs. Emerson who was holding him as a slave in Missouri. It is of the utmost importance to note that Goode [Emerson's attorney] raised no doubts about the constitutionality of the Ordinance of 1787 or of the Missouri Compromise, nor was any issue made of Dred Scott's citizenship or of his right to sue. Equally significant is that the defense did not deny to Dred Scott his right to freedom by virtue of residence in free territory. This case clearly did not raise constitutional questions. It was a *bona fide* suit involving only one issue—freedom— and the technical validity of the evidence presented.[16]

While issues can be raised at oral argument, which in the nineteenth century was usually lengthy, there was no oral argument in *Scott v. Emerson*.[17] True, the last brief filed in *Scott v. Emerson* suggested the tone and scope of the eventual opinion.[18] But the issues to be addressed were decided long before this last-minute brief. After thorough investigation of the primary materials, Walter Ehrlich has written:

> These [first] briefs were filed on March 8, 1850, in time for the regular March term. But the schedule was unusually heavy due to the transfer of many cases from the Jefferson City docket, and the court was unable to take up the case during this term. By the time the court convened in October 1850, for its next regular session in St. Louis, a decision had been reached. This decision, however, was based not upon the unbiased and genuine arguments and points of law that attorneys had presented in their briefs, but rather upon the judges' own prejudicial views toward the question that by now had become the main issue of a bitter and partisan struggle in Missouri—slavery in the territories. *Here, for the first time, politics was injected into the case, not by the parties, but by the judges of the Missouri Supreme Court in their intended decision.*[19]

In fact, this tentative opinion agreed to in 1850 by the preelection court of Napton, Birch, and Ryland would have injected even more issues and was even more wide-ranging and radical than the final opinion.[20] The election intervened. After only Ryland was elected—to serve with Scott and Gamble—the court issued *Scott v. Emerson* in 1852. As Dennis Boman has observed:

> In their explication of the court's decision in *Scott v. Emerson,* scholars have not accounted for the fact that Judge William Scott's opinion was not as far-reaching as the one Napton had prepared. Given his strongly held proslavery and states' rights views, it is at first surprising that Judge Scott did not rule, as Napton had intended, that the Ordinance of 1787 and the Missouri Compromise were unconstitutional. Moreover, scholars have not accounted for Ryland's concurrence despite his intention to write a dissenting opinion to Napton's earlier decision. However, with Gamble's determination to rule according to law and precedent in freedom suit cases, Judge Scott, unlike his predecessor Napton, did not have a colleague to support his more

radical decision. All of these facts point to a Scott-Ryland compromise in conference. This interpretation best explains Scott's
"restraint" in not addressing the issue of congressional power and
Ryland's agreement to overturn three decades of precedent in
freedom suits.[21]

This compromise reflected the dominant political factions, anti-Benton and
pro-Benton. The preelection court had two strong anti-Benton judges—
Napton and Birch—motivated to publish a decision against Benton before
his election in January 1851.[22] After Benton was defeated and the postelec-
tion court had only one strong anti-Benton judge (Scott) and one pro-
Benton judge (Ryland), the opinion became less radical.[23] Collegiality and
politics did soften the final opinion in *Scott v. Emerson*. Even so, that opinion injected issues beyond those raised by the parties.

Adherence to precedent, stare decisis, is another cornerstone of the judicial process in the United States. Justice Benjamin N. Cardozo in his
famous lectures on judging wrote:

> *Stare decisis* is at least the everyday working rule of our law. I
> shall have something to say later about the propriety of relaxing
> the rule in exceptional conditions. But unless those conditions
> are present, the work of deciding cases in accordance with
> precedents that plainly fit them is a process similar in its nature
> to that of deciding cases in accordance with a statute. It is a
> process of search, comparison, and little more. . . .
>
> One of the most fundamental social interests is that law be
> uniform and impartial. There must be nothing in its action that
> savors of prejudice or favor or even arbitrary whim or fitfulness.
> Therefore in the main there shall be adherence to precedent.[24]

Justice Lewis Powell, in another legendary lecture, outlined specific merits of
stare decisis: easing the burden on judges, lawyers, and litigants; providing stability in law; and enhancing public legitimacy and respect for the judiciary.[25]
And, as Taney once put it, this was the rule in the nineteenth century:

> The case of the *Thomas Jefferson* did not decide any ques-
> tion of property, or lay down any rule by which the right of
> property should be determined. If it had, we should have felt

ourselves bound to follow it notwithstanding the opinion we have expressed. For every one would suppose that after the decision of this court, in a matter of that kind, he might safely enter into contracts, upon the faith that rights thus acquired would not be disturbed. In such a case, *stare decisis* is the safe and established rule of judicial policy, and should always be adhered to.[26]

The Missouri Supreme Court, shortly before *Scott v. Emerson,* announced that stare decisis was "peculiarly applicable" where property investment was involved.[27]

In *Scott v. Emerson,* the Missouri Supreme Court overruled a long line of precedent, without discussing or analyzing the cases.[28] For three decades before *Scott v. Emerson,* Missouri courts granted freedom to slaves on the basis of residence in free states.[29] In *Winny v. Whitesides,* an enslaved woman was taken from Carolina to Illinois, residing there for three or four years. The owner then took her to Missouri, where she sued for freedom. In 1824, the Missouri Supreme Court held:

We are clearly of opinion that if, by a residence in Illinois, the plaintiff in error lost her right to the property in the defendant, that right was not revived by a removal of the parties to Missouri. . . . The sovereign power of the United States has declared that "neither slavery nor involuntary servitude["] shall exist there; and this court thinks that the person who takes his slave into said territory, and by the length of his residence there indicates an intention of making that place his residence and that of his slave, and thereby induces a jury to believe that fact, does, by such residence, declare his slave to have become a free man.[30]

In *LaGrange v. Chouteau* four years later, the Missouri Supreme Court articulated the doctrine: "Any sort of residence contrived or permitted by the legal owner, upon the faith of secret trusts or contracts, in order to defeat or evade the [Northwest] ordinance [of 1787], and thereby introduce slavery *de facto,* would doubtless entitle a slave to freedom, and should be punished by a forfeiture of title to the property."[31] The same focus appeared in *Ralph v. Duncan* in 1833: "The object of the ordinance of 1787, was to prohibit the introduction of slaves into the Territory of which the present State of Illinois constitutes a part, and the master who permits his slave to go there to hire himself, offends against the law as much as one who takes his slave along with himself to reside there."[32]

In *Julia v. McKinney*, decided that same year, the owner worked the slave in Illinois, then sold her in St. Louis. The Missouri Supreme Court ruled: "The Constitution of Illinois does not regard the intention to introduce or not to introduce slavery, but prohibits the act. If a person says he does not intend to introduce slavery, yet if he does introduce it *de facto*, can the innocent intent save him from the forfeiture? We think it cannot, unless he can also show that his case raises a reasonable and necessary exception."[33] Exceptions were merely traveling with slaves through free territory without unnecessary delay,[34] or a slave's escape.[35]

In *Rachael v. Walker* in 1836—on facts almost identical to *Scott v. Emerson*—an army officer purchased Rachael in St. Louis, took her to free soil (Fort Snelling until 1831, then Prairie du Chien until 1834), and returned to St. Louis. The court declared Rachael free, by virtue of the Northwest Ordinance of 1787 and the Missouri Compromise act of 1820.[36] Justice Samuel Nelson of the U.S. Supreme Court later asserted that "there is no discrepancy between the earlier and the present [Missouri Supreme Court] cases upon this subject."[37] Even he must promptly concede that *Scott v. Emerson* departed from the decision in *Rachael v. Walker*.[38] Like most commentators, Lea VanderVelde and Sandhya Subramanian note: "Coming after this long line of precedents restricting slaveowners' right to take their slaves onto free soil, the Dred Scott decision seems particularly anomalous—especially when we consider that the Missouri Supreme Court rejected the Scotts' claim to freedom just 16 years after it granted freedom to a plaintiff, Rachael, whose circumstances strikingly resembled the Scotts."[39]

Many commentators, however, ignore that the Missouri Supreme Court drifted toward deserting its line of precedent in the 1840s. In at least three cases, the court interpreted the law contrary to the spirit of its earlier cases.[40] More plainly, Napton wrote in his diary that he and Scott intended in the 1840s to "overrule the old decisions of our court."[41] Unquestionably, the retirements of Judges Mathias McGirk and George Tompkins in 1841 and 1845, respectively, left the precedents at risk.[42]

True, the opinion in *Scott v. Emerson* did cite *Rex v. Allan [The Slave, Grace]* as precedent.[43] However, that 1827 English case was not binding precedent on the Missouri Supreme Court. More important, it was decided after Missouri established its (contrary) doctrine on emancipation by residence in a free state. "For the most part, southern states did not initially follow the *Slave Grace* precedent. Courts in Missouri, Kentucky, and Louisiana continued to free slaves who had lived or worked in free jurisdictions. Well after *Slave Grace,* the Missouri courts continued to liberate slaves who had lived in the North."[44]

Likewise, *Scott v. Emerson* found support in a Kentucky case, *Graham v. Strader,*[45] which the U.S. Supreme Court left standing before *Scott v. Emerson* was handed down.[46] *Strader,* however, fully deferred to state law; it did not require a change in Missouri law; it had no more force than the U.S. Supreme Court's earlier dismissals of appeals from three Missouri freedom suits.[47] Moreover, the facts in *Strader*—temporary trips to free territory, with a later escape—vastly differ from the Scotts' two lengthy periods of residence in free states.

The conflict was not just with Missouri precedent. Justice Nelson was wrong in asserting that "the current of authority, both in England and in this country, is in accordance with the law as declared by the courts of Missouri in the case before us, and we think the court below was not only right, but bound to follow it."[48] More accurate was Gamble's observation that Missouri precedent "is supported by the decisions of the other slave States, including those in which it may be supposed there was the least disposition to favor emancipation."[49] As Don Fehrenbacher observed: "Except in Missouri, as a result of the Dred Scott case, there appears to have been no decision of a southern appellate court that denied a suit for freedom in a clear-cut case of permanent residence on free soil."[50] The consequence of violating stare decisis is clear: "Indeed, if the Missouri Supreme Court had followed thirty years of precedents and held Scott to be free, the case would never have been brought into the federal courts."[51]

Another bedrock of the judicial process is respect for policy judgments of the legislative branch. "A process undisciplined by relation to the rules in precedent or statute . . . leads to unpredictability, vitiating a cardinal purpose in the law if future conduct is to be influenced by law. Worse, it leads to subjectivism or idiosyncrasy at the hands of the men in the long robes."[52] Justice Stephen Breyer wrote recently: "[E]ven if a judge knows what the just result should be, that judge is not to substitute even his juster will for that of the people. In a constitutional democracy a deep-seated conviction on the part of the people . . . is entitled to great respect."[53] This was the rule in the nineteenth century, as Justice Levi Woodbury stated in 1848 for the Taney court:

> [O]ur legislatures stand in a position demanding often the most
> favorable construction for their motives in passing laws, and
> they require a fair rather than hypercritical view of well-intended
> provisions in them. Those public bodies must be presumed to
> act from public considerations, being in a high public trust; and
> when their measures relate to matters of general interest, and can
> be vindicated under express or justly implied powers, and more
> especially when they appear intended for improvements, made
> in the true spirit of the age, or for salutary reforms in abuses, the
> disposition in the judiciary should be strong to uphold them.[54]

The Missouri Supreme Court, shortly before *Scott v. Emerson*, recognized that "successive enactments" and the "years . . . elapsed since the passage of the first act on this subject" entitled the legislative policy to deference.[55]

The legislature enacted the freedom-suit law five times before *Scott v. Emerson*, amending it as late as 1845.[56] Just months after statehood, in a case little noted by modern commentators, the Missouri Supreme Court reversed a technical dismissal of a freedom suit, emphasizing the law's "sole purpose of enabling free persons, held in slavery, to recover their freedom," noting "the spirit of the statute" and concluding that "the object of the Legislature was, to afford to plaintiffs of this description, all opportunity of having the questions of freedom fairly put in issue between the parties."[57] The freedom-suit law was a touchstone in the early cases favoring freedom.[58] As late as the Civil War, the legislature still authorized freedom suits,[59] unlike the state of Louisiana which enacted into law the rule in *Scott v. Emerson*.[60]

In *Scott v. Emerson*, the Missouri Supreme Court ignored the clear expression of policy by the state legislature, not even mentioning the freedom-suit law. True, as David Konig has documented, freedom suits could be based on three general grounds: the slave was manumitted by will or deed;

born free; or resided on free soil.[61] In Missouri—bordered on three sides by free soil—the third ground dominated.[62] "*Scott v. Emerson* was not an absolute rejection of all freedom claims. The decision did imply that Missouri would recognize a claim to freedom based on an 'act of manumission by' a free-state court. . . . But, if *Scott v. Emerson* did not close all doors to freedom in Missouri, it did close a major one."[63] *Scott v. Emerson,* again without discussion, broke a key appellate rule, disregarding the legislature's policy determination in the freedom suit law.

The Missouri opinion ends with an appeal to religion:

> When the condition of our slaves is contrasted with the state of their miserable race in Africa; when their civilization, intelligence and instruction in religious truths are considered, and the means now employed to restore them to the country from which they have been torn, bearing with them the blessings of civilized life, we are almost persuaded, that the introduction of slavery amongst us was, in the providence of God, who makes the evil passions of men subservient to His own glory, a means of placing that unhappy race within the pale of civilized nations.[64]

Invoking religion was not unique to *Scott v. Emerson.* Two years later, its author, Judge Scott, rejected a challenge to Sunday-closing laws, on the basis that the Missouri Constitution "appears to have been made by Christian men. The constitution, on its face, shows that the Christian religion was the religion of its framers. . . . [and] our constitution was framed for a people whose religion was christianity."[65]

In his appeals to religion, Scott ignored that Tompkins—author of many earlier Missouri precedents—also appealed to Christianity, believing its benevolent influence justified his pro-freedom decisions and was restricting slavery throughout the world.[66] Tompkins wrote for the court, after a lengthy discussion of the history of slavery (and Christianity): "Thus we see that in Europe, where slavery once prevailed, it has by the silent influence of the Christian religion alone been abolished."[67] In short, an appeal to religion did not justify the decision in *Scott v. Emerson.*

To today's legal mind, a glaring error is that *Scott v. Emerson* ignored the supremacy clause of the U.S. Constitution, because it paid little attention to a federal law, the Missouri Compromise of 1820. *Scott v. Emerson* dismissed it as a law for the "mere purpose of governing a territory," implying it did not apply to Missouri.[68]

This modern criticism is refuted by a simple fact: the U.S. Supreme Court soon held in *Dred Scott* that the Missouri Compromise act was unconstitutional, not binding on any court. Moreover, the Missouri Supreme Court properly interpreted the federal precedent. The federal Supreme Court was "proslavery" in the 1840s, the "natural result of judge-made doctrines and tendencies that had been developing for two decades."[69] Just months before *Scott v. Emerson,* the U.S. Supreme Court held—in a case cited to and by the Missouri court—that each state had the "undoubted right" to consider as slaves those negroes within its jurisdiction, whatever their status in another state.[70] The Court also ruled that states can bar slaves, either "liberated or fugitive";[71] that the owner's right to recover a slave trumps a state's police and due process powers;[72] and that Congress (probably) cannot regulate the domestic slave trade.[73]

Scott v. Emerson also selected the federal Supreme Court's preferred English case, *Slave Grace.* The Missouri court did not cite *Somerset v. Stewart,*[74] another English case that was one of the "most potent ideological weapons" of the abolitionists.[75] Although the attorneys emphasized *Somerset* in arguing the landmark cases of *The Antelope, The Amistad,* and *Strader v. Graham,*[76] the Supreme Court completely ignored *Somerset* in all three opinions. In *Prigg v. Pennnsylvania,* the Supreme Court discussed *Somerset,* but only to demonstrate the need for the fugitive slave clause.[77] When the Supreme Court did face the English cases, in *Dred Scott,* a majority approved the *Slave Grace* case, rejecting *Somerset* explicitly,[78] just as *Scott v. Emerson* did implicitly.

Viewed from the twenty-first century, *Scott v. Emerson* gives no deference to a federal statute, in violation of the supremacy clause. In the light of the contemporary jurisprudence, however, *Scott v. Emerson* accurately gauged the course of the highest court.

The criticisms presented here—that in *Scott v. Emerson* the Missouri Supreme Court injected arguments, overruled precedent, and ignored the legislature—each have exceptions, but the coalescing of all three shows that the court's decision resulted from a fundamentally wrong judicial process. Ignoring these judicial restraints, the majority judges were left to their personal views about society, which they candidly disclosed:

Times are not now as they were when the former decisions on this subject were made. Since then not only individuals but States have been possessed with a dark and fell spirit in relation to slavery, whose gratification is sought in the pursuit of measures, whose inevitable consequences must be the overthrow and destruction of our government. Under such circumstances it does not behoove the State of Missouri to show the least countenance to any measure which might gratify this spirit. She is willing to assume her full responsibility for the existence of slavery within her limits, nor does she seek to share or divide it with others. Although we may, for our own sakes, regret that the avarice and hard-heartedness of the progenitors of those who are now so sensitive on the subject, ever introduced the institution among us, yet we will not go to them to learn law, morality or religion on the subject.[79]

On the other hand, the epitome of principled judging was Judge Hamilton Gamble. Boman has written:

As one of the justices who later decided Dred Scott's suit, Gamble's representation of both slaves and slaveholders is of considerable interest, if for no other reason than to contrast his role as a lawyer to his decision-making as a judge. As chief justice, he adjudicated the law in strict accord with the constitutions of the United States and Missouri, and in conformity to legal precedent and statute. Moreover, he adhered strictly to precedent in almost every case he heard; even when in his opinion the decision was contrary to true justice in a case.[80]

In sum, *Scott v. Emerson* teaches the value of adhering to the fundamental principles of appellate judging.

Notes

I appreciate the assistance of my clerk, Dione C. Greene, and the dedicated staff of the Eighth Circuit's library.

1. Dred Scott v. John F. A. Sandford, 60 U.S. (19 How.) 393 (1857).

2. See Mark A. Graber, *Dred Scott and the Problem of Constitutional Evil* (New York: Cambridge University Press, 2006), 15–16, 23–28.

3. Scott, a man of color, v. Emerson, 15 Mo. 576 (1852).

4. Scott, 60 U.S. at 452–54. See also 459 and 465–68 (opinion of Nelson, J.), 494 (opinion of Campbell, J.). Justice John McLean's dissent quotes both opinions in *Scott v. Emerson* and poses as the final important principle: "Are the decisions of the Supreme Court of Missouri, on the questions before us, binding on this court, within the rule adopted" (534, 552–54, 563–64). Justice Benjamin R. Curtis's dissent refuses to recognize *Scott v. Emerson* as authority, quoting the state-court dissent (601–4).

5. An appeal of the grant of a new trial was dismissed because the case was not final in the trial court. Emmerson v. Harriet (of color), 11 Mo. 413 (1848) (Scott, J., for the court). The decision, actually made in Harriet's case, was replicated in Dred's (ibid.); Walter Ehrlich, "History of the Dred Scott Case through the Decision of 1857" (Ph.D. diss., Washington University, 1950), 87n111.

6. Scott, 15 Mo. at 583.

7. Ibid., 583–84.

8. Ibid., 585.

9. Ibid., 585–86, citing cases from England, Massachusetts, and Kentucky: Rex v. Allan [The Slave, Grace], 2 Hagg. 94, 166 Eng. Rep. 179 (Adm. 1827); Commonwealth v. Aves, 35 Mass. (18 Pick.) 193 (1836); and Graham v. Strader, 44 Ky. (5 B. Mon.) 173, 183 (1844).

10. Ibid., 586–87.

11. Ibid., 587–92.

12. Ibid., 591–92.

13. B. E. Witkin, *Manual on Appellate Court Opinions* (St. Paul, Minn.: West Publishing, 1977), 154. See also Karl N. Llewellyn, *The Common Law Tradition: Deciding Appeals* (Boston: Little, Brown, 1960), 29 (noting the benefits of "Issues Limited, Sharpened, and Phrased in Advance," and that an appellate court's reformulation of ill-drawn issues is "both relatively rare and a function of peculiarly sharp pressure from felt need. . . . [T]here is something unfair in putting a decision on a ground which losing counsel has had no opportunity to meet"). For the (extraordinary) exceptions to this rule, see Allan D. Vestal, "Sua Sponte Consideration in Appellate Review," *Fordham Law Review* 27, no. 4 (1959): 477–512.

14. Russell v. Southard, 53 U.S. 139, 159 (1851). See also Cutler v. Rae, 48 U.S. 729, 733 (1849) (separate opinion of Wayne, J.) (noting that the case marks the "first time" the court has decided an important constitutional question, without oral or printed argument, and predicting "it will not occur again").

15. Pacific Railroad v. Governor, 23 Mo. 353, 362 (1856) ("a question about which we express no opinion, especially as it has not been argued on the part of the executive").

16. Walter Ehrlich, *They Have No Rights: Dred Scott's Struggle for Freedom* (Westport, Conn.: Greenwood Press, 1979), 46.

17. Ehrlich, "History of the Dred Scott Case," 118.

18. Brief of Lyman D. Norris, Scott v. Emerson, 577–81. The brief published in *Missouri Reports* is incomplete (Ehrlich, "History of the Dred Scott Case," 119n72). Ehrlich publishes the entire brief in appendix E to his Ph.D. dissertation, "History of the Dred Scott Case," 389–99.

19. Ehrlich, *They Have No Rights,* 57–58 (emphasis in original).

20. Vincent C. Hopkins, *Dred Scott's Case* (New York: Fordham University Press, 1951), 16–17.

21. Dennis K. Boman, *Lincoln's Resolute Unionist: Hamilton Gamble, Dred Scott Dissenter and Missouri's Civil War Governor* (Baton Rouge: Louisiana State University Press, 2006), 85–86. See also Marvin R. Cain, *Lincoln's Attorney General: Edward Bates of Missouri* (Columbia: University of Missouri Press, 1965), 75 ("Gamble's analysis convinced [his brother-in-law and former-law-partner] Bates that the case involved a bargain between two of the justices and the anti-Benton Democrats and Geyer Whigs").

22. William Nisbet Chambers, *Old Bullion Benton: Senator from the New West* (Boston: Little, Brown, 1956), 432. As to Birch's bitter opposition to Benton, see ibid., 346–47, 353–54; Ehrlich, "History of the Dred Scott Case," 109–10; Birch v. Benton, 26 Mo. 153 (1858). As for Napton's differences with Benton, see Ehrlich, "History of the Dred Scott Case," 109.

23. Erhlich, "History of the Dred Scott Case," 115.

24. Benjamin N. Cardozo, *The Nature of the Judicial Process* (New Haven, Conn.: Yale University Press, 1921), 20, 112.

25. Lewis F. Powell Jr., "Leslie H. Arps Lecture, The Association of the Bar of the City of New York (October 17, 1989)," in *Courts, Judges, and Politics: An Introduction to the Judicial Process,* ed. Walter F. Murphy, C. Herman Pritchett, and Lee Epstein (Boston: McGraw-Hill, 2002), 471–72.

26. The Genesee Chief v. Fitzhugh, 53 U.S. 443, 458 (1851). The fullest statement on stare decisis by the Taney Court is Carroll v. Lessee of Carroll, 57 U.S. 275, 286–87 (1853) (involving the bequest of slaves). In a speech to the American Law Institute, Justice Robert Jackson recognized, "Nowhere today is the precedent so decisive of litigation as it is supposed to have been in the eighteenth and nineteenth centuries." Robert H. Jackson, "Decisional Law and Stare Decisis," *American Bar Association Journal* 30 (June 1944): 334.

27. Payne v. St. Louis County, 8 Mo. 473, 476 (1844) (Napton, J., for the court).

28. Scott, 15 Mo. at 582, 584, 586. The closest Judge Scott comes to discussing or analyzing the earlier cases are blanket references: (1) the summary paragraph, "Cases of this kind are not strangers in our courts," preceding the comity discussion; (2) his two references to the "old cases" while ridiculing the length of residence/hiring required for emancipation; and (3) the allusion in the conclusion to the "times" when "the former decisions on this subject were made."

29. Gamble, in dissent, summarizes the key cases (Scott, 15 Mo. at 590). McLean recites the summary in his dissenting opinion (Scott, 60 U.S. at 550–52),

repeatedly noting the duration of the precedent, twenty-eight (or "nearly thirty") years (Scott, 60 U.S. at 554, 555, 556, 563, 564).

30. 1 Mo. 472, 475–76 (1824). The court reiterates this doctrine in *Milly v. Smith,* 2 Mo. 36, 39 (1828), that "slaves carried into Illinois with a view to residence, and staying there long enough to acquire the character of residents, do by virtue of such residence become free"; and in *Vincent v. Duncan,* 2 Mo. 214, 216 (1830), that "if the owner of slaves took them with him into Illinois, with intent to reside there, and did reside there, keeping his slaves, it was a fraud on the ordinance, and the slave became free. If he stay in Kentucky, and send his slave over to Illinois to reside there, it is equally a violation of the provisions of the ordinance."

31. 2 Mo. 20, 22 (1828). Those born and held as slaves *before* the ordinance were not entitled to freedom owing to residence within the Northwest Territory. Theoteste v. Chouteau, 2 Mo. 144, 145 (1829). Slaves' children born *after* the ordinance passed did not continue as slaves within the Northwest Territory. Merry v. Tiffin, 1 Mo. 725, 725–26 (1827); Chouteau v. Hope, 7 Mo. 428, 429 (1842) (limited by the post-*Scott* case of Calvert v. Steamboat Timoleon, 15 Mo. 595, 597 [1852]). This was an exception to the rule that "a person born of a slave is a slave." Lee v. Sprague, 14 Mo. 476, 477 (1851).

32. Ralph v. Duncan, 3 Mo. 194, 195 (1833). Later, the former slave was allowed to recover the value of his services while the freedom suit pended. Gordon v. Duncan, 3 Mo. 385, 387 (1834).

33. Julia v. McKinney, 3 Mo. 270, 274 (1833). The losing attorney was Hamilton R. Gamble. See Boman, *Lincoln's Resolute Unionist,* 72–73.

34. LaGrange, 2 Mo. at 22; Wilson v. Melvin, 4 Mo. 592, 597 (1837) ("The true test would be . . . whether Melvin [the slave owner] made any unnecessary delay in Illinois, before he took his slaves to St. Louis to be hired out").

35. Nat v. Ruddle, 3 Mo. 400, 401 (1834); Robert v. Melugen, 9 Mo. 170, 172 (1845).

36. 4 Mo. 350, 352–54 (1836). The losing attorney was Gamble (ibid., 350, 351); Boman, *Lincoln's Resolute Unionist,* 73–75.

37. Scott, 60 U.S. at 466.

38. Ibid. Justice John Campbell, concurring, tried to reconcile *Scott v. Emerson* with *Winny v. Whitesides,* claiming a lack of domicile in free territory by Scott's owner (494–95).

39. Lea VanderVelde and Sandhya Subramanian, "Mrs. Dred Scott," *Yale Law Journal* 106, no. 4 (1997): 1093n252. See also Louise Weinberg, "Methodological Interventions and the Slavery Cases; or, Night-Thoughts of a Legal Realist," *Maryland Law Review* 56, no. 4 (1997): 1344 (*Scott v. Emerson* was a "dramatic about-face," a "very different view," which "changed the ground rules in the middle of Scott's case, suddenly jettisoning" its comity and freedom rules).

40. Dennis K. Boman, "The Dred Scott Case Reconsidered: The Legal and Political Context in Missouri," *American Journal of Legal History* 44 (October 2000):

417–20, citing Rennick v. Chloe, 7 Mo. 197 (1841); Chouteau v. Pierre 9 Mo. 3 (1845); and Charlotte v. Chouteau 11 Mo. 193 (1847). The last case, *Charlotte v. Chouteau,* says it plainly:

> Whatever may be the policy of other governments, it has not been the policy of this State, to favor the liberation of negroes from that condition in which the laws and usages have placed the mass of their species. On the contrary, our statute expressly throws the burden of establishing a right to freedom upon the petitioner, and the provision is both wise and humane. Neither sound policy nor enlightened philanthropy should encourage, in a slaveholding State, the multiplication of a race whose condition could be neither that of freemen nor of slaves, and whose existence and increase, in this anomalous character, without promoting their individual comforts or happiness, tend only to dissatisfy and corrupt those of their own race and color remaining in a state of servitude.

Ibid., 200 (quoted to conclude Emerson's brief, Scott, 15 Mo. at 581).

The slave won in one case, due to the opposing attorney's error at trial (not objecting to jury instructions). Randolph v. Alsey, 8 Mo. 656 (1844). See also Boman, *Lincoln's Resolute Unionist,* 79. But other cases show the hardening attitude. Peter v. King, 13 Mo. 143, 145 (1850) (freed slave's agent does not prove his authority to recover for the ex-slave's services); Nat v. Coons, 10 Mo. 543, 546 (1847) (strictly interpreting Missourian's will, made in Mississippi, to deny freedom); Eaton v. Vaughan, 9 Mo. 743, 748–49 (1846) (approving punitive damages on steamboat captain who negligently transports a runaway slave); cf. Maria v. Atterberry, 9 Mo. 369, 376–77 (1845) (supreme court reverses trial court for requiring too much proof that Kentuckian freed slave).

41. Boman, "Dred Scott Case Reconsidered," 421.

42. David Thomas Konig, "The Long Road to *Dred Scott:* Personhood and the Rule of Law in the Trial Court Records of St. Louis Slave Freedom Suits," *UMKC Law Review* 75, no. 1 (2006): 77.

43. Scott, 15 Mo. at 586, citing Rex v. Allan [The Slave, Grace].

44. Paul Finkelman, *Dred Scott v. Sandford: A Brief History with Documents* (Boston: Bedford Books, 1997), 21.

45. Scott, 15 Mo. at 586, citing Graham, 44 Ky. at 183.

46. Ibid., 577, 579, 581 (argument of attorney Norris, citing Strader v. Graham, 51 U.S. [10 How.] 82 [1850]).

47. Lagrange v. Chouteau, 29 U.S. 287, 290 (1830); Menard v. Aspasia, 30 U.S. 505, 517 (1831); Chouteau v. Marguerite, 37 U.S. 507, 510 (1838).

48. Scott, 60 U.S. at 468.

49. Scott, 15 Mo. at 590–91, citing cases from Louisiana, Mississippi, Virginia, and Kentucky.

50. Don E. Fehrenbacher, *The Dred Scott Case: Its Significance in American Law and Politics* (New York: Oxford University Press, 1978), 60.

51. Paul Finkelman, *An Imperfect Union: Slavery, Federalism, and Comity* (Chapel Hill: University of North Carolina Press, 1981), 236.

52. Charles D. Breitel, "The Lawmakers," *Columbia Law Review* 65, no. 5 (1965): 774 (author was chief judge of the highest court in New York, the Court of Appeals).

53. Stephen G. Breyer, *Active Liberty: Interpreting Our Democratic Constitution* (New York: Alfred A. Knopf, 2005), 17 (internal quotations marks omitted) (ellipsis in original).

54. Planters' Bank v. Sharp, 47 U.S. 301, 319 (1848).

55. Payne v. St. Louis County, 8 Mo. 473, 476 (1844) (opinion of Napton, J., for the court); see also State ex rel. Gentry v. Fry, 4 Mo. 120, 196 (1835) (opinion of Tompkins, J.) (recognizing "the respectful deference due to the legislative department. . . . A respectful submission to the laws, and a respectful deference to the law making-power").

56. "AN ACT to enable persons held in slavery, to sue for their freedom (June 27, 1807)," *Laws of a Public and General Nature of the District of Louisiana, of the Territory of Louisiana, of the Territory of Missouri, and of the State of Missouri, up to the Year 1824* (Jefferson City: W. Lusk and Son, 1842), 1:96–97; "Act of December 30, 1824," 1825 Mo. Laws (St. Louis: E. Charless, 1825), 1:404–6; "Act of January 27, 1835," *Revised Statutes of Missouri, 1835* (St. Louis: Chambers, Knapp, 1840), 284–86; "Act of February 11, 1841," 1841 Mo. Laws (Jefferson City: Calvin Gunn, 1841), 146; "Act of February 13, 1845," *Revised Statutes of Missouri, 1845* (St. Louis: J. W. Daugherty, 1845), 531–34, also published as (St. Louis: Chambers and Knapp, 1845), 283–84. All Missouri statutes cited here are available in the library of the Supreme Court of Missouri.

57. Susan v. Hight, 1 Mo. 118, 118–19 (1821) (per curiam).

58. Catiche v. Circuit Court, 1 Mo. 608, 609, 613 (1826) (referencing the text and [twice] the object of the freedom suit law, and concluding with the "humanity of the law"); Tramell v. Adam, 2 Mo. 155, 156 (1829) (because freedom statute has "benefits intended for the plaintiff," a court should overlook technical pleading requirements).

59. "Act of November 19, 1855," *Revised Statutes of Missouri, 1855* (Jefferson City: James Lusk, 1856), 1:809–12; Joshua v. Purse, 34 Mo. 209, 209–10 (1863); Lewis v. Hart, 33 Mo. 535, 538–39 (1863). Even after *Scott v. Emerson,* the court, over Scott's dissent, recognized that the freedom-suit law does not require more conclusive proof than other civil cases. Charlotte v. Chouteau, 25 Mo. 465, 483 (1857).

60. Scott, 60 U.S. at 467–68 (opinion of Nelson, J.).

61. Konig, "Long Road to *Dred Scott,*" 68.

62. Ibid.

63. Finkelman, *Imperfect Union,* 227.

64. Scott, 15 Mo. at 587.

65. State v. Ambs, 20 Mo. 214, 216–17, 218–19 (1854).

66. See Boman, *Lincoln's Resolute Unionist,* 68.

67. Marguerite v. Chouteau, 3 Mo. 540, 549 (1834). Similarly, Edward Bates—Gamble's law partner and later Lincoln's attorney general—manumitted a slave for transit to Liberia in the belief that he would spread the Gospel truth. Boman, "Dred Scott Case Reconsidered," 415.

68. Scott, 15 Mo. at 583. Months after *Scott v. Emerson*, the court directly refused to follow the Missouri Compromise act of 1820, on authority of *Scott*. Sylvia v. Kirby, 17 Mo. 434, 434–35 (1853) (Scott, J., for a unanimous court, including Gamble, C.J.).

69. William M. Wiecek, "Slavery and Abolition before the United States Supreme Court, 1820–1860," *Journal of American History* 65, no. 1 (1978): 35, 49.

70. Strader, 51 U.S. at 93–94 (Taney, C.J., for the court), cited to the Missouri Supreme Court by owner's counsel, Scott v. Emerson, 577, 579, 581, and by the court, ibid., 586 (Kentucky decision).

71. Moore v. Illinois, 55 U.S. 13, 18 (1852) (conviction for harboring a Missouri slave in Illinois).

72. Prigg v. Pennsylvania, 41 U.S. 539, 625 (1842).

73. McLean, dissenting in *Dred Scott,* wrote that *Groves* held, "Congress had no power to interfere with slavery as it exists in the States, or to regulate what is called the slave trade among them. If this trade were subject to the commercial power, it would follow that Congress could abolish or establish slavery in every State of the Union." Scott, 60 U.S. at 536–37, citing Groves v. Slaughter, 40 U.S. 449 (1841). The *Groves* opinions are hard to decipher (Wiecek, "Slavery and Abolition," 51–55). McLean's view is, however, consistent with the nineteenth-century commerce clause. "The federal government clearly lacked the power to regulate the domestic slave trade." Randy E. Barnett, "The Original Meaning of the Commerce Clause," *University of Chicago Law Review* 68, no. 1 (2001): 143n202, criticized by Robert J. Pushaw and Grant S. Nelson, "A Critique of the Narrow Interpretation of the Commerce Clause," *Northwestern University Law Review* 96, no. 2 (2002): 702n54.

74. Somerset v. Stewart, 98 Eng. Rep. 499 (K.B. 1772).

75. William M. Wiecek, "*Somerset:* Lord Mansfield and the Legitimacy of Slavery in the Anglo-American World," *University of Chicago Law Review* 42, no. 1 (1974): 86. See generally Alfred W. Blumrosen, "The Profound Influence in America of Lord Mansfield's Decision in Somerset v. Stuart," *Texas Wesleyan Law Review* 13, no. 2 (2007): 645.

76. The Antelope, 23 U.S. 66, 104, 112, 113 (1825) (arguments of counsel); Strader, 51 U.S. at 85–86 (arguments of counsel). In *The Amistad,* 40 U.S. 518, 554 (1841), counsel invoked a case that quoted and followed *Somerset:* Forbes v. Cochrane, 107 Eng. Rep. 450, 453, 458–59 (K.B. 1824).

77. Prigg, 41 U.S. 611–12.

78. Nelson approved *Slave Grace* as superseding *Somerset* (Scott, 60 U.S. at 466–68). Justices James Wayne and Robert Grier concurred in Nelson's opinion

(455, 469) (Grier's explicit position is in Oliver v. Kauffman, 18 F. Cas. 657, 660 [C.C.E.D. Pa. 1850] [Grier, J., on circuit]). Justice Peter Daniel claimed *Slave Grace* "overruled" *Somerset* (485–86). Campbell endorsed *Slave Grace* and criticized *Somerset* (497–500). On the other hand, McLean in dissent discussed *Somerset* at length, claiming *Slave Grace* did not overrule it. (534–35, 548–49). While Curtis's dissent did not cite *Somerset,* "his argument rested on the *Somerset* doctrine that slavery could exist only where sanctioned by positive law." Stuart Streichler, *Justice Curtis in the Civil War Era: At the Crossroads of American Constitutionalism* (Charlottesville: University of Virginia Press, 2005), 142 (citing Scott, 60 U.S. at 627, 624, 625).

79. Scott, 15 Mo. at 586–87.

80. Boman, "Dred Scott Case Reconsidered," 410.

THIRTEEN

Missouri Law, Politics, and the *Dred Scott* Case

Michael A. Wolff

TO GET the Missouri politics of the *Dred Scott* era, let us fast forward a few years to the Civil War. Between 1861 and 1865, many states experienced what many people to the south of St. Louis call the "war between the states" or, more pointedly, "the war of northern aggression." As a border state, Missouri was having a real civil war, from which we are still in recovery. Members of the same families fought one other. Our battles, not as big or as well known as Vicksburg, Shiloh, and Gettysburg, were nonetheless brutal. Acts of terrorism by small cadres abounded.[1]

Missouri was said to have at least three distinct factions: the Charcoals, so called because of their demand for the immediate end of slavery; the Claybanks—unionists, including many slaveholders who favored gradual emancipation, so called because their principles were thought to be "pallid gray"; and, of course, secessionists.[2] President Abraham Lincoln, exasperated in 1863 by the bitter divisions in Missouri, wrote: "It is very painful to me that you in Missouri cannot, or will not, settle your factional quarrel among yourselves. I have been tormented with it beyond endurance for months, by both sides. Neither side pays the least respect to my appeals to your reason."[3] Lincoln, unfortunately, would not live long enough to understand Missouri politics.

The Civil War was, of course, the continuation of politics by other means. It was presaged by the decision of the Supreme Court of the United States in the last of Missouri's slave freedom suits, filed by Dred Scott and his wife Harriet, suits that were very much a product of the contending political forces at play in this state.[4] The case was, at the time of its initial filing in 1846, rather unremarkable. Dred Scott, his wife, Harriet, and their two children sought judgment that, because they had lived in free territory, they no longer were slaves.[5] The decision of the Supreme Court of Missouri in the Scotts' case 155 years ago was, unquestionably, our court's worst decision ever. But if the Supreme Court of Missouri got the decision badly wrong, the U.S. Supreme Court five years later got the case horribly wrong.[6]

A study of this case will teach us a good deal about courts, politics (including the politics of judicial selection), the development of law, and the fateful role court decisions can play in our society. Every case is a story. We appellate judges are not "primary sources" people but are trained, instead, to take and use facts from prior judicial opinions. I think all of us should be mindful that sometimes these previously averred facts may be inaccurate or chosen selectively. For the purpose of putting the *Dred Scott* case in historical perspective, I have read a good amount of history from secondary sources, some written by other contributors to this volume. I am going to be selective, and I hope that my choices will help us set the scene and understand the context of the controversy.

Missouri entered the Union as a result of the Missouri Compromise, a pair of statutes that provided that Missouri would be admitted as a slave state and Maine as a free state, while slavery would be banned in other territories north and west of Missouri in the Louisiana Territory.[7] Slavery similarly had been outlawed in the Northwest Ordinance of 1787, prior to the adoption of the federal Constitution, applying to territories that included what are now the states of Indiana, Illinois, and Wisconsin.[8] By 1860 Missouri's slave population numbered about 115,000, held by more than 24,000 slaveholders, of a total population of more than a million.[9]

Missouri's white population was deeply split on the issue of slavery. During the state's first decades, whites in Missouri grew increasingly concerned about the presence of freed blacks, with many believing that they were responsible for agitating among the slave population and committing crimes.[10] In 1840, the General Assembly of Missouri made it a crime for free blacks to enter Missouri.[11] Their ambivalence toward slavery was shown by the fact that slaves could sue for their freedom.[12] The form of a so-called freedom suit was an action that today we would consider a tort, notably including assault and battery.[13] The statute provided that if the person were enslaved wrongfully, damages in a nominal amount could be awarded.[14] The cases were triable to juries.[15]

What did that say about the status of a slave? He or she could not be mere property. If so, how could he or she have rights, including the right to sue for freedom? Judges in St. Louis, the center of antislavery sentiment, appointed lawyers to represent slaves bringing these suits.[16] With the help of the Missouri State Archives in the Secretary of State's Office and the St. Louis Circuit Clerk's Office, researchers at Washington University and other institutions have found nearly three hundred slave freedom suits in our Missouri court records filed between 1806 and 1857. Many of these suits were successful.[17] From the state's earliest—and calmest—times, Missouri courts applied conflict of laws principles and held that a slave who had traveled to and resided in a free state or territory was freed.[18] The basic notion was that Missouri courts should give respect, or "comity," to the laws of other states or territories.[19] If a slave resided in Illinois, for example, he or she no longer could be considered a slave, because slavery was illegal in Illinois. The act of bringing a slave to free territory was considered an act that emancipated the slave, though courts quibbled about whether the slave and master must "reside" in the free state, not just sojourn or pass through.[20]

What effect, if any, did all this have on the courts? From 1821 until its 1852 *Dred Scott* decision, the Supreme Court of Missouri decided eleven cases affirming the notion that a slave who traveled to and resided in free territory was no longer a slave.[21] These decisions were driven largely by two judges of the state's three-judge supreme court: the first chief justice, Mathias McGirk, and Judge George Tompkins.[22] Both had been appointed to the bench according to Missouri's 1820 constitution, which provided that judges were to be appointed by the governor and confirmed by the Senate, reflecting the system of judicial selection the founding fathers adopted in the federal Constitution some thirty-three years earlier.[23] There were no judicial elections.[24]

McGirk left the bench in 1841, followed by Tompkins in 1845, and decisions of the Supreme Court of Missouri became increasingly adverse to slaves bringing freedom suits.[25] The judges then serving, Judges William Barclay Napton and James Harvey Birch—who had been appointed to the court for life under the original constitutional scheme—were prepared to overrule the earlier cases and to hold that Missouri need not give comity to the law of the free territories.[26] Napton and Birch seemed intent on ending all freedom suits, to declare that Congress had no power to legislate on the subject of slavery in the territories, and to hold that the Missouri Compromise was unconstitutional.[27]

Around the same time, a movement began to select judges for terms of years in elections rather than for life through gubernatorial appointments with Senate confirmation.[28] Some view this change to judicial elections as a product of "Jacksonian democracy," and there is some basis for believing that.[29] It is also quite likely, however, that the movement was seen as a way of not having judges for life who were products of a previously dominant political party or a previous governor.[30] In many states that were moving to elected judiciaries, there were high-profile impeachments of state judges.[31] Many prominent lawyers of the era worried about the legitimacy of the courts where they were staffed with judges with lifetime appointments.[32] In 1848, at the behest of many of the bar's foremost members, the General Assembly proposed to the voters to change the Missouri Constitution to establish judicial elections.[33] Missouri's voters approved the constitutional change in 1849.[34] The judges of the state supreme court thereafter were removed by virtue of the constitutional change, and the court's judges began to be elected starting in 1850.[35]

The strongly proslavery judge, Napton, did not win election,[36] and Birch resigned from the court.[37] All three of the judges serving on the court after the 1851 election were natives of Virginia and were considered proslavery.[38] Judge William Scott, author of the *Dred Scott* majority opinion, previously served on the Supreme Court of Missouri as a result of appointment in 1841.[39] Judge John Ryland had been appointed to the Court in 1849[40] and was elected in 1851.[41] The third judge was Chief Justice Hamilton R. Gamble, a prominent St. Louis lawyer who accepted an invitation from a nearly unanimous bar of St. Louis to run for the supreme court.[42] Gamble refused to campaign for the job, but he felt that it was his duty to make himself available for the position, especially because he had urged the change to judicial elections.[43] He was elected overwhelmingly.[44] Though a slaveholder, he was also a man who put principle above his own preferences and would be the court's dissenter in the *Dred Scott* case.[45]

Who was Dred Scott? A slave, originally owned by the Peter Blow family of St. Louis, he was purchased by Dr. John Emerson prior to Emerson's 1834 assignment as an army surgeon to a military outpost in Rock Island, Illinois.[46] Emerson took Scott to the Rock Island post, where they lived from 1833 to 1836.[47] Thereafter, they moved to Fort Snelling, in the portion of the Louisiana Purchase territory that is now in the state of Minnesota, where they lived from 1836 to 1838.[48]

Who was Harriet Scott? Born Harriet Robinson, a descendant of African slaves, she was either the servant or a slave of Lawrence Taliaferro, the Indian agent stationed at Fort Snelling.[49] Taliaferro brought Harriet to Fort Snelling in 1835.[50] Sometime after Dred Scott arrived with Emerson in 1836, Taliaferro—as a government official—performed a wedding ceremony in which Harriet, then about seventeen years old, was married to Dred, who was then more than forty years old, about twice her age.[51] In the early years of this marriage, four children were born.[52] Two sons died in infancy, and two daughters, Eliza and Lizzie, survived infancy and later became subject to their parents' freedom suit.[53] Eliza was born aboard a steamboat on the Mississippi River north of Missouri, and Lizzie was born at Jefferson Barracks near St. Louis after the Scotts returned to Missouri with Emerson in 1838.[54]

Harriet and Dred Scott sued for their freedom in 1846 in St. Louis Circuit Court, and their case was tried to a jury.[55] In the first trial, the jury found for the defendant, Irene Emerson, the widow of John.[56] The judge in the case, Alexander Hamilton, did something rather unusual, however: he granted a new trial, apparently believing that the jury had decided the issue wrongly.[57] In the second trial—with the jury instructed that, if Dred Scott had lived in free territory, he should be considered free—the jury found for the Scotts.[58] Emerson appealed the circuit court's judgment to the Supreme Court of Missouri, which rendered its decision in 1852.[59]

With three seemingly proslavery judges—Gamble, Ryland, and Scott—elected to the court, it would be easy to say that the switch in doctrine that occurred with the Supreme Court of Missouri's decision in the Scott case is traceable to the change to an elected judiciary, but unfortunately it is too easy. [60] The state's long-serving U.S. senator, Thomas Hart Benton (the Jacksonian Democrat, not the painter of the same name, who was the senator's grandnephew) had become a vocal opponent of the expansion of slavery.[61] In speaking appearances throughout the state in 1849, Benton took the position that, if the issue were a new one, he would not be in favor of introducing slavery into Missouri or, indeed, into the United States.[62] These remarks were controversial, to say the least, and split the Democratic Party.[63]

The Scotts' case was indistinguishable from some of the freedom suits that previously had gone before the Supreme Court of Missouri.[64] But because of the changing times the court's majority in the Scott opinion declined to follow the long line of earlier precedent holding that a slave who resided in free territory was no longer a slave.[65] Interestingly enough, the court based its decision only on conflict of laws principles, a decision on Missouri state law that was the prerogative of the Supreme Court of Missouri to decide.[66] The court did not invoke constitutional principles; specifically, the court did not go where Napton and others had planned to go, that is, to rule that Congress had no power to restrict slavery in the territories and to strike down the federal law known as the Missouri Compromise.[67] To Dred, Harriet, and their children, however, the result— whether based on Missouri law or the U.S. Constitution—was the same. They lost.

The dissenting judge, the slaveholder Hamilton Gamble, said the court should adhere to precedent.[68] Addressing the "temporary public excitement" over the issue of slavery that undoubtedly would cloud the people's judgment, Gamble said: "Times may have changed, public feeling may have changed, but principles have not and do not change; and, in my judgment, there can be no safe basis for judicial decision, but in those principles which are immutable."[69]

When the case was returned to the St. Louis Circuit Court, the Scotts had a new lawyer and a new strategy.[70] Because the Missouri decision was based on state law, there was no avenue of appeal to the U.S. Supreme Court. The Scotts' new lawyer, Roswell Field, filed a new lawsuit in the federal court in St. Louis.[71] The state case was still pending, but apparently only in a technical sense that a final judgment against the Scotts had not yet been rendered in the circuit court on remand.

In their federal court case, the Scotts sued New York resident John F. A. Sanford,[72] who succeeded his sister Irene Emerson as owner of the Scott family. Invoking federal jurisdiction based on diversity of citizenship, the Scotts claimed that they were citizens of Missouri, that Sanford was a citizen of New York, and, therefore, that the federal court had jurisdiction over the case under the federal diversity of citizenship statute.[73] That is one of the ways of maintaining a suit in a federal court. The Scotts' case was tried on the merits in the federal court in St. Louis. The Scotts lost. Then they appealed to the U.S. Supreme Court.

Let me make a civil procedure teacher's comment here. The legal doctrine *res judicata,* Latin for "the matter has been decided," prevents relitigation of cases that already have been decided. In a technical sense, because the state court judgment had not been entered, perhaps it might be said that the doctrine, which is premised on respect for an earlier judgment, did not apply. There certainly was enough legal doctrine around in the 1850s that could have been used to preclude the Scotts' case from being considered a second time in the federal courts. Federal courts in the nineteenth century felt free to apply general principles of common law and were not obligated to follow the common law of states. It was possible, therefore, to hope for a more favorable substantive law by choosing to go to federal court, if there was federal diversity of citizenship jurisdiction.[74]

Remember that the jurisdiction of the federal courts depended on the fact that the Scotts and Sanford were citizens of different states. The first part of the Court's majority opinion was premised on the notion that the Scotts, of African descent, were not and never could be considered citizens of the United States or of the state of Missouri, whether they were free or enslaved.[75] Alas, the populism of President Andrew Jackson lived on, though his presidency had been over for twenty years. A strain of that populism was distinctly racist, both as to American Indians and as to blacks.[76] Chief Justice Roger Taney's majority opinion directly addressed the contradiction between the Court's holding and the language of the Declaration of Independence that states, of course, "that all men are created equal; that they are endowed by their Creator with certain unalienable rights; that among them there is life, liberty, and the pursuit of happiness."[77] The Court's opinion said that it is "too clear for dispute, that the enslaved African race were not intended to be included, and formed no part of the people who framed and adopted this declaration; for if the language, as understood in that day, would embrace them, the conduct of the distinguished men who framed the Declaration of Independence would have been utterly and flagrantly inconsistent with the principles they asserted."[78]

We ought to look at what the founding fathers intended in the words they used. The language just quoted from the *Dred Scott* opinion, however, is a stunningly stark warning that we should be careful how we discern the meaning of the original words of the founders in the various documents that frame our governmental system. It was clear from the language of the Constitution, the Court said in *Scott v. Sandford,* that Congress had no power to "raise to the rank of a citizen anyone born in the United States who, from birth or parentage, by the laws of the country, belongs to an inferior and subordinate class."[79] The Court contrasted the Constitution's predecessor, the Articles of Confederation, which did refer to "*free inhabitants* of each of the states."[80] The Court inferred that the framers of the Constitution explicitly meant to exclude from its protection even those persons who were free at the time it was ratified.[81]

In its majority opinion in *Scott,* the Court went on to say that a state "may give the right to free Negroes and mulattoes, but that does not make them citizens of the States, and still less of the United States. And the provision in the Constitution giving privileges and immunities in other states, does not apply to them."[82] The Court thus concluded that blacks never could become state citizens allowed to sue in the federal courts under the diversity of citizenship statute.[83] As startling as its decision about jurisdiction is, one would think that the opinion should stop there, for if the Court had no jurisdiction owing to a lack of diversity of citizenship, then any other pronouncements in the opinion are what we lawyers call *obiter dictum,* that is, words that are not necessary to the holding in the case. *Dictum* is just the court talking. It is not law. But, of course, lawyers can discuss at some length whether particular phrases in judicial opinions are *dicta* or part of the holding that expresses the law of the case.

Despite its professed lack of jurisdiction, the Supreme Court plunged forth, justifying its further "opinion" as being necessary to correct all errors in the lower court's judgment so that other courts might not be led to "serious mischief and injustice in some future suit."[84] The Court wrote that slaves are property, the same as any other property, and that Congress, therefore, has no power to interfere with the rights of property owners.[85] It then held that the Missouri Compromise, which outlawed slavery in some of the territories, was unconstitutional.[86] Moreover, it wrote, states that had outlawed slavery could not interfere with the property rights of slaveholders.[87] This logic would imply that Missouri's statute that allowed slaves to sue for their freedom also must be void.

The Court's pronouncement was as deeply political as any in our history. Edward Bates, a Missourian who competed with Lincoln for the 1860 Republican nomination, scorned President James Buchanan for urging the Court in a speech in 1857, while the Court was deliberating on the *Dred Scott* case, to strike down the Missouri Compromise.[88] Bates concluded that Buchanan, by asserting that the Missouri Compromise unconstitutionally prohibited slavery in the territories, had reversed the narrow Jacksonian concept of the Supreme Court's role and had exercised a corruptive influence on the justices to win a decision for the slaveholders in his party and to preserve his own political position.[89] The greatest danger to the Union, Bates declared, was that "corrupt and dangerous party"—the Democratic Party—because of its "insistence on keeping the slavery issue in public view."[90]

Across the river in Illinois, that state's great lawyer, Abraham Lincoln, delivered his "House Divided" speech in June 1858 as part of his campaign for the U.S. Senate against Stephen A. Douglas.[91] After his famous opening lines that "a house divided against itself cannot stand" and that "this government cannot endure permanently half slave and half free," Lincoln launched into a history, discussion, and analysis of the *Dred Scott* decision.[92] His single-sentence summary of the entire decision shows his lawyerly gifts; his "brief" of the case was: "If any man choose to enslave another, no third man shall be allowed to object."[93] His opponent Douglas was undercut in his fundamental position on the slavery issue by the Court's decision. Douglas argued for "popular sovereignty," which meant that each state could decide for itself whether to allow slavery.[94] But the *Dred Scott* decision put Douglas in a most awkward position. Douglas believed that the Supreme Court had decided only the question of jurisdiction in the *Dred Scott* case and that all else was mere *obiter dicta*.[95] He refused to admit that the *Dred Scott* pronouncement meant that slavery could go into a territory against the wishes of that territory's inhabitants.[96]

During the Civil War, which followed Lincoln's 1860 election as president and his taking office in 1861, Missouri was split deeply. Its governor, Claiborne Fox Jackson, called a constitutional convention to decide whether Missouri should secede from the Union and join the Confederacy.[97] By then, Hamilton Gamble, the Missouri dissenter in *Dred Scott,* was a private citizen, having left the Supreme Court of Missouri in 1855 because the job did not pay enough.[98] Gamble, a convention delegate, argued strenuously in favor of staying in the Union, though he himself owned slaves, as did many Union loyalists in Missouri.[99] When the convention voted to stay in the Union, Governor Jackson and other Confederate sympathizers in state government fled the state for Texas.[100] The convention elected Gamble as Missouri's provisional governor—though by what authority I do not know—and he served as governor until his death in 1864.[101]

Jackson and his confederates were not the only ones to flee. Near Hannibal, Missouri, at the outbreak of the Civil War, a young man named Samuel Clemens joined a local Confederate militia unit.[102] After about two weeks of field service, during which he nearly was captured by Union forces led by Colonel Ulysses S. Grant, Clemens resigned, explaining that he was "'incapacitated by fatigue' through persistent retreating."[103] Clemens left the state and spent the duration of the war in Nevada and California.[104] For American literature, it was a fortunate choice, for otherwise we might not have Tom Sawyer and Huck Finn to explain us to ourselves, nor would Grant have had Mark Twain's help in editing and publishing his great *Memoirs* shortly before Grant's death in 1885.[105]

What about the Missouri judges? The author of the majority opinion, Judge William Scott, was removed from the Supreme Court of Missouri in 1862 because he refused to swear allegiance to the Union.[106] In fact, three years later (and one year after Gamble's death), one supreme court judge resigned, and the state's provisional governor ordered that the remaining two disloyal supreme court judges be thrown out of office.[107] In his order, the governor charged the commanding brigadier general "with the execution of this order, and will employ such force for that purpose as he may deem necessary, and arrest all persons who may oppose him."[108] He continued that the general should "avoid the use of violent means; but, if in your judgment necessary, do not hesitate to employ all the force it may require."[109]

As provisional governor, Hamilton Gamble, the judge who dissented in the state supreme court's *Dred Scott* decision, proposed a gradual emancipation of slaves in Missouri that would be complete by 1870.[110] That was too slow for President Lincoln, who also was impatient with the radicals' demand for immediate emancipation. The Emancipation Proclamation did not apply to Missouri, which remained in the Union and was not "in rebellion." Gamble went to Washington to win Lincoln's support for the conservative plan. When he failed to get it, he attacked Lincoln as "a mere intriguing, pettifogging, piddling politician." Lincoln did not believe he could solve Missouri's slavery question to anyone's satisfaction, including his own, according to his biographer David Herbert Donald. Lincoln had "no friends in Missouri," he told Attorney General Edward Bates (Gamble's mentor and former law partner).[111]

And what of Dred and Harriet Scott and their family? In the court record, Harriet was described as a washerwoman, and her husband was a porter.[112] Taylor Blow, the son of original master Peter Blow, helped pay for the Scotts' suit for freedom.[113] After the U.S. Supreme Court case was lost, Blow purchased freedom for the Scott family.[114] He posted bond for the Scotts in St. Louis, which was required for freed blacks to remain in Missouri.[115] Dred Scott died the next year, 1858, and Harriet lived until 1876.[116] Some of their descendants are with us today.

We are all heirs to the legacy of Dred and Harriet Scott. Their case is an important reminder, in the words of Judge Gamble, that there is "no safe basis for judicial decision, but in those principles which are immutable."[117] Dred and Harriet Scott are simple symbols of our greatest failure. Past struggles for freedom and equality echo today. History judges courts harshly when they abandon principle under undue political influence.

Let none of us forget our history.

Notes

1. There is a good description of some of the guerrilla activities during the Civil War in Missouri in T. J. Stiles, *Jesse James: Last Rebel of the Civil War* (New York: A. A. Knopf, 2002).

2. David Herbert Donald, *Lincoln* (New York: Simon and Schuster, 1995), 452.

3. Ibid., 452–53.

4. David Thomas Konig, "The Long Road to *Dred Scott:* Personhood and the Rule of Law in the Trial Court Records of St. Louis Slave Freedom Suits," *University of Missouri Kansas City Law Review* 75 (Fall 2006): 58–73.

5. Scott, a man of color, v. Emerson, 15 Mo. 576, 582 (Mo. 1852).

6. Dred Scott v. John F. A. Sandford, 60 U.S. (19 How.) 393 (1857).

7. The statutes known as the Missouri Compromise (1820) were struck down in the *Dred Scott* decision (ibid., 452).

8. Yale Law School, Avalon Project, Northwest Ordinance of 1787, http://www.yale.edu/lawweb/avalon/nworder.htm.

9. See The American Civil War Home Page, "Population of the United States: Border States, Missouri," http://www.civilwarhome.com/population1860.htm.

10. Dennis K. Boman, "The Dred Scott Case Reconsidered: The Legal and Political Context in Missouri," *American Journal of Legal History* 44 (October 2000): 414–15.

11. Ibid, 414–16.

12. Ibid., 405, 406.

13. Ibid., 407.

14. Konig, "Long Road to *Dred Scott,*" 68.

15. Boman, "Dred Scott Case Reconsidered," 406.

16. Ibid.

17. Konig, "Long Road to *Dred Scott.*"

18. See generally Boman, "Dred Scott Case Reconsidered"; Konig, "Long Road to *Dred Scott.*"

19. Konig, "Long Road to *Dred Scott,*" 70.

20. Boman, "Dred Scott Case Reconsidered," 414.

21. Ibid., 414–15.

22. Ibid., 407.

23. See Lawrence M. Friedman, *A History of American Law* (New York: Simon and Schuster, 1973), 340–433.

24. Ibid., 325.

25. Joseph Benson, "Quest for Freedom: The Dred Scott Cases in Missouri and American Legal History" (June 26, 2006) (unpublished manuscript, on file with the U.S. District Court for the Eastern District of Missouri).

26. Ibid.

27. Boman, "Dred Scott Case Reconsidered," 420–23.

28. Friedman, *History of American Law,* 323–24.

29. Adam Goldstein, "Judicial Selection as It Relates to Gender Equality on the Bench," *Cardozo Journal of Law and Gender* 13 (Spring 2007): 373.

30. F. Andrew Hanssen, "Learning about Judicial Independence: Institutional Change in the State Courts," *Journal of Legal Studies* 33, no. 2 (2004): 448.

31. Friedman, *History of American Law,* 325.

32. Hanssen, "Learning about Judicial Independence," 448.

33. "Judges of the Supreme Court of Missouri, 1821–2005," *Official Manual of the State of Missouri* (Jefferson City: Secretary of State, 2005): 232.

34. Ibid.

35. Ibid.

36. Boman, "Dred Scott Case Reconsidered," 423.

37. Ibid., 422.

38. Ibid., 417, 423, 426.

39. Ibid., 417.

40. "Judges of the Supreme Court of Missouri," 246.

41. Boman, "Dred Scott Case Reconsidered," 423.

42. Dennis K. Boman, *Lincoln's Resolute Unionist: Hamilton Gamble, Dred Scott Dissenter and Missouri's Civil War Governor* (Baton Rouge: Louisiana State University Press, 2006), 42.

43. Ibid.

44. Ibid., 43.

45. Boman, "Dred Scott Case Reconsidered," 426.

46. Paul Finkelman, "*Scott v. Sandford:* The Court's Most Dreadful Case and How It Changed History," *Chicago-Kent Law Review* 82, no. 1 (2007): 13–15.

47. Ibid., 14.

48. Ibid., 15.

49. Lea VanderVelde and Sandhya Subramanian, "Mrs. Dred Scott," *Yale Law Journal* 106, no. 4 (1997): 1041.

50. Ibid., 1046.

51. Ibid., 1042.

52. Ibid.

53. Ibid., 1057.

54. Ibid.

55. Finkelman, "*Scott v. Sandford,*" 22.

56. Ibid., 23.

57. Affidavit filed by Samuel M. Bay, July 10, 1847, and George W. Goode's appeal to the Missouri Supreme Court to overturn Hamilton's decision for retrial (Dred Scott documents in the archive files of the Supreme Court of Missouri).

58. Boman, "Dred Scott Case Reconsidered," 421.

59. Scott, a man of color, v. Emerson, 15 Mo. 576 (1852).

60. Bowman, "Dred Scott Case Reconsidered," 408, 413, 423.

61. For a description of the split in Missouri's Democratic Party on the issue of states' rights and slavery, a controversy that centered for a time on Senator Benton, see Dennis K. Boman, *Abiel Leonard: Yankee Slaveholder, Eminent Jurist, and Passionate Unionist* (Lewiston, N.Y.: E. Mellen Press, 2002), 145–58.

62. Boman, "Dred Scott Case Reconsidered," 417.

63. See also Boman, *Abiel Leonard.*

64. Ibid., 408–13.

65. Ibid., 422.

66. Scott, 15 Mo.

67. Boman, "Dred Scott Case Reconsidered," 422.

68. Scott, 15 Mo. at 589.

69. Ibid., 591–92 (Gamble, J., dissenting).

70. Finkelman, "*Scott v. Sandford*," 23–24.

71. The Scotts had many lawyers over the years, many of them prominent in the bar in St. Louis, and most worked without fee. The argument in the Supreme Court of the United States was presented by Montgomery Blair, later to be Lincoln's postmaster general and a close confidant of the president. George H. Shields, "The Old Bar of St. Louis," in *The History of the Bench and Bar of Missouri*, ed. A. J. D. Stewart, 2d ed. (St. Louis: Legal Pub., 1898), 116, cited in Benson, "Quest for Freedom," 44.

72. The defendant is identified by the Supreme Court as John F. A. Sandford. His name was Sanford.

73. Finkelman, "*Scott v. Sandford*," 23–24.

74. Cf. Swift v. Tyson, 41 U.S. 1 (1842); Erie Railroad v. Tompkins, 304 U.S. 64 (1938).

75. Scott, 60 U.S. at 396–97.

76. See generally Gerard N. Magliocca, "Preemptive Opinions: The Secret History of *Worcester v. Georgia* and *Dred Scott*," *University of Pittsburgh Law Review* 63, no. 3 (2002): 487–587.

77. Scott, 60 U.S. at 409–10.

78. Ibid., 410.

79. Ibid., 417.

80. Ibid., 418. Emphasis in original.

81. Ibid., 419–20. The majority opinion is cited in contemporary arguments about the reach of the Second Amendment. The majority in *Dred Scott* would not impute to the founding fathers the intent that blacks should be given the right "to keep and carry arms wherever they went" (ibid., 417). See Robert J. Cottrol and Raymond T. Diamond, "The Second Amendment: Toward an Afro-Americanist Reconsideration," *Georgetown Law Journal* 80, no. 2 (1991): 309–61.

82. Scott, 60 U.S. at 422.

83. Scott, 60 U.S.

84. Ibid., 430.

85. Ibid., 451–52.

86. Ibid., 405–6.

87. Ibid.

88. Marvin R. Cain, *Lincoln's Attorney General: Edward Bates of Missouri* (Columbia: University of Missouri Press, 1965), 101–2.

89. Ibid.

90. Ibid.

91. Albert K. Woldman, *Lawyer Lincoln* (New York: Carroll and Graf, 1936), 258–59.

92. Ibid.

93. Ibid.

94. Donald, *Lincoln,* 454.

95. Ibid.

96. Woldman, *Lawyer Lincoln,* 259.

97. Boman, *Lincoln's Resolute Unionist,* 99.

98. Ibid., 93.

99. Ibid., 105.

100. Ibid., 114.

101. Ibid., 115, 236–37.

102. Charles Neider, ed., *The Autobiography of Mark Twain* (New York: Harper Perennial, 1999), 133–34.

103. Ibid.

104. Ibid.

105. Ibid., 310–16.

106. See "Judges of the Supreme Court of Missouri."

107. Preface, 35 Mo. iii–vi (1865) contains the ordinance of the state convention, which was authorized by a vote of the people to amend the state constitution, vacating the offices of the supreme court judges as of May 1, 1865. The preface also contained the orders of the governor, acting as commander in chief of the military, for removal of judges refusing to leave office (iv–v).

108. "Special Order," 35 Mo. v.

109. "Letter from Gov. Fletcher to Gen. Coleman," June 14, 1865, ibid., v.

110. Boman, *Lincoln's Resolute Unionist,* 214.

111. Donald, *Lincoln,* 454. See also Cain, *Lincoln's Attorney General.*

112. "May Term of Court," *St. Louis County Court Record* 9 (1858). The record reflects that a bond of $1,000 each was secured by Taylor Blow as security, and the court ordered that "Dred Scott and Harriet Scott be severally licensed to remain in the State during good behaviour." The same record indicates that other "free negroes" had been jailed and brought to court lacking bonds and licenses. For them, the court ordered "that the Marshal inflict on the bare back of each of them ten lashes, and that they forthwith depart the State." This record was found by Clayton attorney Charles M. M. Shepherd and furnished to the author.

113. VanderVelde and Subramanian, "Mrs. Dred Scott," 1122n141.

114. Ibid.

115. Ibid.

116. Finkelman, "*Scott v. Sandford,*" 48n82.

117. Scott, 15 Mo. at 592.

FOURTEEN

The Strange Career of *Dred Scott*

From Fort Armstrong to Guantánamo Bay

Paul Finkelman

THIS BOOK emerged from a conference commemorating the one hundred and fiftieth anniversary of the *Dred Scott* decision, held, appropriately in St. Louis at Washington University. Dred Scott's case began in St. Louis, of course, and after ultimately losing his appeal in the U.S. Supreme Court his new owner manumitted him, and he lived the rest of his life in that city. Yet, if St. Louis was the appropriate venue for a conference on the case, was it appropriate to have a conference on the case?

The case involved Dred Scott's claim to freedom, based on his residence in a free state (Illinois) and a federal territory (present-day Minnesota) where slavery was banned under the Missouri Compromise, which had been passed in 1820. In *Dred Scott* the Supreme Court held three things: that blacks could never be citizens of the United States and, therefore, could never sue in federal court as citizens of a state; that Congress had no power to regulate the territories beyond setting up a minimalist form of government; and that the Bill of Rights was applicable to all federal territories and thus neither Congress nor a territorial government could ban slavery in the territories, because this would be an unconstitutional taking of property in violation of the Fifth Amendment.

How do we celebrate, or even commemorate, this case? The notion that we should commemorate the *Dred Scott* case is curious. No decision of the U.S. Supreme Court is more reviled or condemned. More than a century and a half after announcing the decision, Chief Justice Roger B. Taney's "opinion of the court" remains anathema to almost anyone familiar with the case. After Taney died, the Senate refused to appropriate funds for a commemorative bust, accepting Senator Charles Sumner's argument that "If a man has done evil during life he must not be complimented in marble." Sumner declared that Taney's "wicked opinion" was "more thoroughly abominable than anything of the kind in the history of courts." It was "a most unrighteous judgment" in which "every principle of Liberty was falsified." Rather than commemorate Taney, he urged that the space remain empty, where a bust of the departed chief justice might have been placed, "to speak in warning to all who would betray liberty." Sumner argued that "the name of Taney is to be hooted down the page of history."[1]

Since that time, the reputation of Taney has been contested, and despite valiant efforts by friends, independent scholars, and even Justice Felix Frankfurter his reputation has never been truly rehabilitated.[2] To this day justices rarely cite Taney's jurisprudence and even more rarely acknowledge his opinion in *Dred Scott*. If cited at all, it is mentioned as a poster child for bad decision making by the Court.

Almost no one today defends Taney's opinion or the racism on which it was built. *Dred Scott* is a universally condemned decision. Everyone— even those unschooled in constitutional law—knows that *Dred Scott* was a bad decision. For example, during the 2004 presidential debates, President George W. Bush offered up the *Dred Scott* case when asked to name a Supreme Court decision he opposed.[3] No one at the time imagined that he had actually read the case, or that he even knew anything about it. The reporters at the debate did not ask a follow-up question, which might have required Bush to explain what was wrong with the decision. Perhaps this was because they did not want to embarrass a sitting president who was not known for being well read or intellectually sophisticated. But they may have also believed there was no reason for a follow-up question. Everyone knew that *Dred Scott* was a bad decision. Indeed, the president's answer illustrates how *Dred Scott* has come to symbolize bad jurisprudence, or even "evil" in constitutional law.[4]

Almost all modern scholars and jurists agree that the decision was not merely wrong, but pernicious and just plain bad. Charles Evans Hughes argued that *Dred Scott* was one of "three notable instances [in which] the Court has suffered severely from self-inflicted wounds."[5] Similarly, Alexander Bickel of Yale Law School called it a "ghastly error."[6]

For more than a century justices have cited *Dred Scott* as the ultimate bad decision, citing it almost always in dissent, not for authority, but as a way of attacking those with whom they disagree on the Court.[7] When the Supreme Court voted 8–1 to uphold racial segregation in *Plessy v. Ferguson* (1896) Justice John Marshall Harlan, the lone dissenter, compared the Court's decision to *Dred Scott:* "In my opinion, the judgment this day rendered will, in time, prove to be quite as pernicious as the decision made by this tribunal in the *Dred Scott* case."[8] A half century later Justice Hugo Black dissented from a majority opinion in which North Carolina was allowed to deny full faith and credit to a Nevada court decree in a divorce case. Black noted that the underlying basis for the North Carolina decision (and implicitly the Supreme Court's decision upholding that result) was "the assumption that divorces are an unmitigated evil, and that the law can and should force unwilling persons to live with each other." Black analogized this Court's attempt to solve the issue of divorce to the Taney Court's attempt to solve the problem of slavery. Thus, Black wrote, "today's decision will no more aid in the solution of the problem than the *Dred Scott* decision aided in settling controversies over slavery."[9]

More recently Justices William Brennan and Antonin Scalia have accused majorities of acting like the *Dred Scott* Court. While dissenting in a death penalty case Brennan quoted *Dred Scott* to illustrate the way racism has long been a factor in American law. Brennan noted that the justices had only recently "sought to free ourselves from the burden of this history."[10] Similarly, Scalia complained in *Planned Parenthood of Southeastern Pennsylvania v. Casey* that the Court's decision was based not on "reasoned judgment" but only on "personal predilection," and he then quoted Justice Benjamin R. Curtis's dissent in *Dred Scott* to support his position.[11]

Justices have also used *Dred Scott* when they have opposed judicial nega-
tion of state or federal law, even when the particular justice might be sympathetic to a different outcome. *Washington v. Glucksberg,* which upheld
Washington State's ban on assisted suicide, illustrates this. Justice David
Souter dragged *Dred Scott* out from under the jurisprudential rock where
it is usually kept to argue that the Court should be cautious about second-
guessing a legislature. Souter wrote:

> *Dred Scott* was textually based on a Due Process Clause (in the
> Fifth Amendment, applicable to the National Government), and
> it was in reliance on that Clause's protection of property that
> the Court invalidated the Missouri Compromise. This substan-
> tive protection of an owner's property in a slave taken to the
> territories was traced to the absence of any enumerated power
> to affect that property granted to the Congress by Article I of
> the Constitution, the implication being that the Government
> had no legitimate interest that could support the earlier congres-
> sional compromise. The ensuing judgment of history needs no
> recounting here.[12]

Thus, while Souter might have personally opposed the Washington State
law, he used *Dred Scott* to explain why he could not support striking down
the law. Souter believed that this would have been the equivalent of overturning the Missouri Compromise. While this may be a highly exaggerated analysis, it nevertheless underscores how justices have used *Dred Scott*
to illustrate their unbending opposition to some jurisprudential move, in
this case the judicial interference with state laws.

Judges who cite *Dred Scott* today often see the decision as the product
of an overly ideological and reactionary judge—Chief Justice Taney—who
willingly overturned settled law in order to shape public policy to his own
views. The decision is further condemned for its poor scholarship and
weak legal reasoning. Modern judges and legal theorists with diametrically
opposed views on how to interpret the Constitution use *Dred Scott* as the
ultimate "bad" decision. Thus, originalists argue that Taney reached an
erroneous decision because he failed to follow the intent of the framers;
opponents of originalism point out—correctly, I think—that this is perhaps the most originalist opinion in the Court's history.[13]

The Case Itself

The initial response to *Dred Scott* was more complex than the modern view. Republicans famously attacked the decision, and some, like Abraham Lincoln, successfully exploited it to their political advantage. Northern Democrats were generally pleased with the outcome, although it put their leading candidate for the 1860 presidential election, Stephen A. Douglas, in an awkward position.[14] Almost all southern whites were thrilled by the decision, although a few fire-eaters predicted, correctly, that the case would not end antislavery activism. Northern abolitionists met the decision with mixed emotions. All attacked Taney, but some welcomed the opinion because it exposed the proslavery nature of the Constitution or because they believed it would stimulate more antislavery activism. Frederick Douglass deplored Taney's racism but predicted, correctly, that the decision would enhance the struggle for freedom. To understand these responses, a brief overview of the case is in order.

Scott was born a slave in Virginia sometime between 1795 and 1800. Around 1830 his owner, Peter Blow, moved to St. Louis, where he died in 1832. Shortly after Blow's death, Dr. John Emerson, a captain and surgeon in the U.S. Army, purchased Scott.

In December 1833 the army sent Emerson to Fort Armstrong, in present-day Rock Island, Illinois. At the time army officers were expected to provide their own personal servants, and thus Emerson brought Scott with him, despite the fact that both the Northwest Ordinance of 1787 and the Illinois Constitution of 1818 prohibited slavery in Illinois. Yet, despite the Ordinance of 1787 and the state constitution, hundreds of blacks remained in slavery in Illinois into the 1830s. These people had been held as slaves before statehood or were the descendants of slaves living in Illinois before 1787. At this time no Illinois court had ever ruled on the status of these slaves, although in other parts of the Old Northwest slaves gained their freedom directly under the ordinance, or with statehood. While some people lingered in slavery in Illinois until the 1840s, however, it was generally understood that no new slaves could be brought into the state.[15] Under Illinois law Scott had a claim to freedom while in the state, but he failed to assert it.

Had Emerson lived inside Fort Armstrong and kept Scott on the base he might have claimed that he was exempt from local law, because he was in federal service while in Illinois and living on federal land. Such an argument would have mirrored Chief Justice John Marshall's opinion in *McCulloch* v. *Maryland*.[16] In concluding that Maryland could not tax the Bank of the United States, Marshall argued that an alternative result would allow the states to tax military bases, which would undermine the ability of the national government to maintain the army. The same logic could have applied to the status of military personnel on military bases. Surely, Emerson might have argued, an Illinois sheriff could not enter a military base to serve a writ of habeas corpus on a slaveholding officer if that officer had not taken his slave off the base.[17]

This theoretical right to hold a slave at Fort Armstrong did not actually apply to Emerson, since he had in fact purchased land off the base and lived on it with Scott. Between 1834 and 1836 Emerson purchased land in Illinois and built a cabin on it. He almost certainly used Scott to help build this cabin. These facts further supported a claim to freedom for Scott because Emerson appeared to be establishing some sort of residence or permanency in the state, even though he was in the army.

Thus, Scott might have sued for his freedom in Illinois, claiming he had been brought to the state, held there as a slave under the state's jurisdiction, and made to work as a slave. But, whatever claims to freedom Scott might have had in Illinois, he never exercised them there. Perhaps he had no interest in trying to support himself on the rough Illinois frontier. Or perhaps he did not even know he might have a right to be free. In any event, by the end of 1836 Scott was no longer in Illinois. In 1836 the army transferred Emerson to Fort Snelling, in what was then the Wisconsin Territory and later became the state of Minnesota. Emerson brought Scott with him.

Congress had banned slavery in this region in the Missouri Compromise of 1820 and reaffirmed the ban in the Wisconsin Enabling Act of 1836. Once again, Scott was in a place where slavery was illegal, and once again he did not seek his freedom. Shortly after arriving at Fort Snelling, Scott married Harriet Robinson, a slave owned by Major Lawrence Taliaferro, the fort's Indian agent. Taliaferro was also a justice of the peace, and in that capacity he performed a marriage ceremony for the two slaves. Some modern scholars have made much of this fact,[18] arguing that the marriage ceremony proves that Scott was free when living at Fort Snelling. This analysis is based on the fact that slaves could not legally marry, and thus, if a justice of the peace performed their marriage ceremony, it must be because Dred Scott and Harriet Robinson were free. This argument, however, is ultimately unimpressive because there is no actual connection between the ceremony performed by Taliaferro and a legal marriage contract. Throughout the South slave owners often solemnized slave unions with ceremonies. Southern masters understood that stable slave families were likely to produce children, which would increase the wealth of master. They also understood that married slaves were less likely to run away. Furthermore, many masters were evangelical Christians who believed in formal marriages for their slaves. It was quite common, for example, for ministers to officiate at weddings for slaves. Like justices of the peace, ministers had the legal power to perform marriages. This does not mean, however, that such slave unions were legally recognized marriages, or that allowing slaves to exchange vows before a minister or a justice of the peace constituted a de facto emancipation. A serious understanding of the law of slavery undermines the claim that the wedding performed by Taliaferro had any legal significance for Dred or Harriet Scott. They were still slaves, and still subject to the whim of their master, who could have sold them apart or even forced them to live apart without selling them. Slaves and masters alike understood that slave unions existed for the convenience of the master and were never legal marriages.

Another indication that the Scotts were not free came in the spring of 1837, when Emerson was transferred to Jefferson Barracks in St. Louis, but left Dred and Harriet Scott at Fort Snelling, where they were hired out. Obviously Emerson could not have hired out the Scotts and kept the rental income if he did not own them. Furthermore, his fellow officers, who paid Emerson, would not have given the rental income to him if they thought Dred and Harriet Scott were free. More important, Taliaferro, who was among the most influential men at Fort Snelling, would surely have intervened to protect the recently manumitted Scotts if they were free. But neither Taliaferro nor anyone else lifted a finger to help Dred and Harriet Scott gain their liberty, because everyone there understood that they were in fact slaves.[19]

Harriet and Dred Scott might have had a claim to freedom because they had been rented out in a free jurisdiction. Under the laws of most free states, and even under the laws of a number of slave states, the hiring of a slave in a free state constituted an unlawful attempt to import the system of slavery into a free jurisdiction. Thus, even if Emerson might have claimed an exemption from federal law while he was at Fort Snelling, on the grounds that as an army officer he was not only entitled to a servant but was expected to have one, he could certainly not have argued that as an officer he was entitled to rent out a slave in a territory where slavery was banned under federal law while he was not even in that territory. Yet, whatever claims the Scotts might have had to freedom, Dred Scott did not exercise them at this time. Moreover, no one at the base, including Talia-ferro (the one person who might have thought they were free because he had married them) helped the Scotts assert their freedom. At Fort Snelling, whether under the direct control of Taliaferro, Emerson, or someone who hired their services from Emerson, Dred and Harriet Scott were slaves.

After a brief stay in St. Louis, Emerson was transferred once again, this time to Fort Jessup in Louisiana. There he met and married Eliza Irene Sanford in the spring of 1838. Emerson now needed his slaves as domestic servants in his new household, and he sent word to Fort Snelling, ordering the Scotts to come to Louisiana. Dred and Harriet Scott then traveled al-most the entire length of the Mississippi River to reach their owner and his new wife. This is perhaps the most astounding aspect of the saga of Dred Scott. No historian has been able to explain why the Scotts would have traveled all alone, more than a thousand miles, to reach Louisiana. They might have left their steamboat in St. Louis and melted into the large free black community there. They might have landed in the free state of Illinois and made their way north and east to a more secure freedom. They might have stopped off in the Iowa territory, where Quaker communities would have welcomed them. If the Scotts thought they were free, it makes no sense that they dutifully went to the deep South when Emerson commanded them to do so. The only plausible explanation is that the Scotts believed they were slaves and had no desire to live the life of fugitives. Perhaps they expected Emerson to free them at some point or perhaps they just found their service to him to be a better alternative to fending for themselves as runaway slaves in a world where even free blacks had few rights.

In any event, the Scotts reached Louisiana in the spring of 1838, but the following fall Emerson, his wife, and his slaves went back to Fort Snelling. On this journey, Harriet Scott gave birth to their first child, Eliza, while on board a boat on the Mississippi River, between the free territory that later became Iowa and the free state of Illinois. In the spring of 1840 the whole entourage returned to St. Louis, and then Emerson went on to Florida to serve in the Second Seminole War. In the fall of 1842, Emerson returned to St. Louis and left the army. The following spring he left his family and slaves in St. Louis and moved to Davenport, in the Iowa territory, where he died in December 1843.

In 1846 Dred Scott tried to purchase his freedom, but Irene Emerson had no interest in giving up her slaves. A middle-class widow, she needed the Scotts to run her household, and selling them their freedom would only necessitate that she buy more slaves. Unable to buy his freedom, on April 6, 1846, Dred Scott sued for his freedom, and that of his family. The suit was based on his residence in Illinois and the Wisconsin Territory, Harriet's residence in the Wisconsin Territory, and Eliza's birth in a free territory and subsequent residence in the Wisconsin Territory. While the suit was pending Harriet Scott gave birth to her second daughter, Lizzie. Her claim to freedom was based on the claim that her mother was free at the time of Lizzie's birth.

In June 1847 the case finally went to court, but Scott lost on a technicality, because he failed to provide a witness to prove that the defendant, Irene Emerson, was actually his owner. As Don E. Fehrenbacher noted in his Pulitzer Prize–winning study of the case, "The decision produced the absurd effect of allowing Mrs. Emerson to keep her slaves simply because no one had proved that they *were* her slaves."[20] In December, the judge who heard the case granted the Scotts a new trial, but Emerson appealed this ruling to the Missouri Supreme Court. In April 1849 the Missouri Supreme Court upheld the order granting a new trial. The case was docketed for early 1848 but was postponed because of a huge fire and cholera epidemic in St. Louis. Meanwhile, Emerson moved to Springfield, Massachusetts, and left her legal affairs in the hands of her brother, John F. A. Sanford. In January 1850 *Scott v. Emerson* finally reached the St. Louis Circuit Court, where a jury of twelve white men concluded that Dred and Harriet Scott and their two daughters were entitled to their freedom. Sanford, acting on behalf of his sister, appealed to the Missouri Supreme Court.

Under existing precedents, this should have been an easy victory for Scott. Starting in 1824 the Missouri Supreme Court had consistently ruled that slaves gained their freedom through residence in free states.[21] In 1836, while Dred Scott was at Fort Snelling, the Missouri Supreme Court ruled that military officers were *not* exempt from the law of the free states and that, if an officer brought his slave to a free state or territory, that slave became free.[22] By 1850 the Missouri Supreme Court had reached a similar decision in at least a dozen cases.[23] Scores of slaves had been emancipated in St. Louis in cases similar to Dred Scott's.[24] Thus, his victory should have been affirmed.

But it was not. By 1852, when the case finally reached the Missouri Supreme Court, a sea change had taken place in state politics. An elected Supreme Court had replaced an appointed one, and two of the three justices were aggressively proslavery. Thus, in *Scott v. Emerson,* the Missouri Supreme Court reversed the lower court and twenty-eight years of precedents.[25] The Scotts' hopes for freedom were once again dashed. In a frankly political opinion Chief Justice William Scott declared:

> Times are not now as they were when the former decisions on
> this subject were made. Since then not only individuals but
> States have been possessed with a dark and fell spirit in relation
> to slavery, whose gratification is sought in the pursuit of mea-
> sures, whose inevitable consequence must be the overthrow and
> destruction of our government. Under such circumstances it does
> not behoove the State of Missouri to show the least countenance
> to any measure which might gratify this spirit. She is willing to
> assume her full responsibility for the existence of slavery within
> her limits, nor does she seek to share or divide it with others.[26]

The decision by the Missouri Supreme Court probably came as a relief to both Emerson's widow, Irene, and her brother, John Sanford. After nearly six years, the case seemed finally over. But it was not.

In November 1850 Irene Emerson had married Dr. Calvin C. Chaffee, a Springfield, Massachusetts, physician with antislavery leanings who would later serve in Congress as a Know-Nothing (1855–1857) and a Republican (1857–1859). Although no longer in Missouri, Irene Emerson had remained the defendant in Dred Scott's freedom suit before the Missouri state courts while her brother had acted on her behalf in defending the case. With the case finally settled by the Missouri Supreme Court, Irene cut her ties to Dred Scott and either sold him or transferred her ownership to her brother, who was a prosperous businessman in New York City, but with extensive family and professional ties to St. Louis. This set the stage for a federal court case. In 1854 Scott's newest lawyer, Vermont-born Roswell Field, took over the case.[27] Field conceived a rather brilliant strategy—to bring the case into federal court under diversity jurisdiction as set out in Article 3 of the U.S. Constitution. Field argued that Scott was a free person and as such was a "citizen" of Missouri and thus entitled to sue Sanford, a citizen of New York, in federal court. Field's position assumed two points that were as yet unproved: first, that Scott was indeed free and, second, that *if* free, he was also a citizen of Missouri.

By suing in diversity—a suit between citizens of different states—Scott's lawyer assumed the outcome of the case: that Scott was actually free. This was not unusual. In freedom suits Southern state courts regularly accepted a legal fiction that the plaintiff was "free" and therefore had standing to sue. If the court ultimately ruled against the slave plaintiff, the jurisdictional issues disappeared because the defendant continued to own the slave. This is in fact what had happened in Dred Scott's case in the Missouri courts.

In the state case, however, the second issue—the claim of "citizenship"— never arose. A black person did not need be a "citizen" of a state to sue in state court. He or she only had to be "free," or at least have a plausible claim to be free. But this was not true in a diversity suit in federal court. For Scott to sue in federal court, under diversity jurisdiction, the court had to accept the argument that a free black living in Missouri was a citizen of that state and, implicitly, a citizen of the United States.

Although a citizen of New York, Sanford continued to exert control over the Scotts. He also continued to defend the case, because the Scott family constituted a valuable asset. Since early in the litigation, Scott had been in the immediate custody of the sheriff of St. Louis County. The sheriff had been renting Scott and his family out, collecting the rent, and holding the money in escrow until the case was finally settled. By this time a tidy sum of money had accumulated. The winner of the case—either Scott or his owner—would get this money once the case was finally settled. If the Scotts won, they would also become free.

Thus, in 1854, Scott sued John Sanford in federal circuit court for battery and wrongful imprisonment. Scott asked for $9,000 in damages. The complaint and the claim of damages were essentially legal fictions, designed to bring the issue of Scott's freedom into federal court with enough of a damage claim to allow an appeal to the Supreme Court. Scott's goal was, not substantial monetary damages, but only a token sum, which would prove that he was free. Scott's suit was against John Sanford, because at this point Sanford was the one holding Scott in slavery. Historians disagree over whether this was because Irene (Emerson) Chaffee had sold or given Scott to Sanford or because Sanford was simply acting as her agent. The debate is of little importance. Scott sued Sanford, and Sanford never denied he was the appropriate party to be sued. Instead, he responded to the suit. Sanford knew that he was the one holding Scott in slavery. If Scott were legitimately free, Sanford was wrongfully imprisoning him. Sanford's residence in New York allowed for the diversity claim and thus federal jurisdiction for the case. But Scott did not *need* to sue Sanford to get diversity, because if Sanford did not own the Scotts then his sister Irene did, and as Irene Emerson Chaffee she was now a citizen of Massachusetts.

Sanford responded to the new federal case by denying that the federal courts had jurisdiction over the parties because whatever he was—whether slave or free—Dred Scott could not be a citizen of Missouri. To challenge the court's jurisdiction Sanford filed a plea in abatement, asserting that "Dred Scott, is not a citizen of the State of Missouri, as alleged in his declaration, because he is a negro of African descent; his ancestors were of pure African blood, and were brought into this country and sold as negro slaves."[28] This was not a pleading about the substance of the case—whether Scott was free. Rather, Sanford argued that, even if Dred Scott were legally free, he could not vindicate that freedom in a federal diversity suit because free blacks were emphatically *not* citizens of Missouri.

U.S. district court judge Robert W. Wells rejected Sanford's plea, essentially concluding that *if* Dred Scott was free he must be a citizen where he lived. As a slave owner who migrated from Virginia, Wells was not an advocate of black equality or an opponent of slavery. But he did believe that free blacks were entitled to at least some minimal legal rights, including the right to sue in a federal court. In other words, Wells believed that if Scott were free he could sue in federal court to determine if Sanford had illegally harmed him. In reaching this conclusion, Wells did not declare that Scott, or any free black, was entitled to legal, social, or political equality in Missouri or anywhere else in the country. Wells merely held that the term "citizen" in Article 3 of the Constitution was equivalent to a free (not enslaved) resident of a state. If Dred Scott was in fact not a slave, then he met this minimal criterion and was a "citizen" solely for the purpose of suing in federal court.

By rejecting Sanford's plea in abatement, Wells forced Sanford to defend the case on the merits. Sanford responded with a series of pro forma pleas that responded in kind to Scott's pro forma complaint. Scott alleged Sanford had illegally restrained him of his liberty and committed assault and battery on him. Sanford responded that he had not unlawfully harmed Scott and his family. Sanford admitted that he had "restrained them of their liberty" but he asserted "he had a right to do" this because Scott was his slave.[29] Sanford also did not deny that he had "gently laid his hands upon" Scott and his family. In essence, Sanford admitted that he had done all the things of which Scott complained, although with a "humane" spin on the facts. But Sanford argued he was entitled to treat Scott in this manner because he legally owned Scott.

In May 1854 the case went to trial. Wells told the jury that Scott's status was to be determined by Missouri law. Since the Missouri Supreme Court had already decided that Scott was a slave, the federal jury upheld his status as a slave. If an Illinois court or a Wisconsin territorial court had previously declared Scott free, then the result might have been different. Wells might then have held that, under the full faith and credit clause of the Constitution, Missouri was obligated to recognize the judicial proceedings that had emancipated Scott. But no such proceeding had in fact ever taken place in Illinois or in the Wisconsin Territory. Thus, Scott and his family remained slaves.

Dred Scott then appealed to the U.S. Supreme Court, arguing that under the Missouri Compromise, the Wisconsin Enabling Act, and other federal and territorial laws he was free. Because he had won the case, Sanford appealed nothing. Thus, the jurisdictional question—whether free blacks could be citizens for purposes of diversity—was not technically before the Supreme Court. However, Courts always have the right, indeed the obligation, to question their own jurisdiction. In doing so, Taney ruled that blacks, even if born free, could never be citizens of the United States and thus could never sue in federal court. The way Taney framed the issue in his opinion indicates his determination to use the case to decide the status of blacks in America. Taney wrote: "The question is simply this: Can a negro, whose ancestors were imported into this country, and sold as slaves, become a member of the political community formed and brought into existence by the Constitution of the United States, and as such become entitled to all the rights, and privileges, and immunities, guarantied by that instrument to the citizen? One of which rights is the privilege of suing in a court of the United States in the cases specified in the Constitution."[30] In answering this question Taney used some of the most racist language in American jurisprudence, arguing that at the nation's founding blacks were "not included, and were not intended to be included, under the word 'citizens' in the Constitution, and can therefore claim none of the rights and privileges which the instrument provides for and secures to citizens of the United States. On the contrary, they were at that time [1787] considered as a subordinate and inferior class of beings, who had been subjugated by the dominant race, and, whether emancipated or not, yet remained subject to their authority, and had no rights or privileges but such as those who held the power and the Government might choose to grant them."[31] According to Taney, blacks were "so far inferior, that they had no rights which the white man was bound to respect."[32] Thus, he concluded that blacks could never be citizens of the United States, even if they were born in this country and considered to be citizens of the states in which they lived. Taney in effect argued that the Constitution created a kind of dual citizenship—state and federal—and that, while the states might make anyone a citizen, federal citizenship was limited only to whites because it was impossible for Taney to imagine that the Southern founders of the nation would have agreed to the Constitution if blacks were to be citizens.

Taney also held that Congress had no power to ban slavery in the territories because its power to regulate the territories was limited to setting up a basic structure of government. Otherwise, the territories would be treated like colonies, which, Taney argued, ran counter to the fundamental nature of American history. Finally, Taney also argued that, even if Congress could regulate the territories, it could not ban slaves because slaves were a constitutionally protected form of private property and, indeed, a specially protected form of property. He argued that the Bill of Rights applied to federal territories—that in effect the Constitution "followed the flag"[33]—and thus "an act of Congress which deprives a citizen of the United States of his liberty or property, merely because he came himself or brought his property into a particular Territory of the United States, and who had committed no offence against the laws, could hardly be dignified with the name of due process of law."[34]

In reaching this conclusion Taney held that the Missouri Compromise, in force since 1820, was unconstitutional. This was only the second time in U.S. history that the Court had held an act of Congress to be unconstitutional. The last time had been in 1803 when the Court struck down a minor provision of the Judiciary Act of 1803 in *Marbury v. Madison*. But here the Court struck down a major statute—one of the most important in the nation's political history—and one that had been in force for thirty-seven years. This was truly a bombshell and, combined with the racism of Taney's opinion, led to a huge backlash against the decision in much of the North.

What Taney Thought He Had Accomplished

The racism of the decision and its proslavery implications have consigned Taney's opinion to infamy in constitutional law and American history. Abraham Lincoln's incisive criticisms of the opinion in his debates with Stephen A. Douglas in 1858 and in the following two years have further made the case an anathema for constitutional law scholars. But, surely, Taney and the other six justices in the majority did not believe it was an error. To understand the decision we must look at it from the perspective of the chief justice.

Taney's conclusion that blacks could never be citizens of the United States was hardly a new idea for him. As Andrew Jackson's attorney general, Taney had opposed giving blacks passports on the grounds that they could not be citizens. This part of the opinion was hardly an aberration for Taney; it was something he had long believed. More importantly, Taney believed the nation supported him on this. Taney was clearly wrong in asserting that blacks were not citizens at the founding. In 1787 blacks voted in at least six states (Massachusetts, New Hampshire, New York, New Jersey, Pennsylvania, and North Carolina) and thus took part in the ratification of the Constitution. By 1800 Vermont and Tennessee had also enfranchised blacks. Since 1800 free blacks had lost the right to vote in

New Jersey, Pennsylvania, North Carolina, and Tennessee. When New York expanded the vote for whites by eliminating a property requirement, it did not do so for blacks. Blacks were denied the right to vote in fourteen of the fifteen new states admitted from 1803 to 1857. Maine, the one state that did enfranchise blacks, was an offshoot of Massachusetts. In 1857 Illinois, Indiana, and almost every Southern state prohibited black migration. They faced at least some kind of legal discrimination in every state, except perhaps the four in northern New England. In most of the South they could not attend school or even learn to read and write. In all of the South and in some of the North they could not testify against whites.

There had been some significant improvements for the status of blacks in the North in the decade and a half preceding *Dred Scott*. Ohio, for example, repealed most of its black laws in 1849, and Michigan gave blacks the right to vote in school-tax elections. Blacks had held public office in a few Northern states. But Taney did not think these changes mattered much. He saw only the vast discrimination that blacks faced everywhere in the South and in much of the North. Free blacks were equal citizens in a few Northern states, but none were citizens in the South, and in most of the North they were at best second-class citizens. While a few states like Massachusetts might let blacks vote, hold office, or practice law, most did not. Moreover, most whites were not prepared to see blacks sitting in Congress or arguing cases before federal courts. Thus, Taney saw himself as settling, once and for all, the status of free blacks in the nation. Moreover, he believed that he was settling this issue in a way that comported with the views of the vast majority of white Americans. Thus, Taney wrote African Americans out of the Constitution, convinced that this would be supported by most white Americans.

He was of course wrong in his assumptions. Many white Northerners who were conventionally racist and did not want blacks to have significant rights still believed they had some rights. They were shocked by the boldness of Taney's racism and his slanted, one-sided, and often wrong history of the founding. Free blacks had, after all, voted in at least six states when the Constitution was ratified. It was simply impossible for these Northerners—typified by Lincoln—to accept that free blacks had "no rights" under the Constitution. Even some white Southerners were not willing to accept the idea.[35]

While most modern Americans focus on the racism of the decision, that was not the most controversial part for Taney's contemporaries. Many Northerners did not like the racism, but they could have accepted it. Other white Northerners agreed with the racism, as did almost all white Southerners. Far more controversial was Taney's conclusion that the Missouri Compromise was unconstitutional. This was the great bombshell, the reason it has been properly characterized as a "self-inflicted wound." Taney did not have to reach this conclusion. Taney could easily have dismissed the suit with his holding that Scott had no standing to sue as a citizen of Missouri. This would have been the most narrow result and would have quietly disposed of the case.[36] If Scott could not sue, then there was no case before Taney, and he could have simply ended his opinion and affirmed Scott's status as a slave. Alternatively, following the precedent of *Strader v. Graham*[37] the Court could simply have held that the status of anyone (except a fugitive slave) was entirely at the discretion of the state where the person was found, and since Missouri had held Scott was a slave the federal courts had no say in the matter. Initially the Court planned to decide the case this way, and Justice Samuel Nelson of New York drafted an opinion that reflected this view of the law. Nelson's concurring opinion took this position.

But Taney and the Southern majority on the Court were not satisfied with that approach. Taney hoped to use this case to settle the long-standing controversy over slavery in the territories. He saw this case as an opportunity to move the nation forward by ending the debate over slavery in the territories and giving the South a great legal and political victory. In retrospect, it was a disastrous move. But Taney had believed that the majority of Americans wanted him to reach this result.

From the beginning of the nation, slavery had bedeviled American politics. In the Continental Congress delegates debated whether to count slaves when creating quotas for the troops each state needed to supply to the Revolutionary army. Slavery occupied a great deal of the attention of the delegates to the Constitutional Convention. While the Convention met in Philadelphia, the Congress under the Articles of Confederation, meeting in New York, passed the Northwest Ordinance, which banned slavery in the territories north of the Ohio River while implicitly allowing slavery in the Southern territories.[38] In 1819–20 Congress had vitriolic debates over the status of slavery and, in the end, restricted slavery once again in the western territories, by admitting Missouri to the Union as a slave state but otherwise banning the institution north of the 36° 30' parallel, which was the southern boundary of Missouri. This law, the Missouri Compromise, formed the basis of Dred Scott's claim to freedom from his residence at Fort Snelling.

Many Northerners, such as Abraham Lincoln, considered the Northwest Ordinance and the Missouri Compromise to be almost sacred documents, which guaranteed that the spread of slavery into the West would stop. These laws would, as Lincoln put it in his House Divided Speech, "arrest the further spread of [slavery], and place it where the public mind shall rest in the belief that it is in the course of ultimate extinction."[39] The territory of the Old Northwest was successfully organized with a ban on slavery, and by 1850 it had produced five free states: Ohio (1803), Indiana (1816), Illinois (1818), Michigan (1836), and Wisconsin (1848). This was a legacy of the founding that Congress had always respected. From 1820 until 1850 all the territories north of the 36° 30' parallel were also organized with a ban on slavery. This was the implementation of the Missouri Compromise that Lincoln and others held sacred. In 1820 Americans could look forward to a time when the majority of the nation would be dominated by free states in the region that eventually was carved up into Iowa, Minnesota, Kansas, Nebraska, the Dakotas, Montana, Idaho, Oregon, and Washington. After the admission of Missouri, in 1821, the only federal territories where slavery was allowed were the present-day states of Florida, Arkansas, and Oklahoma.

Despite the promise of the Northwest Ordinance and the Missouri Compromise, the Act of 1820 was the *last* significant restriction of the spread of slavery before the Civil War. Following the Missouri Compromise Congress continually expanded the reach of slavery.

In 1821 the United States formally acquired Florida with slavery already there, and statutes creating the Florida Territory placed no limitation on the institution. In 1845 the nation annexed Texas as a vast "Empire for Slavery" that could be divided, if necessary, into a total of five states. Had this happened it would have vastly increased the power of the South in the Senate. In 1846 Congress declared war against Mexico. During and immediately after the war, Northerners in Congress pushed the Wilmot Proviso to ban slavery in the new territories, but it was always blocked in the Senate. In the Compromise of 1850 Congress organized the territories recently acquired from Mexico without regard to slavery, even though some of the territories were north of the 36° 30' parallel. In 1853 Congress authorized the Gadsden Purchase, which added yet more land to the territories where slavery was permitted. Finally, in the Kansas-Nebraska Act of 1854 Congress organized a vast swath of land without a ban on slavery, even though all of that land was part of the territory originally covered by the Missouri Compromise. The 1854 act allowed slavery in all or part of the present-day states of Kansas, Nebraska, South Dakota, North Dakota, Wyoming, Montana, and Idaho. Thus, in 1857 slavery was allowed in almost all the federal territories. It was prohibited in only two territories—Minnesota and Oregon (which included present-day Oregon, Washington, and much of Idaho). Slavery was allowed in all the remaining western territories—the present-day states of Kansas, Nebraska, Colorado, South Dakota, North Dakota, Montana, Wyoming, Nevada, Utah, Arizona, and New Mexico.

The Kansas-Nebraska Act infuriated the majority of Northerners and led to the creation of the Republican Party. Quickly the party gained enormous political strength and, in 1856, ran a popular hero, John C. Frémont, in an aggressive national presidential campaign against the Kansas-Nebraska Act. Frémont won eleven states. The Republicans made the election of 1856 a national referendum on Kansas-Nebraska, and they failed to carry the election.

Since 1850 Congress, the executive branch, and the electorate had consistently supported the spread of slavery into the territories and the piecemeal dismantling of the Missouri Compromise. In 1857, when Taney looked at the expansion of the United States and the growth of slave territories in the nation, he did not see the sacredness of the Missouri Compromise with its implicit limitation on the spread of slavery. Instead he saw an intense expansion of slavery after 1820. Thus, from Taney's perspective, his conclusions about slavery in the territories seemed popular, and his ruling on the Missouri Compromise would not be controversial. On the contrary, he was simply finishing off a process of expanding slavery that began in 1821 with the acquisition of Florida and had continued until the Kansas-Nebraska Act of 1854 and the election of 1856, which confirmed national support for that act. It was of course a disastrous miscalculation.

Dred Scott in History: The Long View

The response to the decision was regional and political. White Southerners mostly loved the decision, although a few cautioned against the idea that it would solve all the South's problems. Democrats in the North liked it because they believed it would destroy the Republican Party and guarantee their political success. Taney declared that Congress could not ban slavery in the territories, and this meant that the raison d'être for the Republican Party was unconstitutional. Taney's opinion undermined Stephen A. Douglas's theory of popular sovereignty, but it also had the potential of taking the whole issue of slavery out of the political debate. If that had happened, the Democrats would have continued their dominance of American politics, which had been in place since the election of Andrew Jackson in 1828.

Of course that did not happen. The Republicans did not pack their tents and leave the field. Instead, they vigorously disputed the legitimacy of Taney's conclusions about federal power in the territories and the right of Congress to prohibit slavery. The most articulate critic of the decision was an obscure lawyer and small-time politician from Illinois who did not even hold a public office. But Abraham Lincoln's attacks on Taney's decision and the other opinions in the case resonated throughout the Midwest and then the entire North. His prediction that the Supreme Court would legalize slavery in the North had rhetorical power and logical appeal. While accepting the Republican nomination for the Senate in 1858 he declared that "ere long" we shall see "another Supreme Court decision, declaring that the Constitution of the United States does not permit a State to exclude slavery from its limits." He warned, "We shall lie down pleasantly dreaming that the people of Missouri are on the verge of making their State free, and we shall awake to the reality instead, that the Supreme Court has made Illinois a slave State."[40]

Northerners found this to be logical. And nothing in *Dred Scott* led them to think otherwise. Justice Samuel Nelson had noted in his concurring opinion, "A question has been alluded to, on the argument: namely: the right of the master with his slave of transit into or through a free State, on business or commercial pursuits, or in the exercise of a Federal, or the discharge of a Federal duty, being a citizen of the United States. . . ." Nelson ominously noted, "This question . . . turns upon the rights and privileges secured to a common citizen of the republic under the Constitution of the United States. When that question arises, we shall be prepared to decide it."[41] The "next" *Dred Scott* decision would legalize taking slave into the North.

Thus, *Dred Scott* made Northerners worry that their way of life was in danger. They might not face tobacco plantations in Pennsylvania, but they might soon face slaves and slavery in their midst. Salmon P. Chase, who would be Lincoln's rival for the Republican nomination in 1860, feared that the successor case to *Dred Scott* would be "a decision in favor . . . of the American slave trade, to be carried on in the free states." Horace Greeley predicted that "we shall see men buying slaves for the New York market. There will be no legal power to prevent it."[42]

Thus, *Dred Scott* stimulated Republicans to fight harder to gain control of Congress and the White House. More important, it led Northerners to join the new party, and thus by 1860 Lincoln could carry all of the free states and win the election. *Dred Scott* did not cause the Civil War, as some commentators have said, but it certainly helped put Lincoln in the White House.

In the end Taney's opinion backfired and gave to those he feared most— the political opponents of slavery—the ammunition they needed to win the election. This did lead to the war and to undermining Taney's reputation. Taney and *his* great case were consigned to historical and jurisprudential oblivion, and deservedly so.

But there is one part of Taney's opinion that ought to be reconsidered on the sesquicentennial of the case. Taney argued that the Missouri Compromise was unconstitutional because it took property away from masters without due process or just compensation. In making this point Taney argued that the Constitution followed the American flag into the territories:

> But the power of Congress over the person or property of a citizen . . . [is] regulated and plainly defined by the Constitution itself. And when the Territory becomes a part of the United States, the Federal Government enters . . . upon it with its powers over the citizen strictly defined, and limited by the Constitution. . . . It has no power of any kind beyond it; and it cannot, when it enters a Territory of the United States, put off its character, and assume discretionary or despotic powers which the Constitution has denied to it . . . and the Federal Government can exercise no power over his person or property, beyond what that instrument confers, nor lawfully deny any right which it has reserved.[43]

Taney went on to argue that neither Congress nor a temporary territorial government could violate the Bill of Rights: "For example, no one, we presume, will contend that Congress can make any law in a Territory respecting the establishment of religion, or the free exercise thereof, or abridging the freedom of speech or of the press, or the right of the people of the Territory peaceably to assemble, and to petition the Government for the redress of grievances."[44] Similarly, Taney asserted that neither Congress nor the local government could abridge "the right to trial by jury, nor compel any one to be a witness against himself in a criminal proceeding."[45] Taney applied this logic to slavery:

> Thus the rights of property are united with the rights of person, and placed on the same ground by the fifth amendment to the Constitution, which provides that no person shall be deprived of life, liberty, and property, without due process of law. And an act of Congress which deprives a citizen of the United States of his liberty or property, merely because he came himself or brought his property into a particular Territory of the United States, and who had committed no offence against the laws, could hardly be dignified with the name of due process of law.[46]

For a century the American flag has flown over a base in Cuba, as well as on other foreign places. It is not absurd to wonder whether more than a century and a half after *Dred Scott* it is not time to revisit this portion of Taney's opinion and salvage a little bit of liberty from a decision that in other ways is a symbol of constitutional evil and a denial of human rights.

Notes

1. *Congressional Globe*, 38th Cong., 2d sess., 1012–17 (February 23, 1865), reprinted in Paul Finkelman, *Dred Scott v. Sandford: A Brief History* (Boston: Bedford Books, 1995), 221–26.

2. Paul Finkelman, "'Hooted Down the Page of History': Reconsidering the Greatness of Chief Justice Taney," *Journal of Supreme Court History* 1994 (1994): 83–102.

3. Commission on Presidential Debates, second Bush-Kerry presidential debate (October 8, 2004), www.debates.org/pages/trans2004c.html.

4. See generally Mark Graber, *Dred Scott and the Problem of Constitutional Evil* (New York: Cambridge University Press, 2006).

5. Charles Evans Hughes, *The Supreme Court of the United States: Its Foundation, Methods, and Achievements* (New York: Columbia University Press, 1928), 50. Hughes considered the other cases to be *Hepburn v. Griswold*, 8 Wall. 603 (1870), and *Pollock v. Farmers' Loan and Trust Company*, 157 U.S. 429 (1895). In Hepburn

the Court held that the United States had unconstitutionally issued paper money during the Civil War. The Court reversed this decision two years later in *The Legal Tender Cases* (*Knox v. Lee* and *Parker v. Davis*), 79 U.S, (12 Wall.) 457 (1872). *Pollock* declared the federal income tax law to be unconstitutional. It was effectively reversed by the Sixteenth Amendment.

6. Alexander M. Bickel, *The Supreme Court and the Idea of Progress* (New Haven, Conn.: Yale University Press, 1978), 41.

7. Justice Felix Frankfurter cited it in a majority opinion, but as a caution to indicate what the courts should not do. Frankfurter asserted that courts should "refrain . . . from avoidable constitutional pronouncements" and thought "the Court's failure in *Dred Scott v. Sandford*" was one of those "rare occasions when the Court, forgetting 'the fallibility of the human judgment,' has departed from its own practice." U.S. v. International Union United Automobile, Aircraft and Agricultural Implement Workers of America (UAW-CIO), 352 U.S. 567, 590–91 (1957).

8. Plessy v. Ferguson, 163 U.S. 537, 559 (1896), (Harlan, J., dissenting).

9. Williams v. North Carolina, 325 U.S. 226, 275 (1945) (Black, J., dissenting).

10. McCleskey v. Kemp, 481 U.S. 279, 343–44 (1987) (Brennan, J., dissenting). McCleskey, an African American, had been sentenced to death in Georgia. In appealing his death penalty McCleskey presented overwhelming evidence that race was a major factor in death sentences and that blacks who killed whites, as McCleskey had, were 4.3 times more likely to be sentenced to death than defendants (white or black) who killed blacks. The Supreme Court rejected these statistics in upholding the death penalty; Brennan dissented, in part citing *Dred Scott.*

11. Planned Parenthood of Southeastern Pennsylvania v. Casey, 505 U.S. 833, 984 (1992), Scalia quoting from Dred Scott v. Sandford, 60 U.S. (19 How.) 393 (1857) (Curtis, J., dissenting). Casey was a case involving abortion rights. Opponents of reproductive choice often compare *Roe v. Wade,* 410 U.S. 113 (1973) to *Dred Scott* on the grounds that both deny liberty to an oppressed group—fetuses and blacks. This is another example of using *Dred Scott* to discredit one's opponents.

12. Washington v. Glucksberg, 521 U.S. 702, 758–59 (1997) (Souter, J., concurring) (internal citations omitted). Oddly enough, Justice Souter is the only Justice in living memory to cite *Dred Scott* favorably. In his dissent in *Seminole Tribe of Florida v. Florida,* 517 U.S. 44 (1995), at 152, he wrote "Regardless of its other faults, Chief Justice Taney's opinion in *Dred Scott v. Sandford,* 19 How. 393, (1857), recognized as a structural matter that '[t]he new Government was not a mere change in a dynasty, or in a form of government, leaving the nation or sovereignty the same, and clothed with all the rights, and bound by all the obligations of the preceding one'" (citing Scott, 60 U.S. at 441).

13. Paul Finkelman, "The Constitution and the Intentions of the Framers: The Limits of Historical Analysis," *University of Pittsburgh Law Review* 50, no. 2 (1989): 349–98.

14. Douglas advocated "popular sovereignty," which would allow the settlers of a territory to decide for themselves whether they wanted to have slavery. Taney's decision applying the Bill of Rights to the territories precluded territorial governments, as well as Congress, from banning slavery in the territories.

15. E.g., State v. Lasalle, 1 Blackf. (Ind.) 60 (1820). On lingering slavery in Illinois and the effect of the Northwest Ordinance, see chaps. two and three of Paul Finkelman, *Slavery and the Founders: Race and Liberty in the Age of Jefferson,* 2d ed. (Armonk, N.Y.: M. E. Sharpe, 2001).

16. McCulloch v. Maryland, 17 U.S. (4 Wheat.) 316 (1819).

17. In *Rachael v. Walker,* 4 Mo. 350 (1836), the Missouri Supreme Court had freed a slave who had been taken to military bases in free states and free territories, but this was based on Missouri law, not the law of the free jurisdiction.

18. E.g., Lea VanderVelde and Sandhya Subramanian, "Mrs. Dred Scott," *Yale Law Journal* 106, no. 4 (1997): 1033; Lea VanderVelde, *Mrs. Dred Scott: A Life on Slavery's Frontier* (New York: Oxford University Press, 2009), 115, 355nn2–3.

19. For a detailed discussion of slaves gaining their freedom through transit or residence in a free state, see Paul Finkelman, *An Imperfect Union: Slavery, Federalism, and Comity* (Chapel Hill: University of North Carolina Press, 1981).

20. Don E. Fehrenbacher, *The Dred Scott Case: Its Significance in American Law and Politics* (New York: Oxford University Press, 1978), 254.

21. Winny v. Whitesides, 1 Mo. 472 (1824).

22. Rachael, 4 Mo. at 350.

23. Finkelman, *An Imperfect Union,* 217–28.

24. David T. Konig, "The Long Road to Dred Scott: Personhood and the Rule of Law in the Trial Court Records of St. Louis Slave Freedom Suits," *University of Missouri Kansas City Law Review* 75, no. 1 (2006): 53.

25. Scott, a man of color, v. Emerson, 15 Mo. 576, 585 (1852).

26. Ibid. at 586.

27. See generally Kenneth C. Kaufman, *Dred Scott's Advocate: A Biography of Roswell M. Field* (Columbia: University of Missouri Press, 1996).

28. Scott v. Sandford, 60 U.S. at 396–97.

29. Fehrenbacher, *Dred Scott Case,* 279 (quoting Missouri U.S. Circuit Court records).

30. Scott v. Sandford, 60 U.S. at 403.

31. Ibid. at 404–5.

32. Ibid. at 407.

33. The Supreme Court would reach a completely different conclusion in the *Insular Cases* after the Spanish American War. Downes v. Bidwell, 182 U.S. 244 (1901); Dorr v. U.S., 195 U.S. 138 (1904); Dowdell v. U.S., 221 U.S. 325 (1911). For a short summary of all these cases, see Paul Finkelman and Melvin I. Urofksy, *Landmark Decisions of the United States Supreme Court,* 2d ed. (Washington, D.C.: CQ Press, 2008), 162–64. More recently, the Court has at least determined that

for some limited purposes, the Constitution has followed the flag at least ninety miles—to the U.S. military base at Guantánamo.

34. Scott v. Sandford, 60 U.S. at 450.

35. See the dissent in *Mitchell v. Wells,* arguing that a Mississippi slave emancipated in Ohio had the right to inherit property in Mississippi, despite the conclusions of *Dred Scott.* Mitchell v. Wells, 37 Miss. 235 (1859). The majority on the Mississippi court also rejected the doctrine of *Dred Scott* in *Shaw v. Brown,* 5 Miss. 246 (1858). Both cases are discussed in Finkelman, *An Imperfect Union,* 232–34, 293–95.

36. See Paul Finkelman, "Was *Dred Scott* Correctly Decided? An 'Expert Report' for the Defendant," *Lewis & Clark Law Review* 12, no. 4 (2008): 1219–52.

37. Strader v. Graham, 51 U.S. (10 How.) 82 (1851).

38. These issues are discussed in Donald L. Robinson, *Slavery in the Structure of American Politics, 1765–1820* (New York: Harcourt Brace Jovanovich, 1970); Staughton Lynd, *Class Conflict, Slavery, and the United States Constitution: Ten Essays* (Indianapolis: Bobbs-Merrill, 1967); and Finkelman, *Slavery and the Founders.*

39. Abraham Lincoln, "'A House Divided': Speech at Springfield, Illinois," June 16, 1858, in Roy P. Basler, ed., *The Collected Works of Abraham Lincoln,* 8 vols. (New Brunswick, N.J.: Rutgers University Press, 1953–1955), 3:461.

40. Ibid., 3:464, 467.

41. Scott v. Sandford, 60 U.S. at 468–69.

42. Both quoted in Finkelman, *An Imperfect Union,* 334.

43. Scott v. Sandford, 60 U.S. at 449–50.

44. Ibid. at 450.

45. Ibid.

46. Ibid.

SELECT BIBLIOGRAPHY

Books

Adams, Charles Francis, ed. The *Works of John Adams, Second President of the United States*. Vol. 9. Boston: Little, Brown, 1854.

————. *Memoirs of John Quincy Adams, Comprising Portions of His Diary from 1795 to 1848*. Vol. 5. Freeport, N.Y.: Books for Libraries Press, 1969.

Allen, Austin. *Origins of the* Dred Scott *Case: Jacksonian Jurisprudence and the Supreme Court, 1837–1857*. Athens: University of Georgia Press, 2006.

Allen, W. B., ed. *George Washington: A Collection*. Indianapolis: Liberty Classics, 1988.

Arenson, Adam. "City of Manifest Destiny: St. Louis and the Cultural Civil War, 1848–1877." Ph.D. diss., Yale University, 2008.

Ayers, Edward L. *Vengeance and Justice: Crime and Punishment in the 19th Century American South*. New York: Oxford University Press, 1984.

Barber, Sotirios, and James E. Fleming. *Constitutional Interpretation: The Basic Questions*. New York: Oxford University Press, 2007.

Beale, Howard K., ed. *The Diary of Edward Bates, 1859–1860*. Washington, D.C.: Government Printing Office, 1933.

Bell, Howard Holman, ed. *Minutes of the Proceedings of the National Negro Conventions, 1830–1865*. New York: Arno Press, 1969.

Bensel, Richard Franklin. *The American Ballot Box in the Mid-nineteenth Century*. New York: Cambridge University Press, 2004.

Benton, Thomas Hart. *Historical and Legal Examination of That Part of the Decision of the Supreme Court of the United States in the Dred Scott Case, Which Declares the Unconstitutionality of the Missouri Compromise Act, and the Self-Extension of the Constitution to Territories, Carrying Slavery along with It*. New York: D. Appleton, 1857.

Bethel, Elizabeth Rauh. *The Roots of African-American Identity: Memory and History in the Antebellum Free Communities*. New York: St. Martin's Press, 1997.

Bickel, Alexander M. *The Least Dangerous Branch: The Supreme Court at the Bar of Politics*. Indianapolis: Bobbs-Merrill, 1962.

————. *The Supreme Court and the Idea of Progress*. New Haven, Conn.: Yale University Press, 1978.

Blair, Francis P., Jr. *The Destiny of the Races of This Continent: An Address Delivered before the Mercantile Library Association of Boston, Massachusetts. On the 26th of January, 1859*. Washington, D.C.: Buell and Blanchard, 1859.

Blaustein, Albert P., and Robert L. Zangrando. *Civil Rights and African Americans: A Documentary History*. Evanston, Ill.: Northwestern University Press, 1991.

Blight, David W. *Race and Reunion: The Civil War in American Memory*. Cambridge, Mass.: Belknap Press of Harvard University Press, 2001.

Bogle, Donald. *Primetime Blues: African Americans on Network Television*. New York: Farrar, Straus and Giroux, 2001.

———. *Toms, Coons, Mulattoes, Mammies, and Bucks: An Interpretive History of Blacks in American Films*. Rev. ed. New York: Continuum, 1989.

Boman, Dennis K. *Abiel Leonard: Yankee Slaveholder, Eminent Jurist, and Passionate Unionist*. Lewiston, N.Y.: E. Mellen Press, 2002.

———. *Lincoln's Resolute Unionist: Hamilton Gamble, Dred Scott Dissenter and Missouri's Civil War Governor*. Baton Rouge: Louisiana State University Press, 2006.

Bork, Robert H. *The Tempting of America: The Political Seduction of the Law*. New York: Free Press, 1990.

Bowman, James. *Honor: A History*. New York: Encounter Books, 2006.

Brandwein, Pamela. *Reconstructing Reconstruction: The Supreme Court and the Production of Historical Truth*. Durham, N.C.: Duke University Press, 1999.

Breyer, Stephen G. *Active Liberty: Interpreting Our Democratic Constitution*. New York: Alfred A. Knopf, 2005.

Brophy, Alfred L. *Reparations Pro and Con*. New York: Oxford University Press, 2006.

Cain, Marvin R. *Lincoln's Attorney General: Edward Bates of Missouri*. Columbia: University of Missouri Press, 1965.

Cardozo, Benjamin N. *The Nature of the Judicial Process*. New Haven, Conn.: Yale University Press, 1921.

Carton, Evan. *Patriotic Treason: John Brown and the Soul of America*. New York: Free Press, 2006.

Castel, Albert. *General Sterling Price and the Civil War in the West*. Baton Rouge: Louisiana State University Press, 1968.

Chambers, William Nisbet. *Old Bullion Benton: Senator from the New West*. Boston: Little, Brown, 1956.

Chase, Salmon Portland. *Reclamation of Fugitives from Service*. Cincinnati: B. P. Donogh, 1847.

———. *Speech of Salmon P. Chase in the Case of the Colored Woman, Matilda*. Cincinnati: Pugh and Dodd, Printers, 1837.

Cherry, Robert. *Who Gets the Good Jobs? Combating Race and Gender Disparities*. New Brunswick, N.J.: Rutgers University Press, 2001.

Clamorgan, Cyprian. *The Colored Aristocracy of St. Louis*. St. Louis, 1858; repr., edited by Julie Winch, Columbia: University of Missouri Press, 1999.

Cobb, T. R. R. *An Inquiry into the Law of Negro Slavery in the United States of America*. Philadelphia: T. and J. W. Johnson, 1858; repr., edited by Paul Finkelman, Athens: University of Georgia Press, 1999.

Coleman, James. *Foundations of Social Theory*. Cambridge, Mass.: Belknap Press of Harvard University Press, 1990.

Currie, David. *The Constitution in the Supreme Court: The First Hundred Years.* Chicago: University of Chicago Press, 1985.

Dain, Bruce. *A Hideous Monster of the Mind: American Race Theory in the Early Republic.* Cambridge, Mass.: Harvard University Press, 2003.

Davis, William C. *The Cause Lost: Myths and Realities of the Confederacy.* Lawrence: University Press of Kansas, 1996.

Delgado, Richard, ed. *Critical Race Theory: The Cutting Edge.* Philadelphia: Temple University Press, 1995.

Donald, David Herbert. *Lincoln.* New York: Simon and Schuster, 1995.

Dworkin, Ronald. *Law's Empire.* Cambridge, Mass.: Harvard University Press, 1986.

———. *Taking Rights Seriously.* Cambridge, Mass.: Harvard University Press, 1978.

Dyson, Michael Eric. *The Michael Eric Dyson Reader.* New York: Basic Civitas Books, 2004.

Ehrlich, Walter. *They Have No Rights: Dred Scott's Struggle for Freedom.* Westport, Conn.: Greenwood Press, 1979.

Entman, Robert M., and Andrew Rojecki. *The Black Image in the White Mind: Media and Race in America.* Chicago: University of Chicago Press, 2000.

Epstein, Richard A. *Forbidden Grounds: The Case against Employment Discrimination Laws.* Cambridge, Mass.: Harvard University Press, 1992.

Ewen, Elizabeth, and Stuart Ewen. *Typecasting: On the Arts and Sciences of Human Inequality.* New York: Seven Stories Press, 2006.

Farber, Daniel. *Lincoln's Constitution.* Chicago: University of Chicago Press, 2003.

Fehrenbacher, Don E. *The Dred Scott Case, Its Significance in American Law and Politics.* New York: Oxford University Press, 1978.

———. *The Slaveholding Republic: An Account of the United States Government's Relations to Slavery.* Edited by Ward M. McAfee. New York: Oxford University Press, 2001.

Finkelman, Paul. *Dred Scott v. Sandford: A Brief History with Documents.* Boston: Bedford Books, 1997.

———. *An Imperfect Union: Slavery, Federalism, and Comity.* Chapel Hill: University of North Carolina Press, 1981.

———. *Slavery and the Founders: Race and Liberty in the Age of Jefferson.* 2d ed. Armonk, N.Y.: M. E. Sharpe, 2001.

———, ed. *Slavery and the Law.* Madison, Wis.: Madison House, 1997.

Finkelman, Paul, and Melvin I. Urofksy. *Landmark Decisions of the United States Supreme Court.* 2d ed. Washington, D.C.: C.Q. Press, 2008.

Foner, Eric. *Free Soil, Free Labor, Free Men: The Ideology of the Republican Party before the Civil War.* New York: Oxford University Press, 1970.

———. *Reconstruction: America's Unfinished Revolution, 1863–1877.* New York: Harper and Row, 1988.

Foner, Philip S., and George E. Walker, eds. *Proceedings of the Black State Conventions, 1840– 1865.* Philadelphia: Temple University Press, 1979.

Fox-Genovese, Elizabeth, and Eugene D. Genovese. *The Mind of the Master Class: History and Faith in the Southern Slaveholders' Worldview.* New York: Cambridge University Press, 2005.

Franklin, John Hope. *The Militant South, 1800–1861.* Cambridge, Mass.: Belknap Press of Harvard University Press, 1956.

Fredrickson, George M. *The Black Image in the White Mind: The Debate on Afro-American Character and Destiny, 1817–1914.* New York: Harper and Row, 1971.

Freehling, William W. *The Road to Disunion.* Vol. 2, *Secessionists Triumphant, 1854–1861.* New York: Oxford University Press, 2007.

Friedman, Lawrence M. *A History of American Law.* 3d ed. New York: Simon and Schuster, 2005.

Gaertner, Samuel L., and John F. Dovidio. *Reducing Intergroup Bias: The Common Ingroup Identity Model.* Philadelphia: Psychology Press, 2000.

Gerteis, Louis S. *Civil War St. Louis.* Lawrence: University Press of Kansas, 2001.

Gienapp, William E. *The Origins of the Republican Party, 1852–1856.* New York: Oxford University Press, 1987.

Gilens, Martin. *Why Americans Hate Welfare: Race, Media, and the Politics of Antipoverty Policy.* Chicago: University of Chicago Press, 1999.

Graber, Mark A. *Dred Scott and the Problem of Constitutional Evil.* New York: Cambridge University Press, 2006.

Greenberg, Kenneth S. *Honor and Slavery.* Princeton, N.J.: Princeton University Press, 1996.

Gross, Ariela J. *Double Character: Slavery and Mastery in the Antebellum Southern Courtroom.* Princeton, N.J.: Princeton University Press, 2000.

Hager, Ruth Ann. *Dred and Harriet Scott: Their Family Story.* St. Louis: St. Louis County Library, 2010.

Hahn, Steven. *A Nation under Our Feet: Black Political Struggles in the Rural South from Slavery to the Great Migration.* Cambridge, Mass.: Harvard University Press, 2003.

Hamilton, Daniel W. *The Limits of Sovereignty: Property Confiscation in the Union and the Confederacy during the Civil War.* Chicago: University of Chicago Press, 2007.

Harris, William C. *Lincoln's Rise to the Presidency.* Lawrence: University Press of Kansas, 2007.

Higginbotham, A. Leon, Jr. *Shades of Freedom: Racial Politics and Presumptions of the American Legal Process.* New York: Oxford University Press, 1996.

Hill, Frederick Trevor. *Decisive Battles of the Law; Narrative Studies of Eight Legal Contests Affecting the History of the United States between the Years 1800 and 1886.* New York: Harper and Brothers, 1907.

Hill, Thomas E., Jr. *Respect, Pluralism, and Justice: Kantian Perspectives.* New York: Oxford University Press, 2000.

Hobson, Charles F., and Robert A. Rutland, eds. *The Papers of James Madison.* Vol. 12. Charlottesville: University Press of Virginia, 1979.

Holland, Antonio Frederick. *Nathan B. Young and the Struggle over Black Higher Education.* Columbia: University of Missouri Press, 2006.

Holman, Howard. *A Survey of the Negro Convention Movement, 1830–1861.* New York: Arno Press, 1969.

Hopkins, Vincent C. *Dred Scott's Case.* New York: Fordham University Press, 1951.

Horton, James Oliver, and Lois E. Horton, eds. *Slavery and Public History: The Tough Stuff of American Memory.* New York: New Press, 2006.

Hughes, Charles Evans. *The Supreme Court of the United States: Its Foundation, Methods, and Achievements.* New York: Columbia University Press, 1928.

Jackson, Ronald L., II. *Scripting the Black Masculine Body: Identity, Discourse, and Racial Politics in Popular Media.* Albany: State University of New York Press, 2006.

Jaffa, Harry V. *Crisis of the House Divided: An Interpretation of the Issues in the Lincoln-Douglas Debates.* Garden City, N.Y.: Doubleday, 1959.

Jones, James M. *Prejudice and Racism.* New York: McGraw-Hill, 1997.

Jordan, Winthrop D. *White over Black: American Attitudes toward the Negro, 1550–1812.* Chapel Hill: University of North Carolina Press, 1968.

Kaplan, Sidney, and Emma Nogrady Kaplan. *The Black Presence in the Era of the American Revolution.* Rev. ed. Amherst: University of Massachusetts Press, 1989.

Kaufman, Kenneth C. *Dred Scott's Advocate: A Biography of Roswell M. Field.* Columbia: University of Missouri Press, 1996.

Kern-Foxworth, Marilyn. *Aunt Jemima, Uncle Ben, and Rastus: Blacks in Advertising, Yesterday, Today, and Tomorrow.* Westport, Conn.: Greenwood Press, 1994.

Kinder, Donald R., and Lynn M. Sanders. *Divided by Color: Racial Politics and Democratic Ideals.* Chicago: University of Chicago Press, 1996.

Krause, Sharon R. *Liberalism with Honor.* Cambridge, Mass.: Harvard University Press, 2002.

Kremer, Gary R. *James Milton Turner and the Promise of America: The Public Life of a Post–Civil War Black Leader.* Columbia: University of Missouri Press, 1991.

Llewellyn, Karl N. *The Common Law Tradition: Deciding Appeals.* Boston: Little, Brown, 1960.

Louie, Miriam Ching Yoon. *Sweatshop Warriors: Immigrant Women Workers Take On the Global Factory.* Cambridge, Mass.: South End Press, 2001.

Loury, Glenn C. *The Anatomy of Racial Inequality.* Cambridge, Mass.: Harvard University Press, 2002.

Lowenthal, David. *The Heritage Crusade and the Spoils of History.* New York: Cambridge University Press, 1998.

Lynd, Staughton. *Class Conflict, Slavery, and the United States Constitution: Ten Essays.* Indianapolis: Bobbs-Merrill, 1967.

Manning, Chandra. *What This Cruel War Was Over: Soldiers, Slavery, and the Civil War.* New York: Vintage Books, 2007.

Mansfield, Harvey C. *Manliness.* New Haven, Conn.: Yale University Press, 2006.

May, Robert E. *The Southern Dream of a Caribbean Empire, 1854–1861.* Baton Rouge: Louisiana State University Press, 1973.

McDonald, Forrest. *States' Rights and the Union: Imperium in Imperio, 1776–1876.* Lawrence: University Press of Kansas, 2000.

McDonald, Terrence J., ed. *The Historic Turn in the Human Sciences.* Ann Arbor: University of Michigan Press, 1999.

McPherson, James M. *Abraham Lincoln and the Second American Revolution.* New York: Oxford University Press, 1990.

———. *Battle Cry of Freedom: The Civil War Era.* New York: Oxford University Press, 1988.

———. *Ordeal by Fire: The Civil War and Reconstruction.* 2d ed. New York: McGraw-Hill, 1992.

———. *The Struggle for Equality: Abolitionists and the Negro in the Civil War and Reconstruction.* Princeton, N.J.: Princeton University Press, 1964.

Miller, William Ian. *The Mystery of Courage.* Cambridge, Mass.: Harvard University Press, 2000.

Mishel, Lawrence R., Jared Bernstein, and Sylvia A. Allegretto. *The State of Working America, 2004/2005.* Ithaca, N.Y.: ILR Press, 2005.

Morris, Thomas D. *Free Men All: The Personal Liberty Laws of the North, 1780–1861.* Baltimore: Johns Hopkins University Press, 1974.

Morrison, Michael A. *Slavery and the American West: The Eclipse of Manifest Destiny and the Coming of the Civil War.* Chapel Hill: University of North Carolina Press, 1997.

Moses, Shelia P., and Bonnie Christensen. *I, Dred Scott: A Fictional Slave Narrative Based on the Life and Legal Precedent of Dred Scott.* New York: Margaret K. McElderry Books, 2005.

Neely, Mark E., Jr. *The Fate of Liberty: Abraham Lincoln and Civil Liberties.* New York: Oxford University Press, 1991.

———. *The Last Best Hope of Earth: Abraham Lincoln and the Promise of America.* Cambridge, Mass.: Harvard University Press, 1993.

Neider, Charles, ed. *The Autobiography of Mark Twain.* New York: Harper Perennial, 1999.

Neighbour, Mary E. *Speak Right On: Dred Scott: A Novel.* New Milford, Conn.: Toby Press, 2006.

Nell, William C. *The Colored Patriots of the American Revolution.* Boston: Robert F. Wallcut, 1855; repr., New York: Arno Press, 1968.

————. *Services of Colored Americans in the Wars of 1776 and 1812*. Boston: Prentiss and Sawyer, 1851; repr., New York: AMS Press, 1976.

Newmyer, R. Kent. *John Marshall and the Heroic Age of the Supreme Court*. Baton Rouge: Louisiana State University Press, 2001.

Nisbett, Richard E., and Dov Cohen. *Culture of Honor: The Psychology of Violence in the South*. Boulder, Colo.: Westview Press, 1996.

Novick, Peter. *That Noble Dream: The "Objectivity Question" and the American Historical Profession*. New York: Cambridge University Press, 1988.

Obama, Barack. *Dreams from My Father: A Story of Race and Inheritance*. New York: Times, 1995.

Ogbar, Jeffrey O. G. *Hip Hop Revolution: The Culture and Politics of Rap*. Lawrence: University Press of Kansas, 2007.

Ogbu, John U. *Minority Education and Caste: The American System in Cross-Cultural Perspective*. New York: Academic Press, 1978.

Parrish, William E. *Frank Blair: Lincoln's Conservative*. Columbia: University of Missouri Press, 1998.

————. *Missouri under Radical Rule*. Columbia: University of Missouri Press, 1965.

Patterson, Orlando. *Slavery and Social Death*. Cambridge, Mass.: Harvard University Press, 1982.

Peterson, Merrill D., ed. *The Portable Thomas Jefferson*. New York: Penguin Books, 1975.

Peterson, Norma L. *Freedom and Franchise: The Political Career of B. Gratz Brown*. Columbia: University of Missouri Press, 1965.

Potter, David M. *The Impending Crisis, 1848–1861*. Edited by Don E. Fehrenbacher. New York: Harper and Row, 1976.

Putnam, Robert. *Making Democracy Work: Civic Traditions in Modern Italy*. Princeton, N.J.: Princeton University Press, 1993.

Ramsay, David. *The History of the American Revolution*. Philadelphia: R. Aitken and Son, 1789; repr., edited by Lester H. Cohen, Indianapolis: Liberty Classics, 1990.

Rehnquist, William H. *Centennial Crisis: The Disputed Election of 1876*. New York: Knopf, 2004.

Richardson, Heather Cox. *The Death of Reconstruction: Race, Labor, and Politics in the Post–Civil War North, 1865–1901*. Cambridge, Mass.: Harvard University Press, 2001.

Robertson, Lindsay G. *Conquest by Law: How the Discovery of America Dispossessed Indigenous Peoples of Their Lands*. New York: Oxford University Press, 2005.

Robinson, Donald L. *Slavery in the Structure of American Politics, 1765–1820*. New York: Harcourt Brace Jovanovich, 1970.

Robinson, Randall. *The Debt: What America Owes to Blacks*. New York: Dutton, 2000.

Rome, Dennis. *Black Demons: The Media's Depiction of the African American Male Criminal Stereotype.* Westport, Conn.: Praeger, 2004.

Rosenzweig, Roy, and David P. Thelen. *The Presence of the Past: Popular Uses of History in American Life.* New York: Columbia University Press, 1998.

Sen, Amartya. *Development as Freedom.* New York: Knopf, 1999.

Sewell, Richard H. *Ballots for Freedom: Antislavery Politics in the United States, 1837–1860.* New York: Oxford University Press, 1976.

Shaffer, Arthur H. *To Be an American: David Ramsay and the Making of the American Consciousness.* Columbia: University of South Carolina Press, 1991.

Shalhope, Robert E. *Sterling Price: Portrait of a Southerner.* Columbia: University of Missouri Press, 1971.

Simon, James F. *Lincoln and Chief Justice Taney: Slavery, Secession, and the President's War Powers.* New York: Simon and Schuster, 2006.

Spooner, Lysander. *The Unconstitutionality of Slavery.* Boston: B. Marsh, 1845.

Stampp, Kenneth M. *And the War Came: The North and the Secession Crisis, 1860–1861.* Baton Rouge: Louisiana State University Press, 1970.

Steiner, Bernard C. *Life of Roger Brooke Taney: Chief Justice of the United States Supreme Court.* Baltimore: Williams and Wilkins, 1922.

Stiles, T. J. *Jesse James: Last Rebel of the Civil War.* New York: A. A. Knopf, 2002.

Stowe, Harriet Beecher. *Dred: A Tale of the Great Dismal Swamp.* Boston: Phillips, Sampson, 1856.

Thernstrom, Abigail, and Stephan Thernstrom. *No Excuses: Closing the Racial Gap in Learning.* New York: Simon and Schuster, 2003.

Ture, Kwame (Stokely Carmichael), and Charles V. Hamilton. *Black Power: The Politics of Liberation in America.* New York: Vintage Books, 1992.

Urofsky, Melvin, and Paul Finkelman. *A March of Liberty: A Constitutional History of the United States.* 2d ed. New York. Oxford University Press, 2002.

VanderVelde, Lea. *Mrs. Dred Scott: A Life on Slavery's Frontier.* New York: Oxford University Press, 2009.

Vorenberg, Michael. *Final Freedom: The Civil War, the Abolition of Slavery, and the Thirteenth Amendment.* Cambridge: Cambridge University Press, 2001.

Wallance, Gregory J. *Two Men before the Storm: Arba Crane's Recollection of Dred Scott and the Supreme Court Case That Started the Civil War.* Austin, Tex.: Greenleaf Book Group Press, 2006.

Watson, Harry L. *Liberty and Power: The Politics of Jacksonian America.* New York: Farrar, Straus and Giroux, 1990.

Watts, Steven. *The Magic Kingdom: Walt Disney and the American Way of Life.* Columbia: University of Missouri Press, 2001.

Wiencek, Henry. *An Imperfect God: George Washington, His Slaves, and the Creation of America.* New York: Farrar, Straus and Giroux, 2003.

Witkin, B. E. *Manual on Appellate Court Opinions.* St. Paul, Minn.: West Publishing, 1977.

Woldman, Albert K. *Lawyer Lincoln*. New York: Carroll and Graf, 1936.

Wood, Gordon S. *The Purpose of the Past: Reflections on the Uses of History.* New York: Penguin Press, 2008.

Woodward, C. Vann. *Reunion and Reaction: The Compromise of 1877 and the End of Reconstruction.* Boston: Little, Brown, 1951.

Wyatt-Brown, Bertram. *The Shaping of Southern Culture: Honor, Grace, and War, 1760s– 1880s.* Chapel Hill: University of North Carolina Press, 2001.

———. *Southern Honor.* New York: Oxford University Press, 1982.

Selection or Book Chapter in Anthology

Blight, David W. "They Knew What Time It Was: African-Americans and the Coming of the Civil War." In *Why the Civil War Came,* edited by Gabor S. Boritt, 51–77. New York: Oxford University Press, 1996.

Bobo, Lawrence, and James R. Kluegel. "Status, Ideology, and Dimensions of Whites' Racial Beliefs and Attitudes: Progress and Stagnation." In *Racial Attitudes in the 1990s: Continuity and Change,* edited by Steven A. Tuch and Jack K. Martin, 99–105. Westport, Conn.: Praeger, 1997.

Cover, Robert M. "Nomos and Narrative." In *Narrative, Violence, and the Law: The Essays of Robert Cover,* edited by Martha Minow, Michael Ryan, and Austin Sarat, 95–172. Ann Arbor: University of Michigan Press, 1993.

Finkelman, Paul. "The Centrality of Slavery in American Legal Development." In *Slavery and the Law,* edited by Paul Finkelman, 4–26. Madison, Wis.: Madison House, 1997.

Gaertner, Samuel L., and John F. Dovidio. "The Aversive Form of Racism." In *Prejudice, Discrimination, and Racism,* edited by John F. Dovidio and Samuel L. Gaertner, 61–89. Orlando, Fla.: Academic Press, 1986.

Gerteis, Louis. "Shaping the Authentic: St. Louis Theater Culture and the Construction of American Social Types, 1815–1860." In *St. Louis in the Century of Henry Shaw: A View beyond the Garden Wall,* edited by Eric Sandweiss, 212–15. Columbia: University of Missouri Press, 2003.

Gordon, Robert W. "The Past as Authority and as Social Critic: Stabilizing and Destabilizing Functions of History in Legal Argument." In *The Historic Turn in the Human Sciences,* edited by Terrence J. McDonald, 339–78. Ann Arbor: University of Michigan Press, 1999.

Hancock, Scott. "'Tradition Informs Us': African Americans' Construction of Memory in the Antebellum North." In *Slavery, Resistance, Freedom,* edited by Gabor S. Boritt and Scott Hancock, 51–56. New York: Oxford University Press, 2007.

Johnson, William R., and Derek Neal. "Basic Skills and the Black-White Earnings Gap." In *The Black-White Test Score Gap,* edited by Christopher Jencks and Meredith Phillips, 480–98. Washington, D.C.: Brookings Institution Press, 1998.

Loury, Glenn. "A Dynamic Theory of Racial Income Differences." In *Women, Minorities, and Employment Discrimination,* edited by Phyllis Ann Wallace and Annette M. Lamond, 153–87. Lexington, Mass.: Lexington Books, 1977.

Powell, Lewis F., Jr. "Leslie H. Arps Lecture, The Association of the Bar of the City of New York (October 17, 1989)." In *Courts, Judges, and Politics: An Introduction to the Judicial Process,* edited by Walter F. Murphy, C. Herman Pritchett, and Lee Epstein, 471–72. Boston: McGraw-Hill, 2002.

Russell, Thomas D. "Slave Auctions on the Courthouse Steps: Court Sales of Slaves in Antebellum South Carolina." In *Slavery and the Law,* edited by Paul Finkelman, 329–64. Madison, Wis.: Madison House, 1997.

Sen, Amartya. "Capability and Well-Being." In *The Quality of Life,* edited by Martha C. Nussbaum and Amartya Sen, 30–53. New York: Oxford University Press, 1993.

Shields, George H. "The Old Bar of St. Louis," In *The History of the Bench and Bar of Missouri,* edited by A. J. D. Stewart, 116. 2d ed. St. Louis: Legal Pub., 1898.

Periodicals

Adams, Terri M., and Douglas B. Fuller. "The Words Have Changed but the Ideology Remains the Same: Misogynistic Lyrics in Rap Music." *Journal of Black Studies* 36, no. 6 (2006): 938.

Aleinikoff, Alexander. "A Case for Race Consciousness." *Columbia Law Review* 91, no. 5 (1991): 1060–1125.

Alexander, Larry, and Frederick Schauer. "On Extrajudicial Constitutional Interpretation." *Harvard Law Review* 110, no. 7 (1997): 1359–87.

Allen, Austin. "Rethinking *Dred Scott:* New Context for an Old Case." *Chicago-Kent Law Review* 82, no. 3 (2007): 141–76.

Amar, Akhil Reed. "Foreword: The Document and the Doctrine." *Harvard Law Review* 114, no. 1 (2000): 26–134.

Arenson, Adam. "Freeing Dred Scott: St. Louis Confronts an Icon of Slavery, 1857–2007." *Common-Place* 8, no. 3 (2008), http://www.common-place.org/vol-08/no-03/arenson/.

Armour, Jody. "Stereotypes and Prejudice: Helping Legal Decisionmakers Break the Prejudice Habit." *California Law Review* 83, no. 3 (1995): 733–72.

Arrow, Kenneth. "What Has Economics to Say about Racial Discrimination?" *Journal of Economic Perspectives* 12, no. 2 (1998): 91–100.

Auchampaugh, Philip. "James Buchanan, the Court, and the *Dred Scott* Case." *Tennessee Historical Magazine* 9 (1929): 236.

Barnett, Randy E., "The Original Meaning of the Commerce Clause." *University of Chicago Law Review* 68, no. 1 (2001): 101–47.

Baugh, John. "It Ain't About Race: Some Lingering (Linguistic) Consequences of the African Slave Trade and Their Relevance to Your Personal Historical Hardship Index." *Du Bois Review: Social Science Research on Race* 3, no. 1 (2006): 145–59.

———. "Linguistic Contributions to the Advancement of Racial Justice within and beyond the African Diaspora." *Language and Linguistics Compass* 1, no. 4 (2007): 331–49.

Bednar, Jenna, and William N. Eskridge Jr. "Steadying the Court's 'Unsteady Path': A Theory of Judicial Enforcement of Federalism." *Southern California Law Review* 68, no. 6 (1995): 1480.

Blumrosen, Alfred W. "The Profound Influence in America of Lord Mansfield's Decision in Somerset v. Stuart." *Texas Wesleyan Law Review* 13, no. 2 (2007): 645–58.

Boman, Dennis K. "The Dred Scott Case Reconsidered: The Legal and Political Context in Missouri." *American Journal of Legal History* 44 (October 2000): 405–28.

Borchard, Edwin. "The Supreme Court and Private Rights." *Yale Law Journal* 47, no. 7 (1938): 1051–78.

Borjas, George. "Ethnic Capital and Intergenerational Mobility." *Quarterly Journal of Economics* 107, no. 1 (1992): 123–50.

Boudin, Louis B. "Truth and Fiction about the Fourteenth Amendment." *New York University Law Quarterly Review* 16, no. 1 (1938): 19–82.

Bracey, Christopher A. "Dignity in Race Jurisprudence." *University of Pennsylvania Journal of Constitutional Law* 7, no. 3 (2005): 669–720.

Breitel, Charles D. "The Lawmakers." *Columbia Law Review* 65, no. 5 (1965): 749–77.

Brophy, Alfred L. "Let Us Go Back and Stand upon the Constitution: Federal-State Relations in *Scott v. Sandford*." *Columbia Law Review* 90, no. 1 (1990): 192–225.

———. "Reconsidering Reparations." *Indiana Law Journal* 81, no. 3 (2006): 811–49.

———. "Reparations Talk: The Tort Law Analogy in Reparations." *Boston College Third World Law Journal* 24, no. 1 (2004): 81–138.

Brown-Nagin, Tomiko. "Race as Identity Caricature: A Local Legal History Lesson in the Salience of Intraracial Conflict." *University of Pennsylvania Law Review* 151, no. 6 (2003): 1913–76.

Calabresi, Steven G. "The Originalist and Normative Case against Judicial Activism: A Reply to Professor Randy Barnett." *Michigan Law Review* 103, no. 6 (2005): 1081–98.

Corwin, Edward S. "The Doctrine of Due Process of Law before the Civil War." *Harvard Law Review* 24, no. 5 (1911): 366–85.

———. "The Doctrine of Due Process of Law before the Civil War (continued)." *Harvard Law Review* 24, no. 6 (1911): 460–79.

———. "The Dred Scott Decision, in the Light of Contemporary Legal Doctrines." *American Historical Review* 17, no. 1 (1911): 52–69.

Cottrol, Robert J., and Raymond T. Diamond. "The Second Amendment: Toward an Afro-Americanist Reconsideration." *Georgetown Law Journal* 80, no. 2 (1991): 309–61.

Davis, Peggy C. "Law as Microaggression." *Yale Law Journal* 98, no. 8 (1989): 1559–77.

Devine, Patricia G., and Andrew J. Elliot. "Are Racial Stereotypes Really Fading? The Princeton Trilogy Revisited." *Personality and Social Psychology Bulletin* 21, no. 11 (1995): 1139–50.

Dilliard, Irving, and James Milton Turner. "Dred Scott Eulogized by James Milton Turner: A Historical Observance of the Turner Centenary: 1840–1940." *Journal of Negro History* 26, no. 1 (1941): 1–11.

Dixon, Travis L., and Daniel Linz. "Overrepresentation and Underrepresentation of African Americans and Latinos as Lawbreakers on Television News." *Journal of Communication* 50, no. 2 (2000): 131–54.

Dovidio, John F., and Samuel L. Gaertner. "Aversive Racism and Selection Decisions: 1989 and 1999." *Psychological Science* 11, no. 4 (2000): 315–19.

Dovidio, John F., Samuel L. Gaertner, and Kerry Kamakami. "Implicit and Explicit Prejudice and Interracial Interaction." *Journal of Personality and Social Psychology* 82, no. 1 (2002): 62–68.

Edwards, Harry T. "The Growing Disjunction between Legal Education and the Legal Profession." *Michigan Law Review* 91, no. 1 (1992): 34–78.

Eisgruber, Christopher L. "*Dred* Again: Originalism's Forgotten Past." *Constitutional Commentary* 10, no. 1 (1993): 37–65.

Ely, James W., Jr. "The Oxymoron Reconsidered: Myth and Reality in the Origins of Substantive Due Process." *Constitutional Commentary* 16, no. 2 (1999): 315–45.

Fallon, Richard H., Jr. "Executive Power and the Political Constitution." *Utah Law Review* 2007, no. 1 (2007): 1–23.

Finkelman, Paul. "Civil Rights in Historical Context: In Defense of *Brown*." *Harvard Law Review* 118, no. 3 (2005): 973–1029.

———. "The Constitution and the Intentions of the Framers: The Limits of Historical Analysis." *University of Pittsburgh Law Review* 50, no. 2 (1989): 349–98.

———. "'Hooted Down the Page of History': Reconsidering the Greatness of Chief Justice Taney." *Journal of Supreme Court History*, 1994, 83–102.

———. "*Scott v. Sandford:* The Court's Most Dreadful Case and How It Changed History." *Chicago-Kent Law Review* 82, no. 1 (2007): 3–48.

———. "Was *Dred Scott* Correctly Decided? An 'Expert Report' for the Defendant." *Lewis and Clark Law Review* 12, no. 4 (2008): 1219–52.

Foran, William A. "John Marshall as Historian." *American Historical Review* 43, no. 1 (1937): 51–64.

Gilliam, Franklin D., Jr., and Shanto Iyengar. "Prime Suspects: The Influence of Local Television News on the Viewing Public." *American Journal of Political Science* 44, no. 3 (2000): 560–73.

Goldin, Claudia Dale. "The Economics of Emancipation." *Journal of Economic History* 33, no. 1 (1973): 66–85.

Goldstein, Adam. "Judicial Selection as It Relates to Gender Equality on the Bench." *Cardozo Journal of Law and Gender* 13 (Spring 2007): 369–406.

Goluboff, Risa. "'Let Economic Equality Take Care of Itself': The NAACP, Labor Litigation, and the Making of Civil Rights in the 1940s." *UCLA Law Review* 52, no. 5 (2005): 1393–1486.

Graglia, Lino A. "Interpreting the Constitution: Posner on Bork." *Stanford Law Review* 44, no. 5 (1992): 1019–50.

Graham, Howard Jay. "The Conspiracy Theory of the Fourteenth Amendment." *Yale Law Journal* 47, no. 3 (1938): 393–402.

———. "Justice Field and the Fourteenth Amendment." *Yale Law Journal* 52, no. 4 (1943): 859.

Greenwald, Anthony G., and Linda Hamilton Krieger. "Implicit Bias: Scientific Foundations." *California Law Review* 94, no. 4 (2006): 945–67.

Greenwald, Anthony G., Debbie E. McGhee, and Jordan L. K. Schwartz. "Measuring Individual Differences in Implicit Cognition: The Implicit Association Test." *Journal of Personality and Social Psychology* 74, no. 6 (1998): 1464–80.

Hanssen, Andrew F. "Learning about Judicial Independence: Institutional Change in the State Courts." *Journal of Legal Studies* 33, no. 2 (2004): 431–73.

Harrison, John. "Substantive Due Process and the Constitutional Text." *Virginia Law Review* 83, no. 3 (1997): 493–558.

Henry, Patrick J., and David O. Sears. "The Symbolic Racism Scale." *Political Psychology* 23, no. 2 (2002): 254–58.

Horton, James O. "Patriot Acts: Public History in Public Service." *Journal of American History* 92, no. 3 (2005): 801–10.

Hunt, Cecil J., II. "In the Racial Crosshairs: Reconsidering Racially Targeted Predatory Lending under a New Theory of Economic Hate Crime." *University of Toledo Law Review* 35, no. 2 (2003): 211–315.

Jackson, Robert H. "Decisional Law and Stare Decisis." *American Bar Association Journal* 30 (June 1944): 334–35.

Johannsen, Robert W. "Stephen A. Douglas, 'Harper's Magazine,' and Popular Sovereignty." *Mississippi Valley Historical Review* 45, no. 4 (1959): 606–31.

———. "Stephen A. Douglas and the South." *Journal of Southern History* 33, no. 1 (1967): 26–50.

Jones, James M. "Psychological Knowledge and the New American Dilemma." *Journal of Sociological Issues* 54, no. 4 (1998): 641–62.

Kang, Jerry. "Trojan Horses of Race." *Harvard Law Review* 118, no. 5 (2005): 1489–1593.

Kelly, Alfred H. "Clio and the Court: An Illicit Love Affair." *Supreme Court Review,* 1965, 119–58.

Kinder, Donald R., and David O. Sears. "Prejudice and Politics: Symbolic Racism versus Racial Threats to the Good Life." *Journal of Personality and Social Psychology* 40, no. 3 (1981): 414–31.

Konig, David Thomas. "The Long Road to *Dred Scott:* Personhood and the Rule of Law in the Trial Court Records of St. Louis Slave Freedom Suits." *University of Missouri Kansas City Law Review* 75, no. 1 (2006): 53–80.

Krieger, Linda Hamilton. "The Content of Our Categories: A Cognitive Bias Approach to Discrimination and Equal Employment Opportunity." *Stanford Law Review* 47, no. 6 (1995): 1161–1248.

Krieger, Linda Hamilton, and Susan T. Fiske. "Behavioral Realism in Employment Discrimination Law: Implicit Bias and Disparate Treatment." *California Law Review* 94, no. 4 (2006): 997–1062.

Lawrence, Charles R., III. "The Id, the Ego, and Equal Protection: Reckoning with Unconscious Racism." *Stanford Law Review* 39, no. 2 (1987): 317–88.

Lung, Shirley. "Exploiting the Joint Employer Doctrine: Providing a Break for Sweatshop Garment Workers." *Loyola University Chicago Law Journal* 34, no. 2 (2003): 291–358.

Magliocca, Gerard N. "Preemptive Opinions: The Secret History of *Worcester v. Georgia* and *Dred Scott.*" *University of Pittsburgh Law Review* 63, no. 3 (2002): 487–587.

Milburn, Page. "The Emancipation of the Slaves in the District of Columbia." *Records of the Columbia Historical Society* 16 (1913): 96–119.

Miller, Eric L. "Reconceiving Reparations: Multiple Strategies in the Reparations Debate." *Boston College Third World Law Journal* 24, no. 1 (2004): 45–79.

Nelles, Walter. "Towards Legal Understanding: II." *Columbia Law Review* 34, no. 6 (1934): 1041–75.

Ogbu, John U. "Understanding Cultural Diversity and Learning." *Educational Researcher* 21, no. 8 (1992): 5–14.

Ogletree, Charles J. "Repairing the Past: New Efforts in the Reparations Debate in America." *Harvard Civil Rights–Civil Liberties Law Review* 38, no. 2 (2003): 279–320.

Prygoski, Philip J. "War as Metaphor in Federal Indian Law Jurisprudence: An Exercise in Judicial Activism." *Thomas M. Cooley Law Review* 14, no. 3 (1997): 491–532.

Pushaw, Robert J., and Grant S. Nelson. "A Critique of the Narrow Interpretation of the Commerce Clause." *Northwestern University Law Review* 96, no. 2 (2002): 695–719.

Rabinowitz, Howard N. "More Than the Woodward Thesis: Assessing the Strange Career of Jim Crow." *Journal of American History* 75, no. 3 (1988): 842–56.

Ramsdell, Chas. W. "The Natural Limits of Slavery Expansion." *Mississippi Valley Historical Review* 16, no. 2 (1929): 151–71.

Raskin, Jamin B. "*Roe v. Wade* and the *Dred Scott* Decision: Justice Scalia's Peculiar Analogy in *Planned Parenthood v. Casey.*" *American University Journal of Gender and Law* 1, no. 1 (1993): 61–85.

Reid, John Phillip. "Law and History." *Loyola of Los Angeles Law Review* 27, no. 1 (1993–94): 193–224.

Roper, Donald M. "In Quest of Judicial Objectivity: The Marshall Court and the Legitimation of Slavery." *Stanford Law Review* 21, no. 3 (1969): 532–39.

Rose, Carol M. "Property and Expropriation: Themes and Variations in American Law." *Utah Law Review*, 2000, no. 7: 1504–17.

Schauer, Frederick. "Community, Citizenship, and the Search for National Identity." *Michigan Law Review* 84, no. 7 (1986): 1504–17.

Scherr, Arthur. "Governor James Monroe and the Southampton Slave Resistance of 1799." *Historian* 61, no. 3 (1999): 577–78.

Smith, Earl. "William Cooper Nell on the Fugitive Slave Act of 1850." *Journal of Negro History* 66, no. 1 (1981): 37–40.

Spaulding, Norman W. "Constitution as Countermonument: Federalism, Reconstruction, and the Problem of Collective Memory." *Columbia Law Review* 103, no. 8 (2003): 1992–2015.

Stanley, J. Lemons. "Black Stereotypes as Reflected in Popular Culture, 1880–1920." *American Quarterly* 29, no. 1 (1977): 102–16.

Stephens, Alexander H. "Cornerstone Address," March 21, 1861. In *Southern Pamphlets on Secession, November 1860–April 1861,* edited by Jon L. Wakelyn, app. B. Chapel Hill: University of North Carolina Press, 1996.

Stevens, Walter B. "Lincoln and Missouri." *Missouri Historical Review* 10, no. 2 (1916): 64.

Summers, Clyde W. "Contingent Employment in the United States." *Comparative Labor Law and Policy Journal* 18, no. 4 (1997): 503–22.

Tomlins, Christopher L. "Framing the Field of Law's Encounters: A Historical Narrative." *Law and Society Review* 34, no. 4 (2000): 911–72.

VanderVelde, Lea, and Sandhya Subramanian. "Mrs. Dred Scott." *Yale Law Journal* 106, no. 4 (1997): 1033–1122.

Vestal, Allan D. "Sua Sponte Consideration in Appellate Review." *Fordham Law Review* 27, no. 4 (1959): 477–512.

Vorenberg, Michael. "Imagining a Different Reconstruction Constitution." *Civil War History* 51, no. 4 (2005): 416–26.

Ware, Leland. "A Comparative Analysis of Unconscious and Institutional Discrimination in the United States and Britain." *Georgia Journal of International and Comparative Law* 36, no. 1 (2007): 89–157.

Weinberg, Jonathan. "The Artist and the Politician—George Caleb Bingham." *Art in America* 88, no. 10 (2000): 138–45.

Weinberg, Louise. "*Dred Scott* and the Crisis of 1860." *Chicago-Kent Law Review* 82, no. 1 (2007): 97–139.

———. "Methodological Interventions and the Slavery Cases; or, Night-Thoughts of a Legal Realist." *University of Maryland Law Review* 56, no. 4 (1997): 1316–70.

West, Robin. "Rights, Capabilities, and the Good Society." *Fordham Law Review* 69, no. 5 (2001): 1901–32.

Westley, Robert. "Many Billions Gone: Is It Time to Reconsider the Case for Black Reparations?" *Boston College Law Review* 40, no. 1 (1998): 429–76.

Wiecek, William M. "Slavery and Abolition before the United States Supreme Court, 1820–1860." *Journal of American History* 65, no. 1 (1978): 34–59.

———. "*Somerset:* Lord Mansfield and the Legitimacy of Slavery in the Anglo-American World." *University of Chicago Law Review* 42, no. 1 (1974): 86–146.

Woodhouse, Barbara Bennett. "Dred Scott's Daughters: Nineteenth Century Urban Girls at the Intersection of Race and Patriarchy." *Buffalo Law Review* 48 (Fall 2000): 669–701.

Yanich, Danilo. "Crime Creep: Urban and Suburban Crime on Local TV News." *Journal of Urban Affairs* 26, no. 5 (2004): 535–63.

Young, Donna E. "Racial Releases, Involuntary Separations, and Employment At-Will." *Loyola of Los Angeles Law Review* 34, no. 2 (2001): 351–438.

Cases

The Amistad, 40 U.S. 518 (1841).

The Antelope, 23 U.S. (10 Wheat.) 66 (1825).

Ayotte v. Planned Parenthood of N. New England, 546 U.S. 320 (2006).

Bailey v. Poindexter's Executor, 14 Gratt. 132 (Va. 1858).

Beebe v. State, 6 Ind. 501 (1855).

Birch v. Benton, 26 Mo. 153 (1858).

Booten v. Pinson, 77 W. Va. 412 (1915).

Borino v. General Registrars of Voters, 86 Conn. 622 (1913).

Brown v. Board of Education, 347 U.S. 483 (1954).

Calvert v. Steamboat Timoleon, 15 Mo. 595 (1852).

Carroll v. Lessee of Carroll, 57 U.S. 275 (1853).

Catiche v. Circuit Court, 1 Mo. 608 (1826).

Causeway Medical Suite v. Ieyoub, 109 F. 3d 1096 (5th Cir. La. 1997).

Charlotte v. Chouteau, 11 Mo. 193 (1847).

Chouteau v. Hope, 7 Mo. 428 (1842).

Chouteau v. Marguerite, 37 U.S. 507 (1838).

Chouteau v. Pierre, 9 Mo. 3 (1845).

The Civil Rights Cases, 109 U.S. 3 (1883).

Commonwealth v. Aves, 35 Mass. 193 (1836).

Cutler v. Rae, 48 U.S. 729 (1849).

Des Moines Joint Stock Land Bank v. Nordholm, 217 Iowa 1319 (1933).

Doe v. Kamehameha Schools, 295 F. Supp. 2d 1141, (D. Haw. 2003), aff'd en banc 470 F. 3d 827 (9th Cir. 2006).

Dorr v. U.S., 195 U.S. 138 (1904).

Dowdell v. U.S., 221 U.S. 325 (1911).

Downes v. Bidwell, 182 U.S. 244 (1901).

Dred Scott v. Sandford, 60 U.S. (19 How.) 393 (1857).

Eaton v. Vaughan, 9 Mo. 743 (1846).

Emmerson v. Harriet, 11 Mo. 413 (1848).

Erie Railroad v. Tompkins, 304 U.S. 64 (1938).

Ex parte Anonymous, 803 So. 2d 542 (Ala. 2001).

Ex parte Rhodes, 202 Ala. 68 (1918).

Forbes v. Cochrane, 107 Eng. Rep. 450 (K.B. 1824).

Fullilove v. Klutznick, 448 U.S. 448 (1980).

Genesee Chief v. Fitzhugh, 53 U.S. 443 (1851).

Gentry v. Fry, 4 Mo. 120, 196 (1835).

Gibbons v. Ogden, 22 U.S. (9 Wheat.) 1 (1824).

Gideon v. Wainwright, 372 U.S. 335 (1963).

Girard v. Diefendorf, 54 Idaho 467 (1934).

Gonzales v. Carhart, 550 U.S. 124, 127 S. Ct. 1610 (2007).

Gordon v. Duncan, 3 Mo. 385 (1834).

Graham v. Strader, 44 Ky. 173 (1844).

Gratz v. Bollinger, 539 U.S. 244 (2003).

Griffin v. Illinois, 351 U.S. 12 (1956).

Griswold v. Connecticut, 381 U.S. 479 (1965).

Groves v. Slaughter, 40 U.S. 449 (1841).

Grutter v. Bollinger, 539 U.S. 306 (2003).

Harris v. McCrae, 448 U.S. 297 (1980).

Hepburn v. Griswold, 8 Wall. 603 (1870).

Home Building and Loan Association v. Blaisdell, 290 U.S. 398 (1934).

Johnson v. M'Intosh, 21 U.S. 543 (1823).

Joshua v. Purse, 34 Mo. 209 (1863).

Julia v. McKinney, 3 Mo. 270, 274 (1833).

Knox v. Lee, 79 U.S. (12 Wall.) 457 (1872).

Koy v. Schneider, 110 Tex. 369, 378 (Tex. 1920).

Lagrange v. Chouteau, 29 U.S. 287 (1830).

Lee v. Sprague, 14 Mo. 476, 477 (1851).

The Legal Tender Cases, 79 U.S. (12 Wall.) 457 (1872).

Lewis v. Hart, 33 Mo. 535 (1863).

Lochner v. New York, 198 U.S. 45 (1905).

Loving v. Virginia, 388 U.S. 1 (1967).

Luther v. Borden, 48 U.S. 1 (1849).

Maher v. Roe, 432 U.S. 464 (1977).

Marguerite v. Chouteau, 3 Mo. 540 (1834).

Maria v. Atterberry, 9 Mo. 369 (1845).

McCleskey v. Kemp, 481 U.S. 279 (1987).

McCulloch v. Maryland, 17 U.S. 316 (1819).

Menard v. Aspasia, 30 U.S. 505 (1831).

Merry v. Tiffin, 1 Mo. 725 (1827).

Metro Broadcasting v. Federal Communications Commission, 497 U.S. 547 (1990).

Milly v. Smith, 2 Mo. 36, 39 (1828).

Mitchell v. Wells, 37 Miss. 235 (1859).

Moore v. Illinois, 55 U.S. 13, 18 (1852).

Nat v. Coons, 10 Mo. 543 (1847).

Nat v. Ruddle, 3 Mo. 400 (1834).

Oliver v. Kauffman, 18 F. Cas. 657 (C.C.E.D. Pa. 1850).

Osborn v. Nicholson, 80 U.S. (13 Wall.) 654 (1872).

Pacific Railroad v. Governor, 23 Mo. 353 (1856).

Parents Involved v. Seattle Schools, 127 S. Ct. 2738 (2007).

Parker v. Davis, 79 U.S. (12 Wall.) 457 (1872).

Payne v. St. Louis County, 8 Mo. 473 (1844).

Peter v. King, 13 Mo. 143 (1850).

Planned Parenthood of Southeastern Pennsylvania v. Casey, 505 U.S. 833 (1992).

Planters' Bank v. Sharp, 47 U.S. 301 (1848).

Plessy v. Ferguson, 163 U.S. 537 (1896).

Pollock v. Farmers' Loan and Trust Company, 157 U.S. 429 (1895).

Prigg v. Pennsylvania, 41 U.S. 539 (1842).

Proprietors of Charles River Bridge v. Proprietors of Warren Bridge, 36 U.S. 420 (1837).

Rachael v. Walker, 4 Mo. 350 (1836).

Ralph v. Duncan, 3 Mo. 194 (1833).

Randolph v. Alsey, 8 Mo. 656 (1844).

Read v. Manning, 1 George 308 (Miss. Err. App 1855).

Regents of the University of California v. Bakke, 438 U.S. 265 (1978).

Rennick v. Chloe, 7 Mo. 197 (1841).

Rex v. Allan, 2 Hagg. 94, 166 Eng. Rep. 179 (Adm. 1827).

Richmond v. Croson, 488 U.S. 469 (1989).

Robert v. Melugen, 9 Mo. 170 (1845).

Roe v. Wade, 410 U.S. 113 (1973).

Russell v. Southard, 53 U.S. 139 (1851).

Scott v. Emerson, 15 Mo. 576 (1852).

Seminole Tribe of Florida v. Florida, 517 U.S. 44 (1995).

Shaw v. Brown, 5 Miss. 246 (1858).

The Slaughterhouse Cases, 83 U.S. 36 (1873).

Somerset v. Stewart, 98 Eng. Rep. 499 (K.B. 1772).

South Carolina v. U.S., 199 U.S. 437 (1905).

State ex rel. Diederichs v. State Highway Commission, 89 Mont. 205 (1931).

State ex rel. Richards v. Moorer, 152 S.C. 455 (1929).

State ex rel. West v. Butler, 70 Fla. 102 (1915).

State v. Ambs, 20 Mo. 214 (1854).

State v. Lasalle, 1 Blackf. 60 (1820).

State v. Mann, 13 N.C. 263 (1830).

Strader v. Graham, 51 U.S. 82 (1851).

Strauder v. West Virginia, 100 U.S. 303 (1880).

Sugarman v. Dougall, 413 U.S. 634 (1973).
Susan v. Hight, 1 Mo. 118 (1821).
Swift v. Tyson, 41 U.S. 1 (1842).
Sylvia v. Kirby, 17 Mo. 434 (1853).
Tapley v. Futrell, 187 Ark. 844 (1933).
Theoteste v. Chouteau, 2 Mo. 144 (1829).
Tramell v. Adam, 2 Mo. 155 (1829).
U.S. v. Amy, 24 F. Cas. 792 (C.C.Va. 1859).
U.S. v. International Union United Automobile, Aircraft and Agricultural Implement Workers of America (UAW-CIO), 352 U.S 567 (1957).
Vincent v. Duncan, 2 Mo. 214 (1830).
Washington v. Glucksberg, 521 U.S. 702 (1997).
West Coast Hotel v. Parrish, 300 U.S. 379 (1937).
White v. Hart, 80 U.S. (13 Wall.) 646 (1872).
Williams v. Mississippi, 170 U.S. 213 (1898).
Williams v. North Carolina, 325 U.S. 226 (1945).
Wilson v. Melvin, 4 Mo. 592 (1837).
Winny v. Whitesides, 1 Mo. 472 (1824).
Worthington v. Mason, 101 U.S. 149 (1879).
Wygant v. Jackson Board of Education, 476 U.S. 267 (1986).
Wynehamer v. People, 13 N.Y. 378 (1856).

CONTRIBUTORS

Austin Allen is Associate Professor of History at the University of Houston-Downtown.

Adam Arenson is Assistant Professor of History at the University of Texas at El Paso.

John Baugh is Margaret Bush Wilson Professor in Arts and Sciences at Washington University in St. Louis.

Duane Benton is Circuit Judge, U.S. Court of Appeals for the Eighth Circuit. Judge, Supreme Court of Missouri, 1991–2004; Chief Justice, 1997–1999.

Christopher Alan Bracey is Professor of Law at George Washington University Law School.

Alfred L. Brophy is Reef C. Ivey II Professor of Law at University of North Carolina Law School.

Paul Finkelman is President William McKinley Distinguished Professor of Law at Albany Law School.

Louis Gerteis is Professor of History at the University of Missouri–St. Louis.

Mark Graber is Professor of Law at the University of Maryland School of Law and Professor of Government at the University of Maryland–College Park.

Daniel W. Hamilton is Professor of Law at the University of Illinois College of Law and is Codirector of the Illinois Legal History Program.

Cecil J. Hunt II is Associate Professor of Law, John Marshall Law School.

David Thomas Konig is Professor of History and Professor of Law at Washington University in St. Louis.

Leland Ware is the Louis L. Redding Chair and Professor of Law and Public Policy at the University of Delaware.

Michael A. Wolff is Judge, Supreme Court of Missouri; Chief Justice, 2005–7. Distinguished Visiting Professor, St. Louis University School of Law.

INDEX

Page numbers in *italics* refer to illustrations.

honor cultures, lying and unmasking in, 161–64
Horton, James, 185
Howard, John, 100
Howe, Mark DeWolfe, 9
Hughes, Charles E., on *Dred Scott* case, 229

"Id, the Ego, and Equal Protection" (Lawrence), 148
ideology, action and, 185
Illinois constitution of 1818, 231
Indiana, 79

Jackson, Andrew, 17
Jackson, Claiborne F., 221
Jackson, Lynne Madison, 3
Jaffa, Harry, 60–61; on Lincoln, 57
Jefferson National Expansion Memorial, 1
Jim Crow, 185
Johnson v. M'Intosh, 15
Jolly Flatboatmen at Port (Bingham), 29–30, *30*
Jones, Barbara Jo, 3
Jones, Joseph Lee, 3
Julia v. McKinney, 199

Kansas-Nebraska Act, 59, 245
Kant, Immanuel, 167
Kelly, Alfred H., 9–10
Kennedy, Anthony, 135
Konig, David, 201–2
Krieger, Linda: *Content of Our Categories*, 149

LaGrange v. Chouteau, 198
Lahee, Eugene H., 34
law of the land clauses, 85–86
Lawrence, Charles: "Id, the Ego, and Equal Protection," 148
Lecompton constitution, 58
Leslie's Illustrated, 28
Leutze, Emmanuel: *Washington Crossing the Delaware*, 18
Lincoln, Abraham, 2; Brown and, 53–54, 62; colonization and, 70; debates with Douglas and, 2, 54–55, 60–61, 62; on *Dred Scott* case, 28–29, 50, 52, 55–56, 246; executive power, assertions of, 52–53; "House Divided" speech, 220–21; on Missouri politics, 222; politics of the possible and, 50–51; preliminary Emancipation Proclamation of 1862 and, 74; proslavery policies and, 56; on

saving the Union, 54; on slavery, race, and sectional politics, 49–50, 55, 59, 61–62. *See also* Emancipation Proclamation
Lochner v. New York, 84, 85, 87, 90
Loving v. Virginia, 165
Lowenthal, David, 20

Macias, Edward S., 3
Madison, Eliza Scott, 3
Madison, James: *Constitution a Pro-Slavery Compact*, 182
Madison, John A., *33*; "Breaking the Chains of Slavery," 37–38
Madison, Lynne Jackson, 40
Madison, Marbury v., 241
Mann, State v., 180
Manning, Chandra, 158–59
Marbury v. Madison, 241
Marsalis, Wynton, 147
Marshall, John, 18, 232; as historian, 15; on Native Americans, 15–16; slavery and, 14–15; on Stono Rebellion, 14–15
Marshall, Thurgood, 3
Maryland, McCulloch v., 232
Mason, Worthington v., 111–12
McCulloch v. Maryland, 232
McGirk, Mathias, 199, 214–15
McKinney, Julia v., 199
Metro Broadcasting v. Federal Communications Commission, 135
Michigan, University of, admissions and, 175
Miller, Eric, 184
Miller, Samuel, 112, 123–24
M'Intosh, Johnson v., 15
Missouri, 68–80; 1864 election and, 76–77; 1865 constitutional convention and, 77; Civil War and, 221; elected judiciary and, 215; Emancipation Proclamation and, 222; freedom suits in, 214–15; political factions in, 212–13; Price raid and, 76
Missouri Compromise of 1820, 19, 194, 199, 232; constitutionality of, 180–82, 220, 241, 242–45; *Dred Scott* case and, 220; expansion of slavery and, 244–45; *Scott v. Emerson* and, 202–3
Missouri State Archives, 186
Mobile Register, 178
Moore, Roy, on substantive due process, 90
Morton, Oliver P., 79
Morton, Samuel, 142

Printed and bound by CPI Group (UK) Ltd, Croydon, CR0 4YY

09/06/2025

14685966-0003